Fast & Fabulous
Hors D'Oeuv

Fast & Fabulous
Hors D'Oeuvres

Michele Braden

Photographs by Craig Lovell

MACMILLAN • USA

Macmillan General Reference
A Simon & Schuster Macmillan Company
1633 Broadway
New York, NY 10019-6785

Library of Congress Cataloging-in-Publication Data

Braden, Michele.
Fast & fabulous hors d'oeuvres / Michele Braden.
—1st Collier Books ed.
p.   cm.
Rev. ed. of: Fast & flashy hors d'oeuvres. 1988.
Includes index.
ISBN 0-02-009185-0
1. Appetizers. I. Braden, Michele. Fast & flashy hors
d'oeuvres. II. Title. III. Title: Fast and fabulous
hors d'oeuvres.
TX740.B645   1992
641.8′12—dc20   92-14893
CIP

Book designed by Richard Oriolo

10 9 8

Printed in the United States of America

*This book is lovingly dedicated to my husband, daughter,
and entire family who inspired, taught, and, most importantly,
believed in me. In particular, my grandmother
who passed her gift on to me.*

CONTENTS

4. Forms   162

5. Wraps   230

Index   315

Contents

ACKNOWLEDGMENTS

The book has been greatly enriched by the generous contributions, efforts, and talents of many.

The Wines—
I had the privilege of working with . . .

Bernardus—Carmel Valley's newest winery tucked away in the peaceful rolling hills. Their French-trained winemaster combines the tradition of Old-World patience and techniques with New-World technology to produce world-class wines. Their emphasis is on uncompromising quality. The first release is scheduled for Fall 1992.

Domaine de Clarck—A small, new Carmel Valley winery that prides themselves on Old-World traditions. Their goal is to let nature's own development of the wines shine through, with as little interference as possible.

Lockwood Vineyard—A new Monterey County winery named after its special soil. Lockwood is a registered geological type more commonly called "chalk rock." Their wines won nineteen awards for excellence prior to their first release. These wines are known for their stunning varietal character and the winery has a strong commitment to environmental integrity.

*The Flower Man—*Dana McVey
A marvelous Monterey landscape contractor who made generous plant contributions.

*The Photographer—*Craig Lovell, Eagle Visions
It is a pleasure to work with such an artist. His painstaking efforts shine through.

*The Computer Guru—*Sarge Furman
Without Sarge, you would all have to read my handwriting.

The Props—
For the most part, the props used in the photography represent some of my cherished possessions. I knew that my passion for interesting culinary and household things would pay off. Whatever I did not have and needed was provided by my great friend and business partner Janet Gendelman and my wonderful neighbors, Ginny and Bill Cooperrider.

The Amazing Editor—Pam Hoenig
Who makes it all work.

The Agent—Hal Lockwood
Without him, I would still be knocking on doors.

Thanks!

INTRODUCTION

Back by popular demand, *Fast & Fabulous Hors D'Oeuvres* is technically the second edition of my first book, *Fast & Flashy Hors D'Oeuvres*, but in reality it is all new; bigger and better . . . simply put, it's Fast & Fabulous. I have done a complete revision, making it even easier for any kind of cook to create magic in their kitchens and stage fun and memorable parties. Furthermore, you will find more than eighty *new* recipes, along with extensive coverage of garnishing, serving, and presentation ideas.

The first edition of this book was so popular that I have actually met people who tried for over a year to get a copy. I can't tell you how many times I would receive calls and letters after doing radio or TV shows from people trying to find this elusive book. Once someone was lucky enough to purchase *Fast & Flashy Hors D'Oeuvres*, they used it, loved it, and wanted to share with their friends and family. I have met so many cooks who were so delighted with the results that they began referring to it as "the hors d'oeuvre bible." now, *Fast & Fabulous Hors D'Oeuvres* is even better!

Hors d'oeuvres are fun party food. In today's lingo, they are often referred to as "apps," a shortened, hipper name taken from the word "appetizers." Regardless of what they are called, they can best be described as palate pleasers and teasers.

It is unfortunate that the mere mention of the word "hors d'oeuvres" often brings fear and dread into the hearts of otherwise fearless culinary troupers. Whether you are looking for a glitzy prelude to an elegant dinner or a complete menu of hors d'oeuvres, they perform an important function. They set the stage, act as an icebreaker, welcome your guests, and immediately let them know that they are important.

Fast & Fabulous Hors D'Oeuvres is designed to transform every occasion into an event, whether it is for a casual gathering of neighbors in the backyard, or a holiday gala. The message of this book is that you *can* have it all—entertaining need not be just for those who sit home and clip coupons. Busy people can throw fabulous parties without quitting their jobs, taking out a second mortgage, or forcing their families to eat peanut butter sandwiches for a month before each party. Being Fast & Fabulous is an attitude and a life-style. It's fearless and flamboyant—a bit of a survival kit for today's busy person who wants to be an innovative cook and a great entertainer.

Don't confuse Fast & Fabulous with fast and tacky. There is no need, nor do I ever call for using prepared convenience foods consisting of inferior ingredients to save time. By using only the freshest, purest, and most fragrant ingredients, you will have tastier, healthier results and more pleasing-looking food that captures the essence of each season.

Fast & Fabulous Hors D'Oeuvres is for people who love to cook, entertain, and just plain party! It is designed to charge your batteries and get your creative juices flowing. The intent is for these recipes to build your confidence and inspire you to create variations of your own. That, after all, is what cooking is about. Never again will you be stumped for a creative hors d'oeuvre, imaginative ideas for presentation, or an attractive garnish. It is especially for busy people who must be time efficient. You will see how you can have and do it all, with flair!

Fearless and flamboyant cooking and entertaining is what Fast & Fabulous is all about. Viewed as a blueprint, it liberates culinary clones and kitchen martyrs. Culinary clones follow recipes as if they were heaven-sent. They forget to use their own judgment and the most important rule, that there are no absolutes in cooking. After all, we are dealing with an art form involving organic ingredients that are impossible to standardize. Have you ever seen two identical cloves of garlic or smelled onions of the exact same strength? Fast & Fabulous cooks involve every sense in the cooking process. The look, aroma, texture, sound, and taste are all essentials in the cooking process. Often I'm confronted with resistance when it comes to tasting the work in progress. People are afraid of ruining their appetites or waistlines. Wrong! I am talking about developing and sensitizing your palate. Only a tiny taste, ¼ to ½ teaspoon, is required. Kitchen martyrs simply leave their organizational skills outside of the kitchen door. Consequently, they end up being servants rather than star performers at their parties.

My Fast & Fabulous methodology is based on the simple principles of organization and advance preparation. Intelligent and successful people rely on these two basic principles in every area of their professional lives, but, for some unknown reason, discard them when it comes to cooking or entertaining. Why would you take time away from your guests to slice bread, unwrap a stick of butter, or make a sauce? Most of these tasks can be taken care of several hours in advance. Let's look at a simple detail such as bread. Slice it earlier in the day and wrap it in foil to keep it fresh, then warm before serving. If this is done while guests are there, not only have you taken time away from your primary role, but you've also created a needless mess in your kitchen. Setting the table and selecting serving pieces and wineglasses are vital to a fabulous dinner party and should be given great consideration. Take care of these items when there isn't much cooking to be done. For example, if there is time two days in advance, do it then, leaving only the flowers for the day of the party. This is where you must think of every possible detail. Set out serving pieces and plates. We have all been in the position of frantically scrounging for plates or a serving spoon, trying to remain outwardly calm in front of guests, while the food is getting cold. The point is, there are precious few items that require last-minute attention.

Fast & Fabulous Hors D'Oeuvres is carefully designed to reinforce this methodology. Every recipe is followed by invaluable tips that may include:

FAST: How far in advance the dish can be prepared and refrigerated or frozen without sacrificing taste or quality.

FLASHY: What to serve it with and ideas for garnishing and presentation.

FABULOUS: Alternatives and variations that will serve as a stimulus to spur you on to your own creations, or how else a dish can be used.

FURTHER: Innovative ways for handling leftovers.

Fast & Fabulous goes further. It is concerned with excellence and style in both food and ambience. It views cooking and entertaining as valuable forms of personal expression, a living, three-dimensional art form, and an essential ingredient for a complete life-style.

This book does not for a minute mean to insinuate that you will be able to prepare hors d'oeuvres or throw a fabulous party without investing any effort. The old adage that all things worthwhile require work is true. The complete party process should be a pleasure, from planning, to preparation, to party. What this book is about is how to approach cooking and parties intelligently and with confidence, without wasting time or leaving tasks for the last minute, thereby sabotaging your efforts.

You will notice that I rely heavily on the food processor and use it whenever possible. It is one of the best ways to cut cooking time. I also view freezers as a real necessity. They cut chilling time in half. There is no greater convenience than to be able to pull out a scrumptious hors d'oeuvre from the freezer.

I hope *Fast & Fabulous Hors D'Oeuvres* will serve as inspiration for many wonderful celebrations, and bring much joy and happiness into your lives.

PLANNING YOUR PARTY

THE COOK'S PARTY STRATEGY

Before we try to unravel the strategy for staging a successful dinner party, it is important to consider the role dinner parties play in today's society. There has always been great importance given to breaking bread with people, but in the nineties this activity has taken on a new meaning. In today's fast-paced, often impersonal world, it becomes necessary to exhibit only one side of our personalities, the serious, controlled adult. The stresses of everyday family life can easily perpetuate this behavior at home. Also, in our big cities, filled with big companies, the individual can easily get lost. These conditions make it more important than ever to distinguish ourselves and express our individuality. The dinner party is a marvelous vehicle for not only expressing our uniqueness, but also for enabling us to utilize our entire personalities, to be playful, humorous, and childlike.

Now, let's deal with strategy. Once you make the decision to give a party, you need to create a guest list. This is a challenge, and could be considered an art in and of itself. It is essential not to simply repay obligations—your party will lack effervescence. A guest list must be a balancing of character types and professions. A group consisting of all introverts or brain surgeons is deadly. One of the most successful parties I have ever given stemmed from the fact that one of my guests was an introvert. I tried very hard to balance that and the results were electric. The professions represented ranged from a psychic to a TV anchorman.

Next comes the menu selection. *Fast & Fabulous Hors D'Oeuvres* provides you with limitless ideas. Designing a menu involves considering a great many factors. The season should shape the menu. Then you need to pay close attention to drama and balance. The last factor influencing your menu is your kitchen and home and the limitations they pose. It will be necessary to adjust the menu to suit your needs. For example, if you have one oven or almost no kitchen counter space, it is important to keep it simple. Pare the menu down and invite only as many guests as can be comfortably entertained.

On the day of the party, schedule time for rest and relaxation. A tired and haggard kitchen martyr cannot be a vivacious host or hostess. The Fast & Fabulous entertainer makes everything appear easy and ensures that everyone has fun!

This is the critical organization. Too many of us just do not know what can be done when. Most recipes leave you guessing by saying that the dish can be prepared in advance. How far in advance is critical. Many of you will be amazed to realize how easy this becomes when you give yourself the necessary advance time. If, for instance, you decide to have a party in three weeks, each weekend several dishes can be partially prepared and frozen. By the time the party comes around, the menu has come together comfortably, allowing you the necessary time and energy to devote to all areas, including the ambience and look of the table. You will find that the entire process was pleasurable.

After all, when tackling any major project professionally, you would not expect to finish it in one day. Why then do we feel that we should be able to awaken on Saturday morning, shop, cook, clean, and be prepared to entertain guests? What an overwhelming task! By the time your guests arrive, you're ready to faint, not party! What a waste of time and money!

I'm convinced that the fear factor associated with entertaining all stems from something as simple as not having the necessary organizational skills. Once you put those skills into practice, you'll find that staging a dinner party no longer seems like an impossible task. Automatically, your confidence level is raised and no matter how busy you are, you see that there is still time for celebration.

It is important to consider your home and its role in a successful party. It is essential to pay close attention to comfort and ambience. Realistically, fun becomes almost impossible when comfort is not considered. Seating and lighting are essential to comfort. If you have ever been packed into a dinner table with the elbows of those on either side jabbing you all evening, you know what I am talking about. Good seating facilitates the free flow of conversation.

Lighting is every bit as important. Bad lighting, whether it is too dim or bright, destroys the atmosphere you have worked so hard to create. You can transform a cold, stark space into a warm, dramatic, or romantic room. Candles are an inexpensive but effective way to create lighting magic. It is amazing to see personalities change and how social interaction is sparked by good lighting.

Flowers and arrangements of fresh greens are invaluable props for creating ambience. They symbolize the celebration of nature and provide a festive aura. If budget is a concern, relax, flowers need not be costly. Most of us have greens or flowers in the garden or on the patio that we can pick. In the fall and winter it's fun to take walks and collect interesting dried weeds and greenery for arrangements. As for flowers, if your garden is not in bloom, ask a friend. Sharing flowers is something most gardeners take delight in. Purchasing exotic flowers and using them individually to create stark and dramatic arrangements is another approach.

Be sure to include the entrance to your home when decorating for a party. This instantly welcomes your guests and establishes a tone. When decorating, I also give as much attention to my kitchen and bathrooms as to my living and dining rooms.

Keep in mind that the rooms in which you stage a party play an important role in establishing the desired mood. For example, the family room has a relaxed warmth, whereas a living room projects more formality and elegance. If you need to use a certain room, but don't want the party to take on the feeling of that particular room, work with your props to create the mood you want. Dress up family rooms with candles and flowers, and try using tinted bulbs in the lamps. Living rooms can be given a more casual feel by using pillows on the floor and arranging the furniture in a more intimate manner. Formal pieces can also be removed.

Don't forget your yard—outdoor parties can be either casual or elegant, and offer the opportunity to turn an open space into a wonderful party set.

The Cook's Shelf

Just as a painter needs a full palette, so does the home cook and entertainer need a well-stocked pantry. These are the items that will help create gastronomical ecstasy for your family and friends, whether preparing for a fabulous party or a midweek dinner.

Don't panic over cost, it's not necessary to purchase everything at once. Collect these items gradually and be a smart shopper. Don't go to the priciest food boutique. Hunt around at discount and import stores and take advantage of sales.

Assorted Dried Herbs and Spices

- *Apple pie spice*
- *Basil*
- *Bay leaves*
- *Caraway seeds*
- *Cardamom*
- *Celery seeds*
- *Chili powder*
- *Chiles (whole, red pepper flakes, and ground cayenne pepper)*
- *Cinnamon*
- *Cumin (ground and seeds)*

- *Curry powder*
- *Dillweed and dill seed*
- *Fennel seeds*
- *Fines herbes*
- *Italian herbs*
- *Mace*
- *Marjoram*
- *Mint leaves*
- *Mustard (ground and seeds)*
- *Nutmeg, whole*
- *Oregano*

- *Paprika, Hungarian sweet*
- *Poultry seasoning*
- *Peppercorns (Szechuan, white, pink, green, and black)*
- *Pumpkin pie spice*
- *Rosemary*
- *Tarragon*
- *Thyme (leaves and ground)*

Assorted Oils

- *Avocado oil*
- *Canola oil*
- *Chinese Sesame oil*

- *Grapeseed oil*
- *Olive oil (extra virgin and pure)*

- *Peanut oil*
- *Walnut oil*

Assorted Olives

- *Spanish olives*

- *Black olives*

- *Greek (calamata) or Italian olives*

Assorted Nuts and Seeds (toasted—see page 27—and stored in the freezer to prevent them from becoming rancid)

- *Almonds*
- *Pecans*
- *Pine nuts*

- *Pistachios*
- *Poppy seeds*
- *Pumpkin seeds*

- *Sesame seeds*
- *Sunflower seeds*
- *Walnuts*

Assorted Marinated or Pickled Items

- Capers
- Marinated artichoke hearts
- Pickled ginger
- Pickled mango
- Greek peperoncini
- (Greek-style pickled peppers)
- Sun-dried tomatoes (in olive oil or just dried)

Assorted Rices, Grains, and Beans

- Arborio rice
- Basmati rice
- Long grain white rice
- Wild rice
- Bulgur
- Couscous
- Polenta (regular and/or instant)
- Pastas (assorted, dried)
- Black beans (dried or canned)
- Garbanzo beans (chick-peas) (dried or canned)
- Great northern beans (dried or canned)

Assorted Sauces and Condiments

- Barbecue sauce, Chinese-style, canned or in jars
- Hoisin sauce, Chinese-style, canned or in jars
- Mango chutney
- Mayonnaise
- Mustard (Dijon-style and coarse ground)
- Peperoncini (pickled peppers)
- Pickled mango or mango pickle
- Plum sauce, Chinese-style, canned or in jars
- Soy sauce
- Tabasco (or any kind of hot pepper sauce)
- Tonkatsu sauce, Japanese-style Worcestershire
- Worcestershire sauce

Assorted Staples

- All-purpose unbleached flour
- Baking powder
- Baking soda
- Brown sugar (light or dark)
- Cake flour
- Cornmeal
- Confectioners' sugar
- Granulated sugar
- Honey
- Unflavored gelatin

Assorted Vinegars

- Balsamic
- Cider
- Raspberry
- Rice wine
- Sherry wine
- Tarragon wine
- White and red wine

Wines for Cooking

- Dry vermouth
- Madeira
- Marsala
- Merlot or any dry red
- Port
- Sherry (dry and regular)

Cheeses (*stored in freezer*)

- *Feta*
- *Mizithera*

- *Mozzarella*
- *Parmesan*

- *Romano*

Miscellaneous

- *Anchovies (tinned and paste)*
- *Black fungus (dried)*
- *Garlic (fresh)*
- *Green chiles, whole, canned*
- *Onions (fresh)*

- *Pancetta (stored in freezer)*
- *Pasilla chiles (dried)*
- *Porcini mushrooms (dried)*
- *Potatoes (fresh)*
- *Prosciutto (stored in freezer)*

- *Refried beans (canned)*
- *Shiitake mushrooms (dried)*
- *Tomatoes, canned or fresh*
- *Tuna, canned*

THE CHEF'S PALATE

It is absolutely crucial for you to understand some of my flavor prejudices. This is just as important as knowing the personal bias of a movie critic or restaurant reviewer.

Okay, let's start with the hors d'oeuvres. It is a natural starting point. This is the crucial point of a party. Its role is awesome! This is when you make your first impressions on your guests. It is also an icebreaker. Most of us are all too aware of those first few awkward minutes when the party momentum needs to be jump-started. Interesting and impressive hors d'oeuvres are called for. Those adorable little cubes of cheese speared with colored frilled toothpicks do not exactly fit the bill. Delicate miniature pastry tartlets, pâtés, magnificently marinated seafood, exotically flavored dipping sauces with crisp, garlicky melbas, or pita chips, not generic chips, do rise to the occasion. I always lean toward offering my guests choices, as I have found this to be an instant icebreaker. This means instead of preparing one hors d'oeuvre, often I will do three. Remember, the perfect hors d'oeuvre teases the palate, never satisfying, always arousing the appetite, "palate pleasers and teasers." I am definitely of the opinion that this can be a party maker or breaker. Be flamboyant; set the tone for the evening.

Unusual, luxurious, and enticing is the goal. As for the pacing, it should be leisurely, allowing everyone the opportunity to truly enjoy the food and company. Speaking of food, I only have one rule. Any discussion of calories, fat, and/or diets is forbidden. End of subject . . . case closed. There is an appropriate time and place for everything. Guilt has no place at a party.

Another prejudice of mine is against hosts/hostesses who are unable to be at the table. You know the types. They are locked away in the kitchen madly trying to keep up with the dishes. The remedy is simple—hire help. This is a necessity and need not be out of reach for anyone's budget. If yours happens to be limited, use your kids, their friends, and/or neighborhood teenagers. However, you must let anyone whom you employ know what is expected. I have been to many parties where the hostess has plenty of professional help, but still is busy doing God-only-knows-what! Don't fall into this trap; it simply projects insecurities.

Now for portion size, my culinary style values abundance. That does not mean that I am waging a one-woman war on anorexia. I want my food to look gracious and generous. I do not want it to appear as if each lettuce leaf is counted. It is a terrible feeling to be at a party and be afraid to take a decent serving. It is always better to have too much than not enough, that old adage that most of us have heard from our mothers and grandmothers. What wisdom!

You will rapidly notice that I gravitate toward big flavors. I would be the first to categorize myself as a flavor junkie. Please adjust the seasoning to your own palate.

Texture is vital to good food. I balanced the textures in each dish I prepare, as well as in the entire menu. The perfect example of poor textural composition is the standard Thanksgiving dinner. Almost everything is mashed or pureed. How boring! Now you are ready to go forth and create parties.

SERVING

Too often we devote all our attention to the food itself and forget about how it is going to be served. Here is where we need to anticipate traffic patterns, the temperature at which different items need to be maintained if they need reheating, and the size and placement of the food and plates, platters and bowls.

I realize that discussing traffic patterns sounds more like the rush-hour commute than party planning, but this is a critical area. No matter how delicious or beautiful the hors d'oeuvres are, if your guests cannot get to them, it all becomes an exercise in futility. It is essential to make sure that all the food and beverages are easily accessible. Try to keep your primary serving tables away from the walls. Guests should be able to get to these tables from both sides. This will keep the party flowing smoothly. It is a good idea to have several tables or serving stations in different areas, plus have some hors d'oeuvres passed. Place these stations in the most spacious areas of your home to avoid overcrowding and a mob scene. Move furniture if necessary and be creative. If the largest area in your home is an entry hall, use it! It is fun to transform unexpected spaces into party areas.

The next point of concern when it comes to serving hors d'oeuvres is the size of the food. Hors d'oeuvres should be finger food and that means small. There's nothing I dislike more than trying to balance a drink in one hand and a small plate in another while attempting to eat a hunk of ham on a huge roll. It's an impossible balancing act. Keep in mind this rule of thumb—everything should be bite-size or close to it. Forks, as far as I'm concerned, have no place at a cocktail party.

Often the way in which a dish is served can be as exciting as the flavors themselves. Don't get me wrong. I am not insinuating that presentation is more important than the food. That would be like an exquisitely wrapped package with a Cracker Jack prize inside. By the same token wonderful food presented on tacky plates or platters loses a great deal of impact. Even though it sounds as if I'm about to delve into the world of garnishing, I am just referring to your choice of plates, platters, baskets, trays, and bowls. Selecting serving pieces and collecting them is fun and only limited by your imagination. The secret is to collect that which allows you to create and express your own style.

Think beyond the expected. Interesting pans and woks can be very effective when used for serving. Remember to use different levels rather than having all your serving pieces for creating visual impact. Using pedestals to elevate plates and platters is extremely effective. Turn stemmed glasses upside down, use bricks, baskets, vases, flowerpots, bowls, and/or copper pots. In short, almost anything except the kitchen sink can be used to create pedestals.

Edible Containers

Edible containers provide a touch of surprise and are a conversation point. Anything that can be hollowed out can be used to hold dips, sauces, spreads, or fillings. The following are a few suggestions:

VEGETABLES AND FRUITS:

Pumpkins	*Eggplant*	*Pineapples*
Beefsteak tomatoes	*Onions*	*Coconuts*
Large zucchini	*Bell peppers (all colors)*	*Cabbages*
Acorn squash	*Melons (any variety)*	

BREADS

Long French and round loaves. Cut the top third off of the loaf. Use your fingers or a fork to pull out as much of the bread as possible, leaving the hollowed out shell. Bake it in a preheated 350°F oven until crisp, about 20 minutes. Use the removed bread to make bread crumbs or croutons. Fill the shell with any hot or cold mixture.

Frozen bread dough containers. Thaw the frozen bread dough and roll it out to a 1-inch thickness. Drape this dough over an upside-down pot. Place this on a cookie sheet and bake in a preheated 350°F oven for about 20 minutes. Remove from the oven and unmold. Brush the inside and outside of the dough with the oil of your choice. Lower the oven temperature to 300°F and bake until crisp, another 30 to 40 minutes.

Planning for Quantity

I have saved the most difficult aspect of serving for the last. I tried desperately to avoid it entirely, but my editor is much too conscientious to even think of allowing that. Like most good Jewish mothers, mine raised me to believe that more is better. God forbid, you should look stingy or worse yet, someone could go hungry. Naturally, she learned this from her mother. When I got married, my husband took great pains to get me to cut down my portion sizes. It didn't work! I have exposed all of this to reinforce the point that I like plentiful. It's ingrained in me. Besides which, I truly believe that not providing generous amounts of food for your guests creates tension rather than a relaxed playful mood.

Okay, let's get down to brass tacks—determining amounts of hors d'oeuvres to serve is like ordering Chinese food. It all depends on the number of dishes and the richness of each of them. The more hors d'oeuvres served, the less you need of each one.

CENTERPIECES

Gone are the days when well-dressed tables consisted of a white cloth with a symmetrical arrangement of two candlesticks flanking a pincushion flower arrangement. Contemporary standards encourage all of us to stretch artistically, use our imaginations, and have fun!

Today's centerpieces have broadened into tablescapes, three-dimensional still lifes. Think of the entire table as a canvas. Fresh and dried flowers and herbs, fresh raw fruits and vegetables, dried beans, potted plants, interesting objects, candles, and fabrics all can be utilized in tablescapes. Think past the usual. Even something as basic as a tablecloth can become even more visually exciting by gathering and bunching it rather than placing it flat on the table. You might even use several cloths, a cloth and a fabulous swatch of fabric or scarf or table runner. Rather than a standard tablecloth, use bedsheets, cotton bedspreads from import stores, interesting cotton throw rugs, quilts, and/or shawls. Then there's always paper. That's right, but not the usual tacky paper tablecloths. I'm referring to tan or white butcher paper. It's fun to decorate them in any way that you would normally decorate a table, or get crazy and use Magic Markers to add color here and there. Have fun, there's no limit.

Working with multiples creates a bold and dramatic look. Try using several pots, vases, or baskets. Place them down the center of the table or scatter them. Candles in proper candlesticks are fine, but remember your options are unlimited. Candle pillars or votives are fabulous placed on a platter in flat baskets, in terra-cotta or china saucers, in terra-cotta flowerpots, in old skillets, on planks of wood, or on glass or masonry bricks.

Two candles are normal. Three or more are visually exciting. They need not be in matching holders or all be the same size. It's fun to work with a variety. Be brave and dare to mix and match to create your own look.

One of my favorite ways of arranging is to combine potted flowers in a basket along with greenery cuttings and a head of broccoli, bunches of grapes, and/or a bunch of asparagus. My inspiration for tables usually comes from the season and the style of food being served. Baguettes and loaves of bread might be scattered directly on the table with candles placed on them. Flowering cabbage and kale could be used instead of flowers. Baskets of eggplant or even the ordinary onion might be the basis of a wonderful centerpiece.

GARNISHING

Garnishing is a real passion of mine. In my opinion, it is almost as important as the flavor of the food. We are a fast-paced, visually oriented society. This makes first impressions extremely important. An ungarnished dish sends out the same message an unset table does when you are expecting dinner guests. It says to your guests that they are not important enough to warrant any extra effort.

Here is where you call upon your artistic talents as well as your sense of the whimsical. The sky's the limit! I'm sure you have noticed, there are several schools of thought when it comes to garnishing. Some people prefer an austere, minimal presentation. This type abides by strict laws limiting the garnishes to the ingredients used in the dish. That is to say, if parsley does not appear in the recipe, there is no possible way it could be used in the garnishing. The other school of thought, of which I am a card-carrying member, embraces abundance and generosity. I want everything to appear lush and lavish. Visual appeal and excitement are what I focus on.

For me, garnishing is approached as an abstract art form. I do not strive to make swans out of cream puffs, cucumber snakes, apple birds, watermelon whales, chocolate ballerinas, not to mention the obligatory piece of parsley or, worse yet, a white doily. Instead, I gravitate toward nontoxic flowers and leaves, fresh herbs, fruits and vegetables, all appreciated for and used to project their own beauty and appeal. It's just not my style to want to make food stuffs into lifelike zoo forms.

The following list includes some of my favorite garnishes. It is not possible to mention every one of them, but hopefully this will start your creative juices flowing.

PARSLEY

The most commonly used and widely available garnish. It has gotten somewhat of a tarnished reputation simply because it is often used without any imagination or thought. It can be used sparingly or with wild abandon, either in clumps or minced. It works with almost everything except brownies!

ALFALFA OR OTHER VARIETIES OF SPROUTS

These can be used as a bed on which to place hors d'oeuvres, or in clumps to create borders as you would parsley.

GREEN ONIONS

Use minced and scattered or turn into green onion flowers by cutting off the root and making many thin cuts through about three-quarters the length of the white part. To get this to fan out, place in a bowl of ice water for about 20 minutes. This can be done up to two days in advance and refrigerated. The green part of the onion can also be handled in the same manner by making very thin cuts down the green portion lengthwise.

LEEK FLOWERS

Cut the root end off the leek and make very thin cuts just as is done with the green onion flowers.

FRESH HERBS

Use minced, or use the leaves scattered, or use cuttings. Herb blossoms are also wonderful for garnishing. Some of my favorites are basil, oregano, chives, mint, sage, rosemary, cilantro, dill, and watercress.

WHOLE RAW VEGETABLES AND/OR FRUITS

Red, green, purple, and/ or yellow bell peppers	*Winter squash*	*Persimmons*
All varieties of chiles	*Baby boy choy*	*Pomegranates*
Heads of garlic	*Tomatoes—all varieties*	*Peaches*
Eggplant—all varieties	*Grapes*	*Plums*
Zucchini	*Apples*	*Kumquats*
	Oranges and tangerines	*Apricots*

| Kiwi | Nectarines | Cherries |
| Pears | Berries | |

TOMATO ROSES

Using a sharp carving knife, cut a wide, thin strip of skin starting at the bottom of the tomato and continuing in a circular fashion to the top. Cut using a back-and-forth sawing motion. To form the rose, start with the end where you finished cutting and wrap the peel around itself. For a greater impact, use several tomato roses grouped together. Place the rose in a plastic bag and refrigerate until you are ready to use it. This can be done up to two days in advance.

CARROT, PARSNIP, AND CUCUMBER CURLS

Peel the vegetable thoroughly. Then press down firmly with the peeler, placing the vegetable down flat on your work surface. Wrap the strips around your finger to form a circular shape. Secure with a toothpick and place in a bowl of ice water to firm the curls up for at least 30 minutes. Remove the toothpicks and place carefully or scatter to garnish platters. Can prepare up to two days in advance if left in the bowl of water to prevent them from drying out.

TWISTED SLICES

This can be done with turnips, cucumbers, zucchini, yellow squash, oranges, lemons, and/or limes. Trim the fruit or vegetable at both ends to prevent it from rolling, then slice into very thin slices by hand, or using an electric slicer or food processor. Stack several slices on your work surface and cut halfway across the fruit or vegetable. Twist and use as desired. This can be done up to two days in advance if refrigerated in a bowl of water to prevent them from drying out.

SOME NONTOXIC FLOWERS FOR GARNISHING

Baby's breath (Gypsophila paniculata)	Johnny-jump-up (Viola tricolor)	Pansy (Viola cornuta)
Cornflower (Centaurea cyanus)	Lilac (Syringa vulgaris)	Poppy (Papaver rhoeas)
Hibiscus (Hibiscus moscheutos)	Marigold (Tagetes)	Rosa (Rosa hybrids)
	Nasturtium (Tropaeolum majus)	

SOME NONTOXIC LEAVES FOR GARNISHING

| Japanese aralia (Fatsia japonica) | Loquat leaves | Herb leaves |
| Grape leaves | Fruit tree leaves | |

CHICKEN BROTH

Yield: about 2 quarts

4 pounds chicken backs, necks,
  and/or wings
4 quarts cold water
1 cup dry sherry or vermouth
1 to 2 bay leaves
4 stalks celery with leaves, cut up
2 to 3 medium-size carrots, cut up
1 large onion, cut up

2 to 4 cloves garlic, minced
4 to 8 fresh parsley sprigs or stems
  from ½ bunch parsley
1 to 2 tablespoons minced fresh
  thyme or 1 teaspoon dried
1 to 2 teaspoons black peppercorns
Salt to taste

1. Place the chicken, water, and wine in a large stockpot and bring to a boil over high heat. Skim off the foam that rises to the top using a fine wire mesh strainer. Continue skimming as the foam rises. This will produce a clear broth.
2. Add the remaining ingredients, except the salt, and reduce the heat to low. Gently simmer, covered, for about 2 to 3 hours. Season with salt.
3. Cool to room temperature, then refrigerate until chilled and the fat rises to the top and congeals. This will take at least 4 hours. Use the freezer to cut the time in half. To speed this process up even more, place about a quart of ice cubes in the hot stock. This will cause the fat to rise to the top and congeal. Remove and discard the fat. Strain through a fine wire mesh strainer to remove all the solids.

FAST: Can prepare up to 3 days in advance and refrigerate or freeze for up to 6 months.

FABULOUS: Seasoned with any fresh or dried herb.

BEEF BROTH

Yield: about 2 quarts

6 pounds beef shank and marrow
  bones
1 to 2 large onions, chopped
1 to 2 medium-size carrots, chopped
3 cups water (approximately)
1 to 2 cups dry red wine
2 to 4 tablespoons tomato paste
3 to 4 stalks celery, with the leaves,
  cut up

4 to 6 cloves garlic, minced
1 to 2 bay leaves
1 teaspoon black peppercorns
1 to 2 tablespoons each minced fresh
  thyme and rosemary or 1 teaspoon
  dried
Salt to taste

1. Place the beef bones, onions, and carrots in a large roasting pan in a preheated 425°F oven until all the ingredients are nicely browned, about 1 hour. Stir from time to time.
2. Transfer the browned ingredients to a large stockpot with enough water to cover. Bring to a boil over high heat and continue boiling while skimming off the foam, using a fine wire mesh strainer.
3. Add all the remaining ingredients, except the salt. Reduce the heat to low and simmer, covered, at least 3 hours or up to 8 hours. Season with salt.
4. Cool to room temperature, then refrigerate until chilled and the fat rises to the top and congeals. This will take at least 4 hours. Use the freezer to cut the time in half. To speed this process up even more, place about a quart of ice cubes in the hot stock. This will cause the fat to rise to the top and congeal. Remove and discard the fat. Strain through a fine wire mesh strainer to remove all the solids.

FAST: Can prepare up to 3 days in advance and refrigerate or freeze for up to 6 months.

FABULOUS: Seasoned with any fresh or dried herb.

SHRIMP STOCK

Yield: about 1 quart

Shrimp shells and tails from 2 pounds
   shrimp
4 cups water
1 cup dry white wine
1 bay leaf
1 to 2 cloves garlic

2 to 4 shallots, minced
3 to 6 sprigs fresh parsley, minced
1 stalk celery with the leaves,
   chopped
Salt and freshly ground white pepper
   to taste

1. Place the shrimp shells and tails in a 2-quart saucepan over medium heat. Cook, stirring, until the shells turn pink and are very fragrant, 3 to 5 minutes.
2. Add the remaining ingredients and bring to a boil over high heat. Reduce the heat to medium and cook, covered, until the flavors develop to your liking, about 1 hour. Strain through a fine wire mesh strainer to remove the shells and tails.

FAST: Can prepare up to 3 days in advance and refrigerate or freeze up to 6 months.

FABULOUS: Seasoned with any fresh or dried herb.

MAYONNAISE

Yield: about 1¼ cups

1 large egg and 1 large egg yolk
1 tablespoon fresh lemon juice
Dash of hot pepper sauce

1 tablespoon Dijon mustard
1 cup extra virgin olive oil
Salt to taste

1. Combine the first 4 ingredients in a food processor fitted with the metal blade or in a blender and process until the egg is fluffy, about 3 minutes.
2. With the machine running add the oil very slowly in a thin stream through the feed tube. When the mayonnaise thickens, the remaining oil can be added at once. Season with salt.

FAST: Can prepare up to 4 days in advance and refrigerate.

FLASHY: Garnished with parsley, a cherry tomato, and/or any nontoxic flowers.

FABULOUS: With peanut, canola, avocado, or grapeseed oil instead of olive oil. Flavored with 2 to 4 tablespoons of drained capers, ½ cup drained marinated artichoke hearts, and/or with 2 to 4 tablespoons of fresh minced herbs.

REFRIED BEANS

*Canned refried beans are fine. I prefer the ones labeled
"vegetarian" since they are not made with
lard. You will notice that my beans are
not fried. There's no reason to . . .
the flavor is great!*

Yield: 5 to 6 cups

1 pound dried pinto, black, or pink
   beans, well rinsed

5 cups water or chicken broth,
   homemade or canned

4 to 6 cloves garlic, minced

½ cup medium-dry sherry

½ to 1 teaspoon ground cumin

½ to 1 teaspoon chili powder

1 teaspoon salt, or more

1 large onion, minced

1. Place the beans in a large bowl and cover with water. Let them soak for 6 hours or overnight.
2. Place the beans along with all of the ingredients in a large pot and bring it to a boil over high heat.
3. Cover with a lid, reduce the heat to the lowest temperature and cook for about 45 minutes to 1 hour.
4. Remove the beans from the liquid using a wire strainer, and puree in a food processor fitted with the metal blade, or mash in a potato ricer. Taste and adjust the seasonings.

FAST: Can prepare up to 4 days in advance and refrigerate, or freeze for up to 3 months.

FLASHY: Served hot or cold.

FABULOUS: Seasoned with chiles and/or oregano (fresh or dried), and/or grated jack or cheddar to taste.

Mango Chutney

Yield: about 1½ cups

1 large mango (page 21), peeled
and cut into small cubes or
chopped
½ cup minced red onion
¼ to ½ cup packed minced fresh
mint leaves

2 tablespoons sugar or to taste
½ to 1 teaspoon salt or to taste
¼ cup balsamic vinegar
Freshly ground white pepper to taste

Combine all the ingredients in a mixing bowl. Taste and adjust the flavors.

FAST: Can prepare up to 4 days in advance and refrigerate or freeze for up to 6 months. Thaw in the refrigerator for 2 days or at room temperature for about 8 hours.

FLASHY: Served in a bowl and garnished with a sprig of mint and/or any nontoxic flower.

FABULOUS: With about ¼ cup minced cilantro and/or minced jalapeño peppers (page 20). With 2 large peaches, 3 to 4 large plums, and/or 2 large nectarines used instead of mangoes.

TERMS AND TECHNIQUES

INGREDIENTS

The following are food items that will help you become a Fast & Fabulous cook and entertainer.

Chinese Ingredients

All of the following items can be purchased in the oriental section or oriental produce section of your supermarket, or in a specialty food store. Occasionally some items will require a trip to a bona fide oriental market.

BARBECUE SAUCE

This sauce is much like hoisin sauce (page 17) and can be used and stored in the same way.

BLACK FUNGUS

Also known as "wood ears." Until very recently it was only available in dried form. When rehydrated it has almost no flavor, but it provides a crunchy texture and black color. To rehydrate black fungus, place it in a small bowl and let it sit, covered with water, until it softens and expands. This will take about 30 minutes. To speed up this process, soften it in a pot of boiling water. When used fresh, it has a delicate, earthy flavor. In folklore, it is prized for its healthful properties, especially in preventing heart disease. I like to use it in rich dishes to help balance fats. It is my insurance policy against cholesterol and falls into the category of "it couldn't hurt."

BOK CHOY

A variety of Chinese cabbage with large dark green leaves and nearly white, smooth stalks. The flavor is refreshing and there is almost no aroma. It is also available in a small size, baby bok choy.

CALIFORNIA PEARL RICE

A short-grained pearl-shaped rice that can be used instead of Japanese or Arborio rice. It is found in the rice section of most supermarkets.

CHINESE PLUM SAUCE

This prepared sauce is like gingered plum jam with chiles. It has an incredibly seductive flavor. For further information on use and storage, refer to hoisin sauce (below).

CHINESE-STYLE BARBECUED PORK

Purchase this delicacy at oriental meat markets. Canadian bacon or ham can be substituted.

CHINESE-STYLE SAUSAGES

These are an absolute treat! They have a unique flavor that is sweet and salty. Use them in dishes or by themselves. In the summer, grill and slice them and serve with mustards and/or any of the Chinese vinegar-type sauces in Chapter 1 as an hors d'oeuvre.

CHINESE FIVE SPICE POWDER

A ground mixture typically consisting of star anise, fennel, clove, cinnamon, and Szechuan peppercorns. When purchasing it, look for a finely ground mixture with a light, earthy color. The darker version is usually an inferior product.

CHINESE SESAME OIL

This is used sparingly as a seasoning, not as a cooking oil. It has a rich, intense flavor but brings out the flavors of the food as well.

CILANTRO

An herb also referred to as Chinese parsley or fresh coriander, cilantro is used in Chinese, Mexican, Middle-Eastern, and Indian cooking.

EGG ROLL WRAPPERS

A large square, thin Chinese pasta-type wrapper.

FERMENTED BLACK BEANS

Also referred to as salted black beans or Chinese black beans and usually purchased in plastic bags. Transfer them to a glass or plastic container and store in the refrigerator for an eternity. They have an intense, salty flavor and impart an earthy richness to dishes.

GINGER ROOT

A pungent root that is indigenous to India and China. It can be refrigerated for about a week before it begins to mold. Fresh ginger should be firm but not wrinkled or dried out. Store it in a jar of sherry or vinegar or freeze it, whole or minced, for up to 6 months.

HOISIN SAUCE

A prepared Chinese sauce with a jamlike consistency. It can be brushed directly on poultry, pork, or beef for barbecuing or broiling. Hoisin sauce also can be used as a seasoning ingredient in sauces or marinades. When it is purchased in a can, transfer the contents to a glass or plastic container and store it in the refrigerator for an eternity.

MIRIN

Sweet sake (rice wine) used only for cooking. It can be found in Asian markets and liquor stores. Pale-dry sherry is a good substitute.

PICKLED GINGER

Also called sushi ginger. I search for the undyed variety—who needs pink ginger? It is pickled in a brine of vinegar, salt, and sugar, which mellows the ginger. Feel free to substitute it for fresh ginger root in any recipe in this book. When using pickled ginger, increase the amount since it is not as potent as the fresh variety.

PICKLED MANGO

An Indian condiment with a pungent flavor. Purchase it in Middle-Eastern or Asian markets.

POTSTICKER WRAPPERS

These resemble a sui mai wrapper (see below) but are thicker. Can be refrigerated for 5 days or frozen for up to 3 months.

RICE WINE VINEGAR

A vinegar with a delightfully mellow and refreshing quality and a slightly sweet flavor. Once you become familiar with it, you will find many interesting ways to use it beyond Chinese cooking. It's excellent in vinaigrettes.

SHIITAKE MUSHROOMS

Also referred to as Black Forest mushrooms or Chinese mushrooms. Their flavor and aroma are rich and earthy and they impart a touch of instant exotica to any dish. Most commonly, they are purchased dried and must be rinsed, then rehydrated in a bowl of warm water. It will take about 20 minutes at room temperature. To speed this process up, place the bowl in the microwave for about 5 minutes or in a saucepan and simmer for about 10 minutes. When softened, remove and discard the stems and squeeze out the excess liquid. The precious soaking liquid should never be discarded; strained through a double thickness of paper towels and stored, it will make a flavorful addition or base for soups and sauces. It can be kept in the refrigerator for a week or frozen indefinitely. The fresh variety are becoming more readily available. I prefer to purchase them dried, because the flavor is more intense.

SUI MAI WRAPPER

A round won ton wrapper. If you can't find them, substitute won ton wrappers (page 19) or potsticker wrappers (see above) and cut them into circles with a wineglass or biscuit cutter. Can be stored in the refrigerator for 5 days or in the freezer up to 3 months.

SWEET RICE

Also referred to as glutinous or sticky rice. This type of rice is opaque and white, rather than translucent. It must be rinsed well, then soaked in warm water for at least two hours or overnight. This removes the coating of starch remaining from the milling process and helps to soften it.

SWEETENED CHILI SAUCE

This sauce has a wonderful, sweet-hot flavor with a catsuplike consistency. For further information on use and storage, see hoisin sauce (page 17).

TONKATSU SAUCE

Japanese-style Worcestershire sauce. Refer to hoisin sauce (page 17) for information on its usage and storage. A great way to achieve bold flavors without adding fats or cholesterol. Can be found in Asian markets or in the Asian section of many supermarkets.

SZECHUAN PEPPERCORNS

These are peppercorns with a unique flavor that is a combination of menthol and heat. They add an interesting flavor to oriental and nonoriental recipes alike. Use them whole or ground.

WON TON WRAPPER

A square, thin Chinese pasta-type wrapper. Can be stored in the refrigerator up to 5 days or the freezer up to 3 months.

Italian Ingredients

BALSAMIC VINEGAR

An Italian vinegar that can be purchased in specialty shops or markets that carry gourmet items. This vinegar is similar to rice vinegar in that it is mild and mellow, with a slightly sweet flavor, and is delicious used both as a seasoning and in salad dressings.

PANCETTA

An Italian cured bacon often coated with coarsely ground black pepper. Can be found at good delicatessens or butcher shops. Store in the freezer for up to a year and cut off what you need while still frozen. Use as a seasoning in small amounts.

PROSCIUTTO

A specially cured Italian-style ham that is a delicacy. It can be used as a cold cut, or to flavor almost anything except fudge cake. Purchase it at any good deli or Italian meat store. It can be stored for up to 3 months.

Miscellaneous Ingredients and Items

BAMBOO SKEWERS

Must be soaked in warm water for at least 30 minutes to prevent them from burning.

BULGUR

Toasted cracked wheat that is available in health food stores or the health food or grain section of supermarkets. It can be cooked like rice or just soaked in water until softened and used for salads.

CALAMATA OLIVES

Cured Greek black olives. Fabulous but salty flavor.

CAPERS

Unopened flower buds of a prickly plant called the caperbush. This bush grows on the mountain slopes bordering the Mediterranean Sea in Italy, Spain, and southern Greece. Capers come packed in brine and can be found in the pickle or gourmet sections of most supermarkets.

CARDAMOM/CARDAMON

Two spellings for the same Indian spice, a member of the ginger family. It can be found in specialty and Indian food stores.

CHÈVRE

A cream-style French goat cheese with a rich herbaceous flavor. This variety is now also being produced in California, New York, Wisconsin, and Vermont.

CHILE PEPPERS

See page 24 for guidelines on handling chile peppers and page 26 for directions on roasting them.

Anaheim chiles. The most common variety available, sold fresh, dried, or canned (as green chiles), it has a long, narrow, and slightly twisted shape and is available in red and green. It has a bittersweet taste and can have a lot of heat to it, although it is usually mild. The flavor becomes much sweeter once it is roasted. Once roasted they can be frozen for up to 1 year.

Ancho/poblano/pasilla chiles. These names are used to refer to a chile that looks like a flattened green bell pepper with a pointed tip and a shiny green or red skin. Normally it is mild but it can surprise you with a great deal of heat. It has a rich earthy flavor and, like Anaheim, improves when it is roasted. Raw it can be refrigerated in a plastic bag for a week. Once roasted they can be frozen for up to 3 months. They can also be purchased dried. To rehydrate them, let them soak in water until softened, about 30 minutes. To speed the process, place in water in a microwave for a few minutes or bring to a boil in a saucepan.

Jalapeño chiles. these fiery peppers are the next most common chile after Anaheims. They are short, somewhat squatty, and have a thick skin. The green variety is more readily available but the red ones are fabulous. Their heat has a delightful hint of sweetness. Jalapeños can be stored in a plastic bag for 1 week.

COUSCOUS

Moroccan pasta (medium-grain semolina).

CRYSTALLIZED GINGER

Candied ginger that can be used in sweet or savory recipes.

DEHYDRATED MASA

Dried ground corn that can be purchased in supermarkets carrying Mexican items.

EXTRA VIRGIN OLIVE OIL (COLD PRESSED)

This is the highest quality olive oil. It has the lowest level of acidity and is the most flavorful.

FENUGREEK

A seasoning used frequently in Greek and Middle-Eastern-style dishes.

FINES HERBES

A premixed herb combination of French origin, consisting of oregano, sage, rosemary, marjoram, and basil. Fines herbes are commonly used in soups, sauces, and marinades.

GRAPESEED OIL

A light monosaturated oil with a high smoking point. It can be used for anything from salads to baking.

GREEN PEPPERCORNS

They are the fresh, immature pepper berries, and can be purchased in the herb or gourmet section of supermarkets. Green peppercorns come freeze-dried or packed in water or brine.

GRUYÈRE CHEESE

A rich and nutty-flavored Swiss cheese.

INSTANTIZED FLOUR

White flour that has been processed in such a way as to make it dissolve instantly. It can be purchased in shaker cans or in bags. When preparing crepes, instantized flour eliminates the necessity of having the batter sit for an hour before using it. In sauce-making there is never the fear of lumps. As a matter of fact, you can whisk this directly into the sauce. Wondra is one brand of instantized flour.

JAMAICAN JERK SEASONING PASTE

A fiery but flavorful seasoning paste found in the gourmet section of supermarkets or in specialty stores. Hot pepper sauce can be substituted but it will not have the same complex flavor.

JICAMA

A tuber originally from Mexico. It resembles a large turnip with a thin sandy-tan skin that is inedible. The flesh is crunchy and can be used raw or cooked.

MANGOES

A fragrant fruit that is originally from Southeast Asia. When ripe the fruit will be soft but the skin should be smooth and tight. The color and the size varies greatly depending on the variety. They will range from very small to very large. The color ranges from green to rose.

MIZITHERA CHEESE

A very tasty white Greek grating cheese that is difficult to find. Substitute Romano or Parmesan.

PAPAYA

A tropical fruit with a yellow, melon-like flesh. It has a large center cavity filled with round black seeds. Select papayas more by feel than appearance. When ripe it will have the same give as an avocado. The coloring will be spotty yellow.

PARCHMENT

Can be found in gourmet and cooks' shops as well as where baking supplies are sold. It frequently is used to line molds, cake pans, and terrines to prevent food from sticking. It makes unmolding a breeze.

PHYLLO

Very thin transparent sheets of pastry commonly used in Greek and Middle-Eastern cooking. It is usually found frozen in supermarkets. Thaw and handle it according to the directions on the package.

PORCINI MUSHROOMS

Very meaty texture when fresh. They resemble domestic mushrooms but are much larger. The caps are tan-to-brown-colored but the flesh is creamy white. Available fresh or dried; more commonly available dried. Fabulous earthy flavor. To rehydrate the dried variety, simply place them in a bowl and cover them with any liquid, from water to broth. Let sit at room temperature for about 1 hour or until soft. To speed up the process, place in a saucepan and boil until tender.

PUMPERNICKEL SQUARES

This refers to thin, firm, European-style pumpernickel bread that you cut into small quarters.

SAFFRON

The most precious and costly spice. It is the stigma of autumn crocus and must be harvested by hand. It gives food a yellow-golden color and an exotic/earthy flavor. Always purchase saffron threads; the powdered form is not as flavorful and often not pure.

SHALLOTS

They resemble tiny brown onions and have a mild onion flavor. To save money, or when you run out of shallots, substitute the whites of green onions (scallions). You will need to use three to six green onions for one shallot.

SUN-DRIED TOMATOES

Italian pear-shaped tomatoes that are salted and dried. They can be very expensive, especially if purchased marinated. I recommend buying them dried in bulk, then marinating them yourself. To soften them for immediate use, place in a plastic or glass jar with a few tablespoons of vinegar, wine, or water. Cover with a lid and place in a microwave for a few minutes until softened. To do this on the stove, place the tomatoes in a saucepan and add an equal amount of the liquid of your choice. Bring to a boil, then gently simmer until tender, about ten minutes. Use as is or cover them with olive oil. Add garlic cloves, bay leaves, peppercorns, and/or fresh or dried herbs of your choice and store in the refrigerator for up to one year. The oil becomes infused with the pungent tomato-herb essence and is wonderful used on bread or in cooking.

TAHINI

A Middle-Eastern sesame seed paste, purchased in the gourmet section of many supermarkets or in health food stores.

TELEME CHEESE

An aged jack cheese with a softer texture and a more complex flavor.

TOMATILLOS

These are also referred to as green Mexican tomatoes. They have a refreshing and slightly tart flavor. Fresh tomatillos are encased in a greenish brown wrapper which must be removed before using. Many supermarkets and most Mexican and South American markets carry them fresh and/or canned.

WALNUT OIL

A very fragrant rich oil that is used sparingly as a seasoning.

WHITE PEPPERCORNS

Milder, richer flavor than black peppercorns. Widely used in delicate light-colored sauces since it does not add black flakes.

ZEST

The flavorful colored part of citrus rind. It is not the bitter-tasting inner white flesh of the fruit. To remove only the zest, use a vegetable peeler or zester, which can be purchased at any store that carries gourmet gadgets.

COOKING TECHNIQUES AND HINTS

Here are a few necessary techniques.

BLANCH

The cooking of vegetables in a large pot of boiling, salted water until they reach the desired degree of tenderness. The vegetables are then removed from the pot and immediately placed under cold running water to stop the cooking process and lock in the color. This technique allows you to prepare the vegetables in advance.

BOILING SHRIMP

(To serve cold.) Bring 2 quarts of water to a boil over high heat. Add about 1 tablespoon of pickling spice or just salt and pepper. Add the shrimp and continue to cook over high heat just until the shrimp turn pink, about 2 minutes. Drain the shrimp in a colander and put in cold water to stop the cooking process. Drain, shell, and enjoy. Shrimp can be cooked up to 2 days in advance and refrigerated or frozen for up to 1 month.

CHILLING TIME

To reduce required chilling time by half, place the food in the freezer.

DEGLAZE

Refers to adding liquid to a hot, degreased cooking pan after sautéing or roasting food in it. The liquid is brought to a boil to capture all the flavor from the remaining brown bits and juices, which should be vigorously scraped. Use this liquid as a sauce or add to a final sauce.

DEGREASE

Degreasing removes the fat from cooked liquids. One of the easiest methods is to refrigerate the item overnight. The next morning you will find a layer of solidified fat that you can easily remove. To remove fat immediately, put ice cubes in the pan or pot with the liquid. The fat will cling to the ice and rise to the top. It is easier if you are able to transfer the liquid to a smaller bowl and then add the ice cubes.

FLASH FREEZE

A technique for safely storing delicate items in the freezer and for economizing on freezer space. Place the items, unwrapped, on cookie sheets and freeze until firm. Remove them from the cookie sheet, place in plastic bags, and return to the freezer.

GRATING JACK CHEESE

To grate jack cheese, partially freeze first.

HANDLING CHILES

Wear plastic gloves when working with chiles to prevent them from burning your skin, and never touch yourself, especially your eyes, after working with chiles until you have washed your hands. If you forget this advice and burn your eyes, flush them with cold water and then put a cold compress over your eyes. For burning skin, place under cold running water, then make a paste using baking soda and water and apply it to the affected area until the burning stops.

HARD-BOILING EGGS

To cook, place the eggs in a saucepan and cover with at least 1 inch of water, adding about 2 teaspoons of salt per quart of water. Bring the water to a boil, cover, remove from the burner, and let sit for 17 minutes. To peel, drain the water out and shake the eggs in the saucepan so the shells crack. Cover with cold water and peel when cool enough to handle.

It seems as if there's always a new food villain. Currently the focus has been on eggs contaminated by the salmonella bacteria. This is of greater concern to pregnant women (because of the risk to the fetus), the elderly, and people already weakened by serious illness or whose immune systems are suppressed. According to the United States Department of Agriculture, the chances of a healthy person being affected are extremely small. They do, however, recommend not eating homemade foods containing raw or lightly cooked eggs. These foods range from mayonnaise to ice cream. The same items are risk-free when commercially prepared because they are pasteurized, which kills the bacteria.

It is very important to follow the safe food-handling practices listed below when using eggs:

- Buy only Grade A or AA eggs from a reputable market that keeps them under refrigeration. Open the carton to make sure the eggs are clean and crack-free. Do not purchase them if the expiration date has passed.
- Make sure you store your eggs in the refrigerator at a temperature no higher than 40°F. Use them before the expiration date. Once they are hard-cooked, they should be used within 1 week. Leftover yolks and whites should be used within 4 days.
- When cooking, eggs should not be left at room temperature for more than two hours.
- Always wash your hands, utensils, and work surfaces with hot, soapy water when working with raw eggs.

You will find that some of my recipes could pose the risk of salmonella. However, the recipes are so delicious and the risk so small that I could not eliminate them. Harold McGee, the author of *The Curious Cook* (Collier Books), provides a microwave method for eliminating salmonella that you might want to look into. The bottom line is that the decision to make any of these dishes is yours, but it is important to be informed and to take into consideration the health of the people who will be enjoying your food.

PEELING CARROTS FASTER

If you are going to cook carrots, do not bother to peel them. After they have been blanched or fully cooked, wipe off the peel while refreshing them. Sometimes it is necessary to use a knife to lightly scrape the skin off.

PEELING TOMATOES

Place tomatoes in a lettuce basket or strainer set in a deep bowl. Pour boiling water over the tomatoes and let stand until the skin can easily be removed, about 30 seconds. Immediately plunge the tomatoes into cold water and drain. Remove and discard the skins.

PREVENTING AVOCADO FROM DISCOLORING

Sprinkle it with lemon juice. When preparing an avocado mixture in advance, place the pit in the bowl and leave it there until serving. This may be an old wives' tale, but it seems to work.

PUREEING GARLIC

Most of you have seen pureed garlic in the produce section of your market, but you can make it yourself. Just peel several heads of garlic and puree them in a food processor fitted with the metal blade, or in a blender, with some olive or vegetable oil. Place in small jars, keeping one in the refrigerator and the rest in the freezer for future use. It will keep for up to 2 weeks in the refrigerator and up to 6 months in the freezer. For a Fast & Fabulous way to peel garlic, hit each clove with the side of a knife or a meat pounder. For an even easier way, just separate the head into cloves and place in a pot of boiling water for about 5 to 10 seconds, then drain and place under cold running water. You should be able to squirt the garlic out of its wrapper with your hands.

REDUCE/REDUCTION

Cooking terms referring to the process of boiling down cooking liquids to concentrate the flavors.

REMOVING BITTERNESS FROM EGGPLANT

As a rule of thumb, the more seeds the eggplant has, the more bitter it is. To remove this bitterness, sprinkle with salt and let sit in a colander to drain for about 1 hour, then rinse.

ROASTING BELL PEPPERS

Cut the peppers in half and remove the seeds and veins. Place them cut-side down on a cookie sheet and bake in a preheated 350° to 400°F oven until charred, 40 to 60 minutes. Remove them from the oven and, when cool enough to handle, remove and discard the skins. At this point they can be stored in the refrigerator for up to 2 weeks or frozen for up to 6 months.

ROASTING CHILES

Place them on a cookie sheet in a preheated 350°F oven until the skin is charred, about 40 to 60 minutes. Put under cold running water and remove their skins. Split in half, remove the seeds, veins, and stem. To freeze, first cool, then place in plastic bags. (They can be frozen for up to 6 months after they are roasted, and skinned, deveined, and seeded after thawing.)

ROASTING GARLIC

To roast garlic, cut the top one third from each head of garlic to expose the cloves. Using your hands, peel away some of the excess skin from around the garlic. Place the heads in a baking pan or heavy skillet and toss with a small amount of olive oil. Cover with a lid and bake in a preheated 250°F oven until the cloves are soft and buttery, about 2 hours, then squeeze the garlic out of its skin. If you are lucky enough to be able to purchase prepeeled garlic cloves, simply toss them in olive oil and bake as directed above. Roasted garlic can be frozen for up to 6 months or refrigerated for at least 5 days.

ROASTING SHALLOTS

Simply cut a small portion of the tip off the shallot and proceed as directed for roasting garlic.

STORING AND MINCING PARSLEY

Mince large quantities of fresh parsley in a food processor fitted with the metal blade. To store it for up to 3 days in the refrigerator, place it in a clean kitchen towel and twist out the excess moisture. Transfer to a container and refrigerate.

STORING NUTS AND SEEDS

To prevent these items from turning rancid, store in the freezer or refrigerator.

SUBSTITUTING FRESH HERBS FOR DRIED

Dried herbs are more potent and concentrated in flavor than fresh. Therefore, you use less than when seasoning with fresh herbs. As a rule of thumb, use three times more fresh herbs than dried. Remember, dried herbs don't last forever, only about a year. If they have lost their aroma or if it is unpleasant, throw them away.

TOASTING SEEDS OR NUTS

Place on an ungreased cookie sheet in a 350°F oven until toasted, about 15 to 20 minutes. Be careful not to burn them.

UNMOLDING GELATIN-BASED DISHES AND OTHER CHILLED ITEMS

First run a knife that has been dipped in hot water around the perimeter of the mold. Place the mold in a basin of warm water for a few seconds (just until the formed mixture begins to pull away from the sides of the mold). Place a plate on top of the mold and invert. Sometimes it is necessary to tap the top of the mold.

1

DUNKS

Do you remember way back, when dips were always limited to prepared ones, purchased in plastic tubs, except for very special occasions? In those instances when a dip was elevated to new heights, we actually took the time to combine dehydrated, artificially flavored packets with sour cream and/or mayonnaise. Because of this tarnished culinary past, I find the mere mention of "dips" as exciting as "Spam on white." That is why I refer to dips as dunks or sauces. Let's sever all ties with the stereotypical dip.

As soon as you prepare your first dunk, you will be thrilled by how effortlessly they go together, not to mention the magical flavors you'll effortlessly create. This makes dunks a great place for novice cooks to jump in and begin to prove themselves. They are confidence builders!

Dunks do not simply represent a category that offers us cooks an easy way out. They provide us with unlimited possibilities for creating tasty and exciting flavor marriages. You will find that some of these recipes can be prepared in a few seconds, none taking more than a few minutes, and all are designed to be made in advance.

This chapter has dunks inspired by many cuisines, and they range from elegant to casual. Most of the recipes can also be used for salad dressings, bread spreads, marinades, and/or entree sauces—the possibilities are limitless.

This chapter contains every variety of dunk imaginable. We start off with cold cream-style sauces and dunks. These are mixtures based on mayonnaise and/or sour cream. Committed fat-watchers can always substitute low-fat yogurt for some or all of the mayonnaise/sour cream. Almost any dunk can be transformed into an elegant offering depending on what is served with it. For instance, hold the packaged chips and go for the cold shrimp. Instant elegance!

Following the exploration of cold cream-style sauces and dunks, we enter the world of vinaigrettes and olive oil-based dunks. They are just as versatile and can be used for everything from dunks and salad dressings to marinades and/or entree sauces. As far as I'm concerned, these are the sauces of the nineties. This is a category that meets all of our criteria—they are cholesterol-free, full-flavored, and made only from high-quality ingredients. Vinaigrettes provide us with a wonderful way to take advantage of the season, as you can build them from any herb in season. More importantly, they can be prepared instantly, and will aid you in creating culinary magic. It's time to take advantage of vinaigrettes and not use them only for salads.

I have also included some dunks based entirely on vinegar sans oil. They are refreshing and a real bargain for fat watchers.

Onward to Mexican-style sauces and dunks—fabulous flavors and safe territory for those in need of strengthening their culinary confidence. These sauces and dunks make great summertime choices, as they require little if any cooking and have a relaxed casual feel to them. As an added bonus, these magical mixtures provide the cook with a limitless range of culinary possibilities while also containing precious few calories. What a culinary bargain! As usual, I have taken creative liberties and used the free-spirited Mexican style as inspiration. This explains why you will find a variety of salsas that wander away from Mexico toward other cuisines. All of them are well-packed with personality and flavors.

From Mexican inspiration we journey to Asian-style dipping sauces. The mysterious East offers noncooks yet another opportunity to build their culinary confidence in a playful way, while providing an unlimited repertoire of intriguing sauces.

After you prepare several of these flavorful mixtures you will be delighted with the culinary options that they offer you. Whether it is carrot sticks, skewers of chicken, or pita chips that need to be dipped, you will have unlimited and unique choices to choose from. Besides dipping, your saucing problems will also be over. Pasta, salads, vegetables, fish, chicken, beef, seafood, or you-name-it will be elevated to new heights by this international array of Fast & Fabulous Dunks.

COLD LEMON TARRAGON SAUCE

*A delicate dunk with a delightful fresh flavor to introduce
an elegant meal.*

Yield: about 2 cups

1 cup mayonnaise, homemade (page
13) or purchased

1 cup sour cream or plain yogurt

Zest of 2 lemons, finely grated

1 teaspoon Dijon mustard

1 tablespoon minced fresh tarragon
leaves or about ½ teaspoon dried

½ to 1 shallot, minced

Salt, ground white pepper, and
fresh lemon juice to taste

Combine all the ingredients in a food processor fitted with the metal blade, in a blender, or in a mixing bowl. Taste and adjust the seasonings.

FAST: Can prepare up to 1 week in advance and refrigerate, or freeze for up to 3 months.

FLASHY: As a dunk for skewers of hot or cold shrimp, lamb, chicken, and/or pork, raw or cold blanched vegetables, especially cold cooked asparagus. Garnished with your choice of fresh or dried tarragon, lemon zest, and/or any nontoxic flowers.

FABULOUS: As an entree sauce with cooked seafood, poultry, veal, or pork.

CAPER SAUCE

Yield: about 2¼ cups

¼ to ½ cup capers, drained and
rinsed

2 cups extra virgin olive oil

½ cup mayonnaise, homemade
(page 13) or purchased, or sour
cream

¼ cup white wine or rice wine
vinegar

Fresh lemon juice to taste

4 to 6 tablespoons minced fresh dill

1 to 2 cloves garlic, minced

Salt and ground white pepper to taste

Combine all the ingredients in a food processor fitted with the metal blade, in a blender, or in a mixing bowl. Taste and adjust the seasonings.

FAST: Can prepare up to 1 week in advance and refrigerate.

FLASHY: Served cold or warm as a dunk for skewers of hot or cold shrimp, lamb, chicken, and/or pork, raw or cold blanched vegetables, especially with cold cooked asparagus. To warm, place in a saucepan over medium-low heat for 5 to 10 minutes, stirring frequently. Garnished with fresh dill and/or any nontoxic flower.

FABULOUS: As an entree sauce on poached salmon, seafood, poultry, lamb, and/or as a sauce for cooked vegetables.

DILL CREAM SAUCE

Another refreshing prelude to a rich meal.

Yield: about 2 cups

¼ cup minced fresh dill or 2 tablespoons dried	1 teaspoon Dijon mustard
4½ teaspoons red wine vinegar	½ cup sour cream
1 hard-boiled egg yolk	Salt and ground white pepper to taste
1 teaspoon sugar	Fresh lemon juice to taste, optional

Combine all the ingredients in a food processor fitted with the metal blade, in a blender, or in a mixing bowl. Taste and adjust the seasonings.

FAST: Can prepare up to 4 days in advance and refrigerate.

FLASHY: As a dunk for hot or cold pieces of cooked seafood, poultry, or lamb. With raw or cooked vegetables. Garnished with fresh dill and/or any nontoxic flower.

FABULOUS: As an entree sauce for seafood, fish, lamb, poultry, or as a sauce for cooked vegetables. As a dunk for boiled baby red potatoes or on baked potatoes.

CURRY SAUCE

A bit of Indian mystique.

Yield: about 2¼ cups

½ cup mayonnaise, homemade
(page 13) or purchased

½ cup sour cream or plain yogurt

1½ teaspoons curry powder or to
taste

¼ teaspoon ground ginger or to
taste

¼ cup minced cilantro (fresh
coriander) or to taste

Fresh lemon juice to taste

Combine all the ingredients in a food processor fitted with the metal blade, in a blender, or in a mixing bowl. Taste and adjust the seasonings.

FAST: Can prepare up to 1 week in advance and refrigerate.

FLASHY: As a dunk for Pita Chips (page 274), raw cauliflower, and/or seafood. Garnished with sprigs of cilantro and/or any nontoxic flower.

FABULOUS: As an entree sauce on lamb, fish, poultry, or on cooked vegetables. As a dressing on seafood, pasta, rice, or bean salad.

DIJON SAUCE

So simple, but so good!

Yield: about 1 cup

1 cup mayonnaise, homemade (page
13) or purchased

1 tablespoon Dijon mustard or to
taste

¼ cup sour cream

Fresh lemon or lime juice to taste

Combine all the ingredients in a food processor fitted with the metal blade, in a blender, or in a mixing bowl. Taste and adjust the seasonings.

FAST: Can prepare up to 1 week in advance and refrigerate.

FLASHY: As a dunk for cooked sausages, chicken, or any raw or blanched vegetable. Garnished with any nontoxic flower and/or fresh parsley sprigs, dill sprigs, and/or lemon zest.

FABULOUS: With soy sauce instead of mustard to create a soy dunk. With minced green onions (scallions), minced fresh ginger, and/or minced parsley to taste added to either version.

PICKLED MANGO SAUCE

This will work your entire palate—sweet, tart, salty,
spicy—and is delicious.

Yield: about 1½ cups

1 cup plain yogurt or sour cream

2 to 4 tablespoons pickled mango
(page 18), depending on how zesty
you want it

1. Combine all the ingredients in a food processor fitted with the metal blade, in a blender, or in a mixing bowl.
2. Taste and add more pickled mango if bland. If it is too zesty, add more yogurt or sour cream.

FAST: Can prepare up to 1 week in advance and refrigerate.

FLASHY: As a dunk for raw or blanched vegetables, Barbecued Pork and Red Cabbage Potstickers (page 254), Curried Carrot Potstickers (page 257), or Chinese Skewered Bites (page 143). Garnished with any nontoxic flower and/or cilantro sprigs.

FABULOUS: As a dressing for spinach, pasta, rice, or potato salad. As an entree sauce for pork, poultry, lamb, and/or seafood.

COLD MADEIRA BLUE CHEESE SAUCE

Wicked on chicken wings.

Yield: about 2½ cups

1 ounce blue cheese or to taste

¼ cup Madeira

1 cup mayonnaise, homemade (page 13) or purchased

1 cup sour cream

1 to 2 cloves garlic

1 to 2 shallots

Salt and ground white pepper to taste

Dash of hot pepper sauce

Dash of Worcestershire sauce

Zest of 2 lemons, finely grated

1. Combine all the ingredients, except for the lemon zest, in a food processor fitted with the metal blade, in a blender, or in a mixing bowl. Process until smooth.
2. Add the zest and process or blend briefly, so as not to destroy all the texture. Taste and adjust the seasonings.

FAST: Can prepare up to 5 days in advance and refrigerate, or freeze up to 3 months.

FLASHY: Served as a dunk for vegetables, cooked hot or cold beef, seafood, turkey, or chicken wings. Garnished with any nontoxic flower, fresh parsley sprigs and/or strips of lemon zest.

FABULOUS: In hollowed-out boiled baby red potatoes, cherry tomatoes, or raw mushroom caps. As an entree sauce with grilled steaks or roast beef. With pink or green peppercorns added.

ANCHOVY BASIL MAYONNAISE

Basil is my favorite summer flavor.

Yield: about 1 cup

2 to 6 cloves garlic, peeled and smashed

1 large egg

1 teaspoon anchovy paste or minced anchovy fillets or to taste

2 to 4 tablespoons minced fresh parsley

1 tablespoon fresh lemon juice or to taste

¼ cup loosely packed minced fresh basil or to taste

½ cup extra virgin olive oil

½ cup peanut oil

Ground white pepper to taste

1. Place the garlic in a saucepan with salted water to cover and bring to a boil. Change the water and repeat. Drain, using a fine-mesh strainer.
2. Combine the garlic with the next 5 ingredients in a food processor fitted with the metal blade, in a blender, or in a mixing bowl using a whisk or electric mixer.
3. Slowly process in the oils through the feed tube while machine is running or drizzle in while mixing and continue mixing until it has a medium-thick consistency. Taste and adjust the seasonings.

FAST: Can prepare up to 5 days in advance and refrigerate.

FLASHY: As a dunk for blanched or raw vegetables, cold seafood, skewers of grilled poultry, pork, lamb, or beef. Garnished with fresh basil and/or any nontoxic flower.

FABULOUS: As an entree sauce for poultry, seafood, or fish.

TARRAGON MAYONNAISE SAUCE

*Fantastic flavors! I came up with this on a hot summer
day to go with skewers
of grilled lamb.*

Yield: about 1 cup

1 cup mayonnaise, homemade (page
  13) or purchased, or more to taste

2 tablespoons tarragon wine vinegar
  or more to taste

4 ounces softened cream cheese,
  optional

1 tablespoon minced fresh tarragon
  or to taste

Combine all the ingredients in a food processor fitted with the metal blade, in a blender, or in a mixing bowl using an electric mixer until smooth. Taste and adjust the seasonings.

FAST: Can prepare up to 7 days in advance and refrigerate.

FLASHY: As a dunk for blanched or raw vegetables, fish, lamb, pork, seafood, or poultry. Garnished with freshly ground black pepper and extra minced fresh tarragon.

FABULOUS: With all or half low-fat plain yogurt instead of the mayonnaise to reduce the calorie count.

WATERCRESS MAYONNAISE

Astringent and refreshing.

Yield: about 1½ cups

1 cup mayonnaise, homemade (page
  13) or purchased

½ to 1 cup loosely packed minced
  watercress leaves

Salt, ground white pepper, and fresh
  lemon juice to taste

½ to 1 shallot, optional

Combine all the ingredients in a food processor fitted with the metal blade, in a blender, or in a mixing bowl. Taste and adjust the seasonings.

FAST: Can prepare up to 3 days in advance and refrigerate.

FLASHY: As a dunk for hot or cold chicken, seafood, or veggies. Garnished with watercress leaves and/or any nontoxic flower.

FABULOUS: With part or all low-fat yogurt in place of the mayonnaise to reduce the fat and calories. As an entree sauce for fish, vegetables, chicken, pork, and/or seafood. With 2 to 4 tablespoons of your favorite vinegar added and used as a salad dressing for any kind of salad.

CHUTNEY MAYONNAISE

1 cup mayonnaise, homemade (page
   13) or purchased
2 tablespoons chutney homemade
   (see Index) or purchased, or to taste

Ground white pepper and fresh lemon
   or lime juice to taste
2 tablespoons minced fresh mint
   leaves

Combine all the ingredients in a food processor fitted with the metal blade, in a blender, or in a mixing bowl. Taste and adjust the seasonings.

FAST: Can prepare up to 5 days in advance and refrigerate.

FLASHY: As a dunk for cold chicken, seafood, or veggies. As a cold sauce for fish, vegetables, chicken, pork, and/or seafood. Garnished with fresh mint leaves and/or any nontoxic flower.

FABULOUS: With part or all low-fat plain yogurt in place of the mayonnaise to reduce the fat and calories. With 2 to 4 tablespoons of your favorite vinegar added and used as a salad dressing for any kind of salad.

ASIAN MAYONNAISE

Yield: about 1 ¼ cups

1 cup mayonnaise, homemade (page
   13) or purchased
2 tablespoons soy sauce or to taste
1 tablespoon minced fresh or pickled
   ginger (pages 17, 18)
1 to 2 green onions (scallions), white
   and green parts, minced

2 to 4 tablespoons minced cilantro
   (fresh coriander), optional
1 tablespoon rice wine vinegar,
   optional

Combine all the ingredients in a food processor fitted with the metal blade, in a blender, or in a mixing bowl. Taste and adjust the seasonings.

FAST: Can prepare up to 5 days in advance and refrigerate.

FLASHY: As a dunk for cold chicken, seafood, or veggies. As a cold sauce for fish, vegetables, chicken, pork, and/or seafood. Garnished with cilantro sprigs, minced green onions, and/or any nontoxic flower.

FABULOUS: With part or all low-fat plain yogurt in place of the mayonnaise to reduce the fat and calories. With 2 to 4 tablespoons of your favorite vinegar added and used as a salad dressing for any kind of salad.

DILL AND CHIVE MAYONNAISE

Yield: about 1½ cups

1 cup mayonnaise, homemade (page 13) or purchased

1 bunch fresh dill, stems removed and minced

¼ cup minced fresh chives or to taste

1 to 2 cloves garlic, minced

½ to 1 shallot, minced

Ground white pepper to taste

Combine all the ingredients in a food processor fitted with the metal blade, in a blender, or in a mixing bowl. Taste and adjust the seasonings.

FAST: Can prepare up to 5 days in advance and refrigerate.

FLASHY: As a dunk for cold chicken, seafood, or veggies. As a cold sauce for fish, vegetables, chicken, pork, and/or seafood. Garnished with fresh dill sprigs, minced chives, and/or chive blossoms.

FABULOUS: With part or all low-fat plain yogurt in place of the mayonnaise to reduce the fat and calories. With 2 to 4 tablespoons of your favorite vinegar added and used as a dressing for any kind of salad.

DOUBLE PEPPER MAYONNAISE SAUCE

Yield: about 1½ cups

3 to 6 dried pasilla chiles, rehydrated (page 20), stemmed, and seeded

2 red bell peppers, roasted, skinned, and seeded (page 26)

1 cup mayonnaise, homemade (page 13) or purchased

Fresh lemon or lime juice to taste

½ cup garlic cloves, roasted (page 26), optional

Combine all the ingredients in a food processor fitted with the metal blade, in a blender, or in a mixing bowl. Taste and adjust the seasonings.

FAST: Can prepare up to 5 days in advance and refrigerate.

FLASHY: As a dunk for cold chicken, seafood, or veggies. As a cold sauce for fish, vegetables, chicken, pork, and/or seafood. Garnished with minced dried pasilla chiles, roasted red peppers, cloves of roasted garlic, and/or any nontoxic flower.

FABULOUS: With part or all low-fat plain yogurt in place of the mayonnaise to reduce the fat and calories. With 2 to 4 tablespoons of your favorite vinegar added and used as a dressing for any kind of salad. With any kind of fresh or dried chile.

COLD CUCUMBER SAUCE

A refreshing choice during a heat wave.

Yield: about 3 cups

1 medium-size to large cucumber, peeled, seeded, and minced

2 cups sour cream or plain yogurt

1 to 2 tablespoons capers, rinsed and drained

¼ to ½ cup minced green onions (scallions), white and green parts

2 tablespoons minced fresh dill or ½ teaspoon dried

Salt, ground white pepper, and fresh lemon juice to taste

1. Combine all the ingredients in a food processor fitted with the metal blade, in a blender, or in a mixing bowl. Taste and adjust the seasonings.
2. Chill for at least 30 minutes before serving.

FAST: Can prepare up to 3 days in advance and refrigerate.

FLASHY: As a dunk for Pita Chips (page 274), Bagel Chips (page 272), or pumpernickel squares. Garnished with minced fresh dill, capers, and/or any nontoxic flower.

FABULOUS: As an entree sauce for seafood, lamb, or poultry, or to dress a potato salad.

COLD PAPAYA CREAM SAUCE

A great choice for summer entertaining.

Yield: about 3 cups

2 cups peeled, seeded, and minced papaya (page 22)

1 cup sour cream

1 tablespoon fresh lime juice

¼ teaspoon salt

1 teaspoon sugar

1 tablespoon Dijon mustard or to taste

2 cloves garlic, pureed (page 25), or to taste

Ground white pepper to taste

Chopped fresh, pickled (page 18), or crystallized ginger (page 21) to taste

Combine all the ingredients in a food processor fitted with the metal blade, in a blender, or in a mixing bowl. Taste and adjust the seasonings.

FAST: Can prepare up to 2 days in advance and refrigerate.

FLASHY: As a dunk for barbecued or broiled pieces of pork, seafood, or lamb. Garnished with toasted sesame seeds (page 27) and/or any nontoxic flower.

FABULOUS: As a sandwich spread on pita, pumpernickel, or sourdough bread.

BACON AND TOMATO DUNK

Here's one for all you BLT fans!

Yield: about 3 cups

10 slices bacon, cooked until crisp,
   drained on paper towels, and
   cooled
3 large, ripe tomatoes, peeled,
   seeded, and finely chopped
1 cup mayonnaise, homemade (page
   13) or purchased

1 tablespoon Dijon mustard
¼ cup minced green onions
   (scallions), white and green parts
¼ cup minced fresh parsley
Dash of hot pepper sauce

Combine all the ingredients in a food processor fitted with the metal blade, in a blender, or in a mixing bowl, taking care to preserve some of the texture. Taste and adjust the seasonings.

FAST: Can prepare up to 4 days in advance and refrigerate.

FLASHY: As a dunk for Pita Chips (page 274), chips, crackers, or Garlic Crouton Rounds (page 270). Garnish with minced green onions, parsley, chopped tomatoes, and/or crumbled bacon.

FABULOUS: With chopped avocado added, and/or used to stuff into cold raw mushrooms, Croustades (page 279), or cold hollowed-out boiled baby potatoes. Also, to dress a rice, bean, or pasta salad.

CAVIAR SAUCE

Divine decadence in minutes.

Yield: about 1½ cups

3 ounces caviar

1 cup sour cream or plain yogurt

2 to 3 large eggs, hard-boiled
(page 24) and chopped

Zest of 1 lemon, finely grated

2 to 4 green onions (scallions), white
and green parts, minced

Fresh lemon juice to taste

Combine all the ingredients in a food processor fitted with the metal blade, in a blender, or in a mixing bowl. Process until smooth, taste and adjust the seasonings.

FAST: Can prepare up to 3 days in advance and refrigerate.

FLASHY: As a dunk for cold boiled baby potatoes, pumpernickel squares, thinly sliced baguettes, any Melba/Crostini (pages 263–273), or Bagel Chips (page 272). As a filling for cherry tomatoes, Croustades (page 279), and/or Belgian endive. Garnished with caviar, minced lemon zest, chopped egg, and/or minced green onions.

FABULOUS: As a dressing for pasta salad, or tossed into hot pasta and served as an appetizer course.

HORSERADISH SAUCE

Yield: about 1¼ cups

1 cup sour cream or plain yogurt

3 tablespoons prepared horseradish or
to taste

Salt, ground white pepper, and
fresh lemon juice to taste

Combine all the ingredients in a mixing bowl or a food processor fitted with the metal blade. Taste and adjust the seasonings.

FAST: Can prepare up to 5 days in advance and refrigerate.

FLASHY: As a dunk for meat, seafood, fish, or poultry, and/or meatballs, shrimp, and fried or boiled potatoes. Garnished with any nontoxic flower and/or minced fresh parsley.

FABULOUS: As an accompaniment to roast beef, ham, or turkey entrees.

COLD SEAFOOD SAUCE

Light and elegant.

Yield: about 3 cups

8 ounces cooked seafood (crabmeat, shrimp, or lobster), minced (page 24)

8 ounces cream cheese, softened

½ cup sour cream

¼ cup mayonnaise, homemade (page 13) or purchased

1 to 2 tablespoons minced fresh dill or 1 teaspoon dried or to taste

1 teaspoon Dijon mustard or to taste

¼ cup minced fresh parsley

¼ cup minced green onions (scallions), white and green parts

Salt, ground white pepper, and fresh lemon juice to taste

Combine all the ingredients in a food processor fitted with the metal blade, in a blender, or in a mixing bowl with an electric mixer. Taste and adjust the seasonings.

FAST: Can prepare up to 2 days in advance and refrigerate.

FLASHY: As a dunk for assorted breads, crackers, celery, endive or romaine leaves, pea pods, or any Melba/Crostini (pages 263–273). Garnished with minced fresh dill, parsley, and/or any nontoxic flower.

FABULOUS: With any seafood or fish, ranging from tuna to lobster, or as a dressing for cold pasta or rice salad. As a filling for crepes, omelets, or pita bread, or on top of English muffins.

COLD SMOKED SALMON SAUCE

The Rolls-Royce of dunks.

Yield: about 3 cups

8 ounces smoked salmon, minced

8 ounces cream cheese, softened

½ cup sour cream or plain yogurt

¼ cup mayonnaise, homemade (page 13) or purchased

1 to 2 tablespoons minced fresh dill or about ½ teaspoon dried

¼ cup minced fresh parsley

¼ cup minced green onions (scallions), white and green parts

Salt, ground white pepper, and fresh lemon juice to taste

Combine all the ingredients in a food processor fitted with the metal blade, in a blender, or in a mixing bowl with an electric mixer. Taste and adjust the seasonings.

FAST: Can prepare for up to 2 days in advance and refrigerate.

FLASHY: As a dunk for Bagel Chips (page 272), pumpernickel squares, and/or thinly sliced cucumber. Garnished with minced fresh dill, parsley, smoked salmon, and/or any nontoxic flower.

FABULOUS: As a dressing for pasta, bean, or rice salads. As a filling for crepes or omelets.

WALNUT PESTO SAUCE

A real Italian treat for summer, full of gusto!

Yield: about 5 cups

1 cup walnuts, toasted (page 27)

2 cups packed fresh basil leaves

½ cup packed minced fresh parsley

½ to 1 cup extra virgin olive oil

1 cup sour cream or plain yogurt

2 cloves garlic or to taste

½ cup freshly grated Parmesan

Salt and ground white pepper to taste

Combine all the ingredients in a food processor fitted with the metal blade or in a blender. Process until the desired texture is reached. Taste and adjust the seasonings.

FAST: Can prepare up to 4 days in advance and refrigerate, or freeze for up to 3 days.

FLASHY: As a dunk for Melba/Crostini (pages 263–273), Pita Chips (page 274), Garlic Crouton Rounds (page 270), or Bagel Chips (page 272). Garnished with fresh basil leaves and/or any nontoxic flower.

FABULOUS: With fish, seafood, or poultry. For a basic pesto, simply eliminate the sour cream. Add mayonnaise to the basic pesto to create a pesto mayonnaise sauce and serve with artichokes, grilled chicken, seafood, pork, or lamb.

MIDDLE-EASTERN VEGETABLE DUNK

Yield: about 3 cups

1 large, ripe tomato, peeled, seeded, and chopped

1 medium-size to large cucumber, peeled, seeded, and chopped

2 to 4 green onions (scallions), white and green parts, minced

¼ cup minced cilantro (fresh coriander)

¼ cup minced fresh parsley

1 to 2 cloves garlic, minced

1 cup sour cream or plain yogurt

Salt, ground white pepper, and fresh lemon or lime juice to taste

Combine all the ingredients in a bowl and refrigerate for at least 1 hour or overnight. Taste and adjust the seasonings.

FAST: Can prepare up to 5 days in advance and refrigerate.

FLASHY: As a dunk for Pita Chips (page 274) or Garlic Crouton Rounds (page 270). Garnished with minced green onions, cilantro, parsley, and/or any nontoxic flower.

FABULOUS: Tossed into pasta, bulgur (page 20), or rice, and served cold. Seasoned with fresh mint leaves.

MIDDLE-EASTERN YOGURT EGGPLANT SAUCE

Yield: about 1½ cups

1 cup minced eggplant

1 teaspoon salt

2 tablespoons extra virgin olive oil

1 cup plain yogurt

2 to 4 green onions (scallions), white and green parts, minced

½ cup minced cilantro (fresh coriander)

1 to 2 cloves garlic, minced

½ teaspoon ground cumin or to taste

¼ cup sesame seeds, toasted (page 27)

Salt, ground white pepper, and fresh lemon or lime juice to taste

1. Place the eggplant in a colander with the salt and let drain for 30 minutes. Rinse and dry with paper towels.

2. Place the eggplant in a mixing bowl and toss with the olive oil.

3. Transfer to an aluminum foil-lined baking sheet. Cook in a preheated 350° to 400°F oven for 15 to 25 minutes, until tender.
4. Transfer the eggplant to a medium-size bowl and add the remaining ingredients and combine thoroughly. Refrigerate until cool. Taste and adjust the seasonings.

FAST: Can prepare up to 5 days in advance and refrigerate.

FLASHY: As a dunk for meatballs, Pita Chips (page 274), or Eastern-style Garbanzo Balls (page 172). Garnished with minced green onions, cilantro, parsley, and/or any nontoxic flower.

FABULOUS: With minced marinated artichoke hearts or Roasted and Marinated Peppers (page 88) mixed in.

OLIVE-OIL BASED DUNKS

ROASTED RED PEPPER SAUCE

This is a favorite of mine. When I prepared it on national television, I splashed it all over the host, Gary Collins.

Yield: 2 to 3 cups

4 large red bell peppers, roasted, seeded, and peeled (page 26)

2 cloves garlic or to taste

1 to 2 cups extra virgin olive oil

Salt, ground white pepper, and fresh lemon or lime juice to taste

1. Combine all the ingredients in a food processor fitted with the metal blade or in a blender and process until smooth.
2. Taste and adjust the seasonings.

FAST: Can prepare up to 4 days in advance and refrigerate, or freeze for up to 6 months.

FLASHY: As a dunk for anything from boiled potatoes to shrimp. Garnished with any nontoxic flower and minced fresh parsley.

FABULOUS: With an equal amount of heavy cream and/or chicken broth instead of the oil and served hot.

TAPANADE SAUCE

*My version of the classic Provençal olive, caper, and
anchovy spread or filling. I have added
tuna and marinated artichoke hearts
along with a few other flavorings.*

Yield: about 3 cups

7½ ounces canned tuna, drained
and flaked

½ cup pitted black olives,
drained, rinsed, and minced

½ cup pitted calamata olives,
drained, rinsed, and minced

2 to 4 tablespoons minced green
onions (scallions), white and
green parts

1 tablespoon green peppercorns or
to taste, minced

3 tablespoons capers, drained,
rinsed, and minced

3 cloves garlic, minced

6 tablespoons fresh lime juice or to
taste

½ teaspoon freshly ground black
pepper

½ cup packed minced fresh Italian
(flatleaf) parsley

2 to 3 tablespoons brandy

1 cup extra virgin olive oil

One 6-ounce jar marinated artichoke
hearts, drained and minced

1. Combine all the ingredients, except the olive oil and artichoke hearts, in a food
processor fitted with the metal blade, in a blender, or in a mixing bowl with an
electric mixer and process until it's a thick paste.
2. Slowly add the olive oil through the feed tube while the machine is running, or mix
in thoroughly.
3. Add the artichoke hearts and process using several quick on-and-off motions, so as
not to destroy their texture, or stir in by hand.

FAST: Can prepare up to 3 days in advance and refrigerate, or freeze for up to 1 month.

FLASHY: As a dunk with any raw or cooked vegetable, or with crackers, any Melba/Crostini
(pages 263–273), Bagel Chips (page 272), or Pita Chips (page 274). Garnished with
minced fresh parsley and/or any nontoxic flower.

FABULOUS: With shrimp, crab, or salmon instead of tuna. With any kind of olive.

ZUCCHINI BASIL SAUCE

A terrific solution for that age-old problem of zucchini glut.

Yield: about 4 cups

2 cups minced zucchini, blanched for about 5 minutes (page 23), drained, and squeezed dry

1 cup extra virgin olive oil

¼ cup freshly grated Parmesan

¼ cup minced green onions (scallions), white and green parts

1 to 2 cloves garlic, minced

1 cup packed fresh basil leaves

¼ cup minced fresh parsley

¼ cup pine nuts, toasted (page 27) and chopped

Salt and ground white pepper to taste

Combine all the ingredients in a food processor fitted with the metal blade, in a blender, or in a mixing bowl with an electric mixer and process until smooth. Taste and adjust the seasonings.

FAST: Can prepare up to 3 days in advance and refrigerate.

FLASHY: As a dunk for any Melba/Crostini (pages 263–273), thinly sliced baguettes, crackers, or vegetables. Garnished with fresh basil leaves and/or any nontoxic flower.

FABULOUS: As an entree sauce on sautéed chicken breasts, fish, or on rice or pasta.

MARINATED ARTICHOKE AND ROASTED RED PEPPER PESTO

Summer magic!

Yield: 2 cups

½ cup marinated artichoke hearts, drained and coarsely chopped

½ cup coarsely chopped roasted red bell peppers (page 26)

¼ to ½ cup extra virgin olive oil

⅓ cup capers, drained, rinsed and coarsely chopped

2 to 4 cloves garlic, coarsely chopped

¼ cup packed, minced fresh Italian (flatleaf) parsley

Fresh lemon juice, salt, and freshly ground black pepper to taste

Fast & Fabulous
Hors D'Oeuvres

Combine all the ingredients in a food processor fitted with the metal blade with several quick on-and-off motions so as not to destroy the texture, or combine in a bowl. Taste and adjust the seasonings.

FAST: Can prepare up to 5 days in advance and refrigerate, or freeze for up to 6 months.

FLASHY: As a spread with crackers, thinly sliced baguettes, and/or any Melba/Crostini (pages 263–273). Garnished with minced fresh Italian parsley and/or any nontoxic flower.

FABULOUS: Mixed into 2 to 3 cups pureed white, pink, or black beans to create a fabulous Mediterranean Bean Spread. Served hot, cold, or at room temperature; on pasta; as a seasoning agent in sauces and soups; or used as a sauce for meat, fish, seafood, poultry, lamb, etc.

PESTO

This is one of my favorite summer flavors. Make extra,
store it in the freezer, and enjoy it
all year long.

Yield: about 3 cups

2 cups packed fresh basil leaves	⅓ cup walnuts, toasted (page 27), or
½ cup packed minced fresh parsley	to taste
2 to 4 cloves garlic	Salt and ground white pepper to
½ cup grated Romano or to taste	taste
½ cup extra virgin olive oil or to taste	

1. Combine the first 5 ingredients in a food processor fitted with the metal blade or in a blender and process until smooth.
2. Process in the walnuts using quick on-and-off motions, so as not to destroy the texture, or blend briefly.
3. Taste and adjust the seasonings.

FAST: Can prepare up to 4 days in advance and refrigerate, or freeze for up to 6 months.

FLASHY: Served at room temperature in a bowl, and garnished with fresh basil leaves and/or any nontoxic flower. As a spread with any Melba/Crostini (pages 263–273) or thinly sliced baguette.

FABULOUS: On hot pasta, in sauces, soups, or stews. For an hors d'oeuvre, spread on thinly sliced baguettes topped with brie or chèvre. With pine nuts, pecans, pistachios, or pumpkin seeds instead of walnuts.

FURTHER: Store leftovers in the freezer and use it as a general seasoning.

CHILE AND
SUN-DRIED TOMATO PESTO

Great summer flavors!

Yield: about 1¾ cups

2   dried red Anaheim chiles,
    rehydrated (page 20), stemmed
    and seeded

3   dried pasilla chiles, rehydrated
    (page 20), stemmed and seeded

½   cup sun-dried tomatoes, softened
    and chopped (page 22)

3   green onions (scallions), white and
    green parts, chopped

1   bunch cilantro (fresh coriander),
    stemmed and chopped

½   cup sour cream or plain yogurt

Salt, ground white pepper, and fresh
    lemon or lime juice to taste

½   cup extra virgin olive oil

1. Place all the ingredients, except the olive oil, in a food processor fitted with a metal
   blade or in a blender and process thoroughly.
2. Slowly add the olive oil through the feed tube while the machine is running and
   process to a thick consistency.

FAST: Can prepare up to 2 days in advance and refrigerate.

FLASHY: As a spread with any Melba/Crostini (pages 263–273) or thinly sliced baguette.
Garnished with a dried pasilla chile, minced cilantro, and/or any nontoxic flower.

FABULOUS: With fresh basil, thyme, or tarragon to taste instead of the cilantro. As an
entree sauce with grilled or roasted beef, pork, chicken, fish, or in soups.

Fast & Fabulous
Hors D'Oeuvres

SUN-DRIED TOMATO
AND ROASTED GARLIC PESTO

A guaranteed hit!

Yield: about 5 cups

2 cups sun-dried tomatoes, softened and minced (page 23)

1 to 2 heads garlic, roasted (page 27)

3 to 6 dried pasilla chiles, rehydrated (page 20), stemmed, seeded, and minced

4 green onions (scallions), white and green parts, minced

¼ cup packed minced fresh parsley

¼ cup pine nuts, toasted (page 27)

One 6-ounce jar marinated artichokes, drained and minced

1 cup extra virgin olive oil

¾ cup crumbled feta cheese

Rosemary leaves, fresh or dried, to taste

Freshly ground black pepper to taste

Hot pepper sauce and fresh lemon or lime juice to taste

Combine all ingredients in a mixing bowl. Taste and adjust the seasonings.

FAST: Can prepare up to 5 days in advance and refrigerate, or freeze up to 6 months.

FLASHY: Served with Garlic Crouton Rounds (page 270) or any Melba/Crostini (pages 263–273). Garnished with crumbled feta, toasted pine nuts, fresh rosemary leaves, minced green onions, parsley, and/or any nontoxic flower.

FABULOUS: With calamata olives and/or any fresh or dried chile instead of pasilla chiles. On beans, rice, or pasta. As a pizza topping or as an omelet filling. As a topping for grilled fish, lamb, or beef. Smothered over jack, feta, teleme, brie, Camembert, muenster, and/or chevre and heated in a preheated 350°F oven for 15 to 25 minutes. With pesto (page 47) mixed in.

ROASTED EGGPLANT WALNUT PESTO

Yield: about 3 cups

One 1-pound eggplant, cubed
1 large red onion, sliced or chopped
¼ cup extra virgin olive oil
1 to 2 large, ripe tomatoes, seeded and cut up
¼ to ½ cup packed minced fresh parsley

½ cup chopped walnuts, toasted (page 27)
2 to 4 tablespoons fresh lemon juice or red or white wine vinegar
Salt and freshly ground black pepper

1. Preheat the oven to 425°F.
2. In a roasting or baking pan, combine the eggplant, onion, and olive oil. Roast in the oven until tender, about 45 minutes.
3. Transfer this mixture to a food processor fitted with the metal blade and puree.
4. Add the remaining ingredients and combine, using several quick on-and-off motions, so as not to destroy the texture. Taste and adjust the seasonings.

FAST: Can prepare up to 3 days in advance and refrigerate, or freeze for up to 1 month.

FLASHY: Served in a crock, pâté terrine, or serving bowl. Garnished with minced fresh parsley, basil leaves, and/or any nontoxic flower.

FABULOUS: Seasoned with fresh basil or oregano, capers, and/or minced marinated artichoke hearts.

CILANTRO PESTO

Yield: about 1½ cups

3 bunches cilantro (fresh coriander), stemmed
½ cup almonds, toasted (page 27)
½ to 1 cup extra virgin olive oil
½ to 1 fresh Anaheim chile (page 20), seeded and deveined (or use several canned, seeded, and deveined chiles)

2 to 4 cloves garlic
Salt to taste
1 tablespoon red wine vinegar or fresh lemon or lime juice to taste

Combine all the ingredients in a food processor fitted with the metal blade or in a blender and process to form a thick paste. Taste and adjust the seasonings.

FAST: Can prepare up to 2 days in advance and refrigerate.

FLASHY: As a spread with any Melba/Crostini (pages 263–273) or a thinly sliced baguette. Garnished with chopped toasted almonds, cilantro, and/or any nontoxic flower.

FABULOUS: With fresh basil, thyme, or tarragon to taste instead of the cilantro. As an entree sauce with grilled or roasted beef, pork, chicken, fish, or with soups.

BASIL PEPPER CHUTNEY

Yield: about 1¼ cups

1 large red bell pepper, cored and
   seeded

¼ cup extra virgin olive oil

½ cup minced red onion

¼ cup packed fresh basil leaves

¼ to ½ red jalapeño pepper (page
   20), seeded, deveined, and
   minced

Salt and fresh lemon or lime juice to
   taste

Combine all the ingredients in a food processor fitted with the metal blade or in a blender using several quick on-and-off motions to keep a chunky texture.

FAST: Can prepare up to 3 days in advance and refrigerate, or freeze for up to 3 months.

FLASHY: Served with any roasted, grilled, or broiled beef, poultry, seafood, pork, and/or lamb.

FABULOUS: Tossed into hot or cold pasta, rice, beans, and/or potato dishes. As a spread combined with 4 to 8 ounces chèvre or cream cheese. Used as a seasoning ingredient in soups, sauces, marinades, or in vegetable dishes.

GINGER PEACH CHUTNEY

Yield: about 1¼ cups

2 large, ripe peaches, coarsely
   chopped

2 tablespoons orange-flavored liqueur

Salt and fresh lime juice to taste

1 to 2 tablespoons minced or pureed
   fresh ginger

2 to 4 tablespoons minced or
   chopped fresh mint leaves

⅛ to ¼ fresh red jalapeño pepper
   (page 20), seeded, deveined, and
   minced

¼ cup raspberry vinegar

Combine all the ingredients in a mixing bowl. Let it sit for at least 1 hour before serving.

FAST: Can prepare up to 3 days in advance and refrigerate, or freeze for up to 3 months.

FLASHY: Served with any roasted, grilled, or broiled beef, poultry, seafood, pork, and/or lamb.

FABULOUS: Tossed into hot or cold pasta, rice, beans, and/or potato dishes. As a spread combined with 4 to 8 ounces chèvre or cream cheese. Used as a seasoning ingredient in soups, sauces, marinades, or in vegetable dishes.

TROPICAL CHUTNEY

Yield: about 4 cups

1   medium-size to large mango
    (page 21), peeled, seeded, and
    coarsely chopped
1   pint-size basket strawberries,
    hulled and coarsely chopped
1   bunch cilantro (fresh coriander),
    stemmed and minced

½   large red onion, minced
¼   cup raspberry vinegar
1   to 2 tablespoon olive oil, optional
Freshly ground black pepper to
    taste

Combine all the ingredients in a mixing bowl and let sit for at least 1 hour before serving.

FAST: Can prepare up to 3 days in advance and refrigerate, or freeze for up to 6 months.

FLASHY: Served hot or cold with roasted, grilled, or broiled beef, poultry, seafood, pork, and/or lamb.

FABULOUS: With fresh basil or dill instead of cilantro. With chopped fresh chiles added. With 1 cup sour cream or low-fat plain yogurt mixed in and served as a dunk. Mixed into pasta, beans, rice, spinach, potato, and/or rice salads.

FIRE AND ICE VINEGAR

A delightful flavored vinegar with both hot and cool seasonings.

Yield: 4 cups

4 cups white wine vinegar

½ to 1 bunch fresh mint, stemmed and coarsely chopped

½ to 1 fresh jalapeño pepper (page 20), deveined, seeded, and minced

Zest of 2 lemons, grated, or fresh lemon grass, chopped

One 2-inch piece fresh ginger, chopped

1. Combine all the ingredients in a covered glass or plastic jar. Let sit at room temperature for at least 4 days.
2. Strain the vinegar through a fine mesh strainer and store in a covered jar or wine bottle.

FAST: Can prepare up to 6 months in advance and store in a cool cupboard.

FLASHY: Used any way you would use any other vinegar.

FABULOUS: Prepared with any herb instead of the mint.

Tarragon Caper Vinaigrette

Yield: about 2¼ cups

½ cup tarragon wine vinegar

¼ cup capers, drained, rinsed, and minced

1¼ cups grapeseed oil or your favorite oil

¼ cup fresh lemon juice

Salt, ground white pepper, and fresh or dried tarragon to taste

1. Combine all the ingredients in a food processor fitted with the metal blade or in a blender and process, or whisk together in a bowl. Taste and adjust the seasonings.
2. Store in the refrigerator in a tightly covered jar. Stir or shake before using.

FAST: Can prepare up to 2 weeks in advance and refrigerate, or freeze for up to 3 months.

FLASHY: As a dunk for raw vegetables, Melba/Crostini (pages 263–273), or thinly sliced baguettes. Garnished by floating fresh tarragon, parsley, and/or any nontoxic flower on top.

FABULOUS: As a marinade or sauce for vegetables, seafood, beef, lamb, poultry, and/or pork. On any salad.

Tarragon Sherry Vinaigrette

If I were stranded on a desert island, this is the dressing I would want! What a fantasy!

Yield: about 2⅔ cups

1 to 2 tablespoons minced fresh tarragon or 1 to 2 teaspoons dried

6 cornichons, finely minced

2 cups extra virgin olive oil

⅓ cup fresh lemon juice

⅓ cup sherry wine vinegar

1 tablespoon Dijon mustard

Salt and freshly ground black pepper to taste

1. Combine all the ingredients in a food processor fitted with the metal blade or in a blender and process, or whisk together in a bowl. Taste and adjust the seasonings.
2. Store in a tightly covered jar in the refrigerator. Stir or shake before using.

FAST: Can prepare up to 2 weeks in advance and refrigerate, or freeze for up to 3 months.

FLASHY: As a dunk for raw vegetables, any Melba/Crostini (pages 263–273), or thinly sliced baguettes. Garnished by floating fresh tarragon, parsley, and/or any nontoxic flower on top.

FABULOUS: As a marinade or sauce for vegetables, seafood, beef, lamb, poultry, and/or pork. On any salad.

CAESAR SAUCE

If anchovies worry you, relax—they just act as a subtle
seasoning, not a pronounced flavor.
Instead of egg, this Caesar is enriched
with feta cheese.

Yield: about 1¾ cups

1 cup extra virgin olive oil

2 tablespoons crumbled feta cheese

1 teaspoon Dijon mustard or to taste

2 cloves garlic, minced, or to taste

4 to 8 anchovy fillets, minced

1 teaspoon Worcestershire sauce

½ cup freshly grated Parmesan or to taste

Fresh lemon or lime juice to taste

Salt and freshly ground black pepper to taste

Combine all the ingredients in a food processor fitted with the metal blade or in a blender and process, or whisk together in a bowl. Taste and adjust the seasonings.

FAST: Can prepare up to 5 days in advance and refrigerate, or freeze for up to 3 months.

FLASHY: As a dunk for romaine, endive, or artichoke leaves, asparagus, broccoli, cauliflower, melba toast, or French bread. Even fingers are sensational dunked in this! Garnished by sprinkling freshly ground black pepper or freshly grated Parmesan over it and/or floating any nontoxic flower on it.

FABULOUS: As a cold sauce for grilled chicken, beef, pork, fish, or lamb, or on any cooked vegetable. As a dressing on any salad.

Balsamic Sun-dried Tomato Vinaigrette

Yield: about 3 cups

2 cups extra virgin olive oil
½ cup sun-dried tomatoes, softened
  (page 22)
2 to 4 cloves garlic

⅔ cup balsamic vinegar
1 shallot
Salt and ground white pepper to taste

1. Combine all the ingredients in a food processor fitted with the metal blade or in a blender until smooth. Taste and adjust the seasonings.
2. Store in a tightly covered jar in the refrigerator. Shake or stir before using.

FAST: Can prepare up to 2 weeks in advance and refrigerate, or freeze for up to 3 months.

FLASHY: As a dunk for raw vegetables, any Melba/Crostini (pages 263–273), or thinly sliced baguettes. Garnished by floating any nontoxic flower on it.

FABULOUS: As a marinade or sauce for vegetables, seafood, beef, lamb, poultry, and/or pork. On any salad.

Tomatillo Vinaigrette

Yield: about 1½ cups

3 large or 6 to 8 small tomatillos,
  cut up (page 23)
1 cup canola or grapeseed oil
2 to 4 cloves garlic
¼ cup mayonnaise, homemade (page
  13) or purchased, or sour cream

Juice of 1 lemon or to taste
Chili powder to taste
Ground cumin to taste
Salt and ground white pepper to taste

Combine all the ingredients in a food processor fitted with the metal blade or in a blender and process until smooth. Taste and adjust the seasonings.

FAST: Can prepare up to 5 days in advance and refrigerate, or freeze for up to 3 months. Shake well or stir before using.

FLASHY: As a dunk for raw vegetables, any Melba/Crostini (pages 263–273), or thinly sliced baguettes. Garnished by floating fresh parsley, cilantro, and/or any nontoxic flower on top.

FABULOUS: As a marinade or sauce for vegetables, seafood, beef, lamb, poultry, and/or pork. On any salad.

BASIL MINT VINAIGRETTE

Yield: about 1½ cups

½ cup packed fresh basil leaves or to
taste

2 to 4 tablespoons minced fresh mint
leaves

2 to 4 cloves garlic

1 cup extra virgin olive oil

2 to 3 tablespoons freshly grated
Parmesan

1 tablespoon Dijon mustard

2 tablespoons anchovy paste or
minced anchovy fillets, optional

Salt, ground white pepper, hot pepper
sauce, and fresh lime juice to
taste

Combine all the ingredients in a food processor fitted with the metal blade or in a blender
and process until smooth. Taste and adjust the seasonings.

FAST: Can prepare up to 5 days in advance and refrigerate, or freeze for up to 3 months.
Shake well or stir before using.

FLASHY: As a dunk for raw vegetables, any Melba/Crostini (pages 263–273), or thinly
sliced baguettes. Garnished by floating fresh basil, mint, and/or any nontoxic flower on top.

FABULOUS: As a marinade or sauce for vegetables, seafood, beef, lamb, poultry, and/or
pork. On any salad.

ANCHOVY LIME DRESSING

Yield: about 1¼ cups

1 cup extra virgin olive
oil

1 to 3 cloves garlic

2 tablespoons Chinese sesame oil

3 anchovy fillets or to taste

Fresh lime juice to taste

¼ cup minced fresh parsley

Salt and ground white pepper to taste

1 tablespoon minced fresh chives or
green onions (scallions), green
part only

2 tablespoons mayonnaise,
homemade (page 13) or purchased

1. Combine all the ingredients in a food processor fitted with the metal blade or in a
blender and process until smooth. Taste and adjust the seasonings.
2. Store in a tightly covered jar in the refrigerator. Shake or stir before using.

FAST: Can prepare up to 2 weeks in advance and refrigerate, or freeze for up to 3 months.
Shake well or stir before using.

FLASHY: As a dunk for raw vegetables, any Melba/Crostini (pages 263–273), or thinly sliced baguettes. Garnished by floating fresh parsley, mint, and/or any nontoxic flower on top.

FABULOUS: With fresh lemon juice or vinegar of your choice instead of the lime juice. As a marinade or sauce for vegetables, seafood, beef, lamb, poultry, and/or pork. On any salad.

GINGER MINT VINAIGRETTE

Yield: about 1½ cups

1 ripe mango, peeled and cut up
   (page 21)
One 1-inch piece fresh ginger, peeled
   and cut up
2 cloves garlic

¼ cup packed fresh mint leaves
¼ cup red or white wine vinegar
⅔ to 1 cup extra virgin olive oil
Hot pepper sauce, salt, and ground
   white pepper to taste

1. Combine all the ingredients in a food processor fitted with the metal blade or in a blender and process until smooth. Taste and adjust the seasonings.
2. Store in a tightly covered jar in the refrigerator. Stir or shake before using.

FAST: Can prepare up to 2 weeks in advance and refrigerate, or freeze for up to 3 months.

FLASHY: As a dunk for raw vegetables, any Melba/Crostini (pages 263–273), or thinly sliced baguettes. Garnished by floating fresh mint leaves and/or any nontoxic flower on top.

FABULOUS: With fresh dill or cilantro instead of the mint. As a marinade or sauce for vegetables, seafood, beef, lamb, poultry, and/or pork. On any salad.

MANGO CHUTNEY VINAIGRETTE

Yield: about 2⅔ cups

2 canned whole green chiles,
   deveined and seeded (page 20)
1 cup extra virgin olive oil
⅓ cup mango chutney, homemade
   (page 15) or purchased

⅓ cup apple cider vinegar
1 clove garlic
1 teaspoon Dijon mustard
1 teaspoon salt
Ground white pepper to taste

1. Combine all the ingredients in a food processor fitted with the metal blade or in a blender and process until a smooth consistency is reached. Taste and adjust the seasonings.
2. Store in a tightly covered jar in the refrigerator. Shake or stir before using.

FAST: Can prepare up to 5 days in advance and refrigerate, or freeze for up to 3 months.

FLASHY: As a dunk for raw vegetables, any Melba/Crostini (pages 263–273), or thinly sliced baguettes. Garnished by floating a whole fresh chile, parsley, mint, and/or any nontoxic flower on top.

FABULOUS: As a marinade or sauce for vegetables, seafood, beef, lamb, poultry, and/or pork. On any salad.

LEMON MUSTARD VINAIGRETTE

Yield: about 2 cups

Fresh lemon juice to taste (about ⅔ cup)
2 cups extra virgin olive oil
1 tablespoon Dijon mustard or to taste

½ to 1 tablespoon minced shallots
Salt and ground white pepper to taste

1. Combine all the ingredients in a food processor fitted with the metal blade or in a blender and process, or whisk together in a bowl. Taste and adjust the seasonings.
2. Store in a tightly covered jar in the refrigerator. Shake or stir before using.

FAST: Can prepare up to 2 weeks in advance and refrigerate, or freeze for up to 3 months.

FLASHY: As a dunk for raw vegetables, any Melba/Crostini (pages 263–273), or thinly sliced baguettes. Garnished by floating fresh parsley and/or any nontoxic flower on top.

FABULOUS: With several cloves of minced garlic, minced fresh or dried dill, oregano, or basil added. As a marinade or sauce for vegetables, seafood, beef, lamb, poultry, and/or pork. On any salad.

HERBED WALNUT VINAIGRETTE

Yield: about 1¼ cups

¼ cup chopped walnuts, toasted
(page 27)

1 cup extra virgin olive oil

⅓ cup sherry wine vinegar

2 to 4 tablespoons minced shallots

¼ cup minced fresh parsley

1 tablespoon capers, drained, rinsed,
and minced

1 to 2 tablespoons fresh thyme
leaves, minced

Salt and ground white pepper to taste

1. Combine all the ingredients in a food processor fitted with the metal blade or in a blender and process, or whisk together in a bowl. Taste and adjust the seasonings.
2. Store in a tightly covered jar in the refrigerator. Shake or stir before using.

FAST: Can prepare up to 5 days in advance and refrigerate, or freeze for up to 3 months.

FLASHY: As a dunk for raw vegetables, any Melba/Crostini (pages 263–273), or thinly sliced baguettes. Garnished by floating fresh parsley, chopped walnuts, thyme, and/or any nontoxic flower on top.

FABULOUS: As a marinade or sauce for vegetables, seafood, beef, lamb, poultry, and/or pork. On any salad.

FENNEL PARMESAN VINAIGRETTE

Yield: about 2⅔ cups

2 to 4 tablespoons fennel seeds

4½ teaspoons anchovy paste or
minced anchovy fillets

4 to 6 cloves garlic, minced

2 cups extra virgin olive oil

⅔ cup balsamic vinegar

2 teaspoons green peppercorns,
drained and minced

½ cup freshly grated Parmesan

1. Combine all the ingredients in a food processor fitted with the metal blade or in a blender and process, or whisk together in a bowl. Taste and adjust the seasonings.
2. Store in a tightly covered jar in the refrigerator. Shake or stir before using.

FAST: Can prepare up to 5 days in advance and refrigerate, or freeze for up to 3 months.

FLASHY: As a dunk for raw vegetables, any Melba/Crostini (pages 263–273), or thinly sliced baguettes. Garnished by floating fresh parsley, fennel leaves, and/or any nontoxic flower on top.

FABULOUS: With sherry wine vinegar instead of balsamic vinegar. With minced fresh rosemary or cilantro instead of fennel seeds. As a marinade or sauce for vegetables, seafood, beef, lamb, poultry, and/or pork. On any salad.

Red Wine Vinaigrette

A classic!

Yield: about 2½ cups

½ cup good quality red wine vinegar

2 cups extra virgin or pure olive oil

2 cloves garlic, minced, or to taste

Salt, freshly ground white and black pepper, and minced fresh or dried herbs to taste

1. Combine all the ingredients in a food processor fitted with the metal blade or in a blender and process, or whisk together in a bowl. Taste and adjust the seasonings.
2. Store in a tightly covered jar in the refrigerator. Shake or stir before using.

FAST: Can prepare up to 2 weeks in advance and refrigerate, or freeze for up to 3 months.

FLASHY: As a dunk for raw vegetables, cold or hot beef, pork, or lamb, any Melba/Crostini (pages 263–273), or thinly sliced baguettes. Garnished by floating fresh parsley and/or any nontoxic flower on top.

FABULOUS: With ¼ to ½ cup crumbled blue, feta, or grated Parmesan cheese, different oils, herbs, vinegars, and/or 2 teaspoons mustard. As a marinade or sauce for vegetables, seafood, beef, lamb, poultry, and/or pork. On any salad.

Balsamic Vinaigrette

Yield: about 3 cups

2 to 4 cloves garlic, minced

2 to 4 teaspoon Dijon mustard

⅔ cup balsamic vinegar

¼ cup apple cider vinegar

2 cups extra virgin olive oil

2 teaspoons salt or to taste

Freshly ground white and black pepper to taste

1. Combine all the ingredients in a food processor fitted with the metal blade or in a blender and process, or whisk together in a bowl. Taste and adjust the seasonings.
2. Store in a tightly covered jar in the refrigerator. Shake or stir before using.

FAST: Can prepare up to 2 weeks in advance and refrigerate, or freeze for up to 3 months.

FLASHY: As a dunk for raw vegetables, cold or hot beef, pork, or lamb, any Melba/Crostini (pages 263–273), or thinly sliced baguettes. Garnished by floating fresh parsley and/or any nontoxic flower on top.

FABULOUS: With about 2 tablespoons minced fresh ginger and/or green onions, the white and green parts. As a marinade or sauce for vegetables, seafood, beef, lamb, poultry, and/or pork. On any salad.

ORANGE TARRAGON VINAIGRETTE

1 cup orange juice

1 sprig fresh tarragon, minced, or
    ¼ to ½ teaspoon dried

4 cloves garlic, minced

2 to 4 tablespoons orange-flavored
    liqueur

½ cup extra virgin olive oil

½ cup peanut oil

¼ cup sherry wine vinegar

2 tablespoons Chinese sesame oil

2 teaspoons white wine Worcester-
    shire sauce, optional

1 teaspoon Dijon mustard or to taste

Salt and ground white pepper to taste

1. Place the orange juice, tarragon, and garlic in a small saucepan and bring to a boil over high heat. Cook until reduced to about ¼ cup.
2. Combine the reduced mixture with the remaining ingredients in a food processor fitted with the metal blade or in a blender and process, or whisk together in a bowl. Taste and adjust the seasonings.
3. Store in a tightly covered jar in the refrigerator. Shake or stir before using.

FAST: Can prepare up to 5 days in advance and refrigerate, or freeze for up to 3 months.

FLASHY: As a dunk for raw vegetables, cold or hot beef, pork, or lamb, any Melba/Crostini (pages 263–273), or thinly sliced baguettes. Garnished by floating minced fresh or dried tarragon and/or any nontoxic flower on top.

FABULOUS: With fresh cilantro, dill, rosemary, or thyme instead of the tarragon. As a marinade or cold sauce for seafood, poultry, pork, lamb, or fish. As a marinade or sauce for vegetables, seafood, beef, lamb, poultry, and/or pork. On any salad.

ASIAN VINAIGRETTE

Yield: about 3 cups

2 cups peanut oil

¼ cup Chinese sesame oil

½ cup soy sauce

¾ cup rice wine vinegar

1 to 4 tablespoons minced fresh
    ginger

2 to 3 shallots or 4 to 6 green
    onions (scallions), white and
    green parts, minced

½ to 1 bunch cilantro (fresh
    coriander), stemmed

Juice of 1 lemon

1 teaspoon Szechuan peppercorns
    (page 19) or to taste

Ground white pepper to taste

1. Combine all the ingredients in a food processor fitted with the metal blade or in a blender and process until smooth. Taste and adjust the seasonings.
2. Store in a tightly covered jar in the refrigerator. Shake or stir before using.

FAST: Can prepare up to 2 weeks in advance and refrigerate, or freeze for up to 3 months.

FLASHY: As a dunk for raw vegetables, cold or hot beef, poultry, or lamb, any Melba/Crostini (pages 263–273), or thinly sliced baguettes. Garnished by floating minced cilantro, green onions, and/or any nontoxic flower on top.

FABULOUS: As a marinade or sauce for vegetables, seafood, beef, lamb, poultry, and/or pork. On any salad.

RASPBERRY VINAIGRETTE

Yield: about 2⅔ cups

⅔ cup raspberry vinegar
2 cups extra virgin olive oil
2 tablespoons minced shallots

Salt, ground white pepper, red wine vinegar, and minced fresh or dried dill to taste

Combine all the ingredients in a food processor fitted with the metal blade or in a blender and process, or whisk together in a bowl. Taste and adjust the seasonings.

FAST: Can prepare up to 5 days in advance and refrigerate, or freeze for up to 3 months.

FLASHY: As a dunk for raw vegetables, cold or hot beef, pork, or lamb, any Melba/Crostini (pages 263–273), or thinly sliced baguettes. Garnished by floating fresh dill and/or any nontoxic flower on top.

FABULOUS: As a marinade or sauce for vegetables, seafood, beef, lamb, poultry, and/or pork. On any salad.

FENNEL MUSTARD VINAIGRETTE

Yield: 1½ cups

1 cup extra virgin olive oil
2 teaspoons fennel seeds
1 to 2 teaspoons Dijon mustard
½ cup rice wine vinegar
2 teaspoons honey

1 tablespoon minced fresh ginger
2 tablespoons mayonnaise, homemade (page 13) or purchased, or plain yogurt
1 to 2 shallots, minced

1. Combine all the ingredients in a food processor fitted with the metal blade or in a blender and process, or whisk together in a bowl. Taste and adjust the seasonings.
2. Store in a tightly covered jar in the refrigerator. Shake or stir before using.

FAST: Can prepare up to 2 weeks in advance and refrigerate, or freeze for up to 3 months.

FLASHY: As a dunk for raw vegetables, hot or cold beef, pork, poultry, lamb, or seafood, any Melba/Crostini (pages 263–273), or thinly sliced baguettes. Garnished by floating minced parsley and/or any nontoxic flower on top.

COLD MUSTARD MINT SAUCE

Great for fat-watchers.

Yield: about 1 cup

2 tablespoons Dijon mustard
3 tablespoons port or dry sherry
⅔ cup balsamic vinegar

2 tablespoons minced fresh mint leaves

1. Combine all the ingredients in a food processor fitted with the metal blade or in a blender and process, or whisk together in a bowl.
2. Shake or stir before using.

FAST: Can prepare up to 7 days in advance and refrigerate, or freeze for up to 6 months.

FLASHY: As a dunk for hot or cold grilled or roasted lamb, beef, pork, or chicken. Served hot or cold. Garnished by floating fresh mint leaves and/or any nontoxic flower on top.

FABULOUS: With pureed roasted garlic (see pages 25, 26) mixed in. With fresh rosemary and/or basil instead of or with the mint. Heated with ¼ to ½ cup heavy cream and served hot.

WARM SHALLOT BLUE CHEESE VINAIGRETTE

Yield: about 1½ cups

1 to 2 shallots, thinly sliced or minced
1 cup extra virgin olive oil
2 tablespoons minced fresh rosemary or to taste
¼ cup balsamic vinegar

2 tablespoons cream sherry
6 to 8 ounces blue cheese, crumbled
1 ripe pear, cored
Salt and freshly ground black pepper to taste

1. Place the shallots and olive oil in a small saucepan and heat over medium-low to medium heat until very fragrant, about 7 minutes.
2. Transfer the shallot oil along with all the remaining ingredients to a food processor fitted with the metal blade or a blender and puree. Taste and adjust the seasonings.
3. Shake or stir before serving.

FAST: Can prepare up to 5 days in advance and refrigerate.

FLASHY: Served hot in a chafing dish or at room temperature. Used as a dunk for cooked seafood, skewers of pork, or chicken. Garnished by floating fresh rosemary and/or any nontoxic flower on top.

FABULOUS: Seasoned with fresh thyme or sage instead of rosemary.

MEXICAN-STYLE DUNKS

PUMPKIN SEED CHILE SALSA

Yield: about 2½ cups

1 cup hulled pumpkin or squash seeds

2 to 6 canned whole green chiles, seeded and deveined (page 20)

2 dried pasilla chiles, rehydrated (page 20), stemmed, and seeded

¼ cup minced cilantro (fresh coriander) or to taste

¼ cup minced green onions (scallions), white and green parts

2 cups peeled, seeded, and chopped tomatoes

2 to 4 cloves garlic, minced

Salt, ground white pepper, and ground cumin to taste

1. Toast the seeds in a heavy frying pan in a preheated 350°F oven until lightly browned, about 10 to 15 minutes. Cool.
2. Combine all the ingredients in a food processor fitted with the metal blade or in a blender. Process briefly, to preserve some of the texture. Taste and adjust the seasonings.

FAST: Can prepare up to 3 days in advance and refrigerate, or freeze for up to 3 months.

FLASHY: Hot or cold as a dunk for Tortilla Chips (page 273), chicken, pork, seafood, and/or beef. Garnished with cilantro and/or any nontoxic flower.

FABULOUS: With toasted almonds, walnuts, or sunflower seeds substituted for the pumpkin seeds. As an entree sauce for poultry, pork, rice, pasta, beans, and/or seafood. With an avocado added.

Salsa Cruda

This is the classic salsa!

Yield: about 3 cups

3 large, ripe tomatoes, chopped

½ cup chopped onions

½ cup packed chopped cilantro (fresh coriander)

2 to 4 canned whole green chiles, seeded, deveined, and minced (page 20)

2 to 4 large tomatillos, husked and chopped (page 23)

2 cloves garlic, minced, or to taste

Fresh red jalapeño pepper, as big a piece as you can handle, seeded, deveined, and minced (page 20)

2 tablespoons extra virgin olive oil

Salt and ground white pepper, dried oregano, and sugar to taste

Combine all the ingredients in a food processor fitted with the metal blade or in a blender and process using several quick on-and-off motions so as not to destroy the texture, or combine in a bowl. A chunky texture is desired. Taste and adjust the seasonings.

FAST: Can prepare up to 5 days in advance and refrigerate, or freeze for up to 1 year.

FLASHY: As a dunk for skewers of pork, seafood, beef, poultry, or with Tortilla Chips (page 273). Garnished with cilantro and/or any nontoxic flower.

FABULOUS: Used to season anything or to use in place of rich sauces. As an entree sauce for beef, pork, poultry, seafood, pasta, or rice.

Mint Salsa

Yield: about 1 cup

1 medium-size red onion, chopped

½ cup packed fresh mint leaves, minced

2 cloves garlic, minced

2 large, ripe tomatoes, seeded and chopped

Fresh lime juice to taste

Salt, sugar, and freshly ground black pepper to taste

Combine all the ingredients in a food processor fitted with the metal blade or in a blender and process using several quick on-and-off motions so as not to destroy the texture, or combine in a bowl. Taste and adjust the seasonings.

FAST: Can prepare up to 4 days in advance and refrigerate, or freeze for up to 6 months.

FLASHY: Served with Tortilla Chips (page 273), Pita Chips (page 274), any Melba/Crostini (pages 263–273), sourdough bread, and/or sausages. Garnished with a sprig of fresh mint and/or any nontoxic flower.

FABULOUS: With any kind of fresh or dried chiles added.

CANTALOUPE SALSA

Yield: about 3 cups

1 bunch cilantro (fresh coriander), stemmed and minced

2 tablespoons sugar

½ fresh red jalapeño, deveined, seeded, and minced (page 20)

2 cloves garlic, minced

¼ to ½ cup minced red onion

½ large cantaloupe, peeled, seeded, and chopped

Salt and fresh lime juice to taste

Combine all the ingredients in a food processor fitted with the metal blade or in a blender and process using several quick on-and-off motions so as not to destroy the texture, or combine in a bowl. Taste and adjust the seasonings.

FAST: Can prepare up to 5 days in advance and refrigerate, or freeze for up to 6 months.

FLASHY: As a dunk for skewers of pork, poultry, seafood, lamb, or beef. Garnished with fresh mint and/or any nontoxic flower.

FABULOUS: As an entree sauce for beef, pork, poultry, seafood, pasta, or rice.

MANGO MINT SALSA

Yield: about 2 cups

1 large, ripe mango, peeled, seeded, and minced (page 21)

3 to 6 green onions (scallions), white and green parts, minced

¼ to ½ medium-size red bell pepper, roasted, peeled, and chopped (page 26)

½ to 1 cup Fire and Ice Vinegar (page 53) or your favorite vinegar

¼ cup packed fresh mint leaves, minced

1 to 3 tablespoons brown sugar, depending on the desired sweetness

Salt and ground white pepper to taste

67

Dunks

1. Combine all the ingredients in a food processor fitted with the metal blade and process using several quick on-and-off motions so as not to destroy the texture, or combine in a bowl. Taste and adjust the seasonings.
2. Let sit for at least 1 hour before serving.

FAST: Can prepare up to 5 days in advance and refrigerate, or freeze for up to 6 months.

FLASHY: As a dunk for Pita Chips (page 274), skewers of pork, poultry, seafood, lamb, or beef. Garnished with fresh mint and/or any nontoxic flower.

FABULOUS: As an entree sauce for beef, pork, lamb, poultry, seafood, pasta, or rice.

EGGPLANT SALSA

Yield: about 3 cups

1 medium-size eggplant, cubed

¼ cup Mango Chutney Vinaigrette (page 58)

¼ to ½ cup packed chopped cilantro (fresh coriander)

1 shallot

1 fresh Anaheim chile, seeded and deveined (page 20)

1 teaspoon dried oregano

3 tablespoons fresh lime juice or to taste

1 tablespoon extra virgin olive oil

¼ cup chopped walnuts or pine nuts, toasted (page 27)

Salt, ground white pepper, and ground cumin to taste

1. Toss the eggplant together with the vinaigrette in a roasting pan or heavy cast-iron skillet. Bake in a preheated 400°F oven until fully cooked, about 30 minutes.
2. Transfer the eggplant to a food processor fitted with the metal blade or in a blender and add the cilantro, shallot, chile, oregano, lime juice, and olive oil. Process until combined but still chunky.
3. Add the nuts and process briefly, so as not to destroy the texture. Taste and season with the salt, pepper, and cumin.

FAST: Can prepare up to 4 days in advance and refrigerate, or freeze for up to 6 months.

FLASHY: Served with chips, crackers, or thinly sliced baguettes, chilled or at room temperature in a bowl, crock, or pâté terrine, and garnished with fresh herbs and nontoxic flowers or leaves.

FABULOUS: With any kind of chile, with garlic, and/or with crumbled feta cheese to taste.

PAPAYA AND TOMATILLO SALSA

Yield: about 2½ cups

1 medium-size, ripe papaya, peeled, seeded, and chopped (page 22)

7 canned whole green chiles or fresh green chiles (page 20), roasted, deveined, seeded, and minced

6 tomatillos or to taste, husked and chopped (page 23)

½ cup rice wine vinegar

Zest and juice of 1 orange

¼ cup packed fresh mint leaves, minced

2 tablespoons Chinese sesame oil

2 to 4 tablespoons brown sugar, depending on the sweetness desired

Salt and hot pepper sauce or Jamaican jerk seasoning paste (page 21) to taste

1. Combine all the ingredients in a food processor fitted with the metal blade or in a blender and process with several quick on-and-off motions so as not to destroy all the texture, or combine in a bowl. Taste and adjust the seasonings.
2. Let sit for at least 1 hour before serving.

FAST: Can prepare up to 5 days in advance and refrigerate, or freeze for up to 6 months.

FLASHY: As a dunk for Tortilla Chips (page 273), poultry, lamb, pork, beef, fish, and/or seafood. Garnished with cilantro (fresh coriander), and/or any nontoxic flower.

FABULOUS: With 1 to 2 tablespoons minced fresh or 2 to 4 tablespoons pickled ginger (page 18), and/or 4 tablespoons minced cilantro. With almost any fresh herb. With ½ cup sour cream. As an entree sauce for beef, pork, lamb, poultry, seafood, pasta, or rice.

MANGO BASIL SALSA

Yield: about 3 cups

1 medium-size, ripe mango, peeled, pitted, and diced (page 21)

1 cup packed fresh basil leaves, minced

2 to 3 cloves garlic, minced

½ teaspoon Jamaican jerk seasoning paste (page 21)

¾ cup extra virgin olive oil

1 cup macadamia nuts, chopped

¼ to ½ cup packed fresh mint leaves, minced

Salt, ground white pepper, and fresh lemon juice to taste

69

Dunks

Combine all the ingredients in a food processor fitted with the metal blade or in a blender and process using several quick on-and-off motions so as not to destroy all the texture, or combine in a bowl. It should be chunky. Taste and adjust the seasonings.

FAST: Can prepare up to 5 days in advance and refrigerate, or freeze for up to 6 months.

FLASHY: As a dunk for French bread or any Melba/Crostini (pages 263–273). Garnished with fresh mint leaves and/or any nontoxic flower.

FABULOUS: As an entree sauce for fish, chicken, beef, pork, pasta, potatoes, or vegetables. With raspberry vinegar instead of the lemon juice.

Italian Basil Salsa

Yield: about 2 cups

8 to 10 ripe pear-shaped tomatoes,
     seeded and chopped
2 to 4 cloves garlic, minced
½ to 1 bunch fresh basil, stemmed
     and minced

¼ to ½ cup minced fresh parsley
¼ cup extra virgin olive oil
Juice of ½ to 1 lemon or lime
Salt and freshly ground black pepper
     to taste

Combine all the ingredients in a food processor fitted with the metal blade and process using several quick on-and-off motions so as not to destroy all the texture, or combine in a bowl. It should be chunky. Taste and adjust the seasonings.

FAST: Can prepare up to 5 days in advance and refrigerate, or freeze for up to 6 months.

FLASHY: As a dunk for French bread, or any Melba/Crostini (pages 263–273). Garnished with fresh basil leaves and/or any nontoxic flower.

FABULOUS: As an entree sauce for fish, chicken, beef, pork, pasta, potatoes, or vegetables. With capers, chopped marinated artichoke hearts, pickled peppers, or minced anchovies to taste mixed in. With chopped cooked shrimp, scallops, or crabmeat mixed in.

ITALIAN SPINACH SALSA

Yield: about 1½ cups

2 to 3 bunches fresh spinach, well
cleaned, or two 8-ounce packages
frozen spinach, thawed, drained,
and chopped

1 cup extra virgin olive oil

¼ cup pine nuts, toasted (page 27)
and chopped

½ to 1 shallot, minced

½ teaspoon dried mixed Italian
herbs, or minced fresh basil to
taste

1. Combine all the ingredients in a food processor fitted with the metal blade or in a
blender and process using several quick on-and-off motions so as not to destroy all
the texture, or combine in a bowl. Taste and adjust the seasonings.
2. Chill for at least 30 minutes before serving.

FAST: Can prepare up to 2 days in advance and refrigerate.

FLASHY: As a dunk for vegetables, Bagel Chips (page 272), or Pita Chips (page 274).
Garnished with fresh basil leaves and/or any nontoxic flower.

FABULOUS: As an entree sauce for fish, seafood, poultry, or on pasta or rice. To dress a
pasta or rice salad, or to stuff baked potatoes.

FETA SALSA

*A happy cross-cultural marriage that is a gift from the
gods!*

Yield: about 5 cups

1 pound feta cheese, crumbled

1 cup extra virgin olive oil

6 green onions (scallions), white
and green parts, minced

½ cup minced fresh parsley

3 to 4 large, ripe tomatoes, peeled,
seeded, and chopped

1 cup Greek or Italian olives, pitted
and coarsely chopped

Juice of 1 lime

1 tablespoon dried oregano

2 to 3 tablespoons chopped fresh dill
or 2 teaspoons dried

Freshly ground white and black
pepper to taste

1. Combine all the ingredients in a food processor fitted with the metal blade and
process using quick on-and-off motions so as not to destroy all the texture. Taste and
adjust the seasonings.
2. Chill for at least 30 minutes before serving.

FAST: Can prepare up to 2 weeks in advance and refrigerate.

FLASHY: With Pita Chips (page 274). Garnished with minced fresh dill, mint, parsley, and/or any nontoxic flower.

FABULOUS: To dress pasta salad or to accompany fish, lamb, or chicken as an entree sauce. With minced fresh mint and/or fresh basil and chopped marinated artichoke hearts.

Mediterranean Salsa

Makes you feel like summer no matter what season it is!

Yield: about 3½ cups

One 16-ounce can Italian plum tomatoes, chopped, or canned Italian-style stewed tomatoes

½ cup marinated artichoke hearts, drained and chopped

½ cup roasted red bell peppers, homemade (page 26) or purchased, chopped

¼ to ½ cup extra virgin olive oil

⅓ cup capers, drained, rinsed, and minced, or more to taste

2 to 4 cloves garlic, minced

¼ cup minced fresh Italian (flatleaf) parsley

Fresh lemon juice, salt, and freshly ground black pepper to taste

Combine all the ingredients in a food processor fitted with the metal blade or in a blender and process with several quick on-and-off motions so as not to destroy all the texture, or combine in a bowl. Taste and adjust the seasonings.

FAST: Can prepare up to 5 days in advance and refrigerate, or freeze for up to 6 months.

FLASHY: Served as a dunk for crackers, thinly sliced baguettes, or any Melba/Crostini (pages 263–273). Garnished with minced fresh parsley, basil, and/or any nontoxic flower.

FABULOUS: Mixed into 2 cups pureed white, pink, or black beans to create a fabulous Mediterranean Bean Spread, served hot, cold, or at room temperature. As an entree sauce on pasta, seafood, pork, poultry, or lamb. As a seasoning agent in sauces and soups.

AVOCADO DIPPING SAUCE

If you think guacamole is good, wait until you taste this!

Yield: about 2 cups

2 large, ripe avocados, peeled,
    pitted, and chopped

2 to 4 large tomatillos or to taste,
    husked and chopped (page 23)

2 to 6 green onions (scallions),
    white and green parts, minced

½ to 1 cup salsa, homemade (see
    Index) or purchased

1 bunch cilantro (fresh coriander),
    stemmed and chopped

½ cup sour cream or plain yogurt

2 cloves garlic, minced

1 to 2 teaspoons ground cumin or to
    taste

Salt, ground white pepper, and fresh
    lemon or lime juice to taste

Combine all the ingredients in a food processor fitted with the metal blade or in a blender, or mix together in a bowl. Taste and adjust the seasonings. The texture can be smooth or chunky.

FAST: Can prepare up to 2 weeks in advance and refrigerate.

FLASHY: With Tortilla Chips (page 273), cold cooked shrimp, and/or spears of jicama. Garnished with sprigs of cilantro and/or any nontoxic flower.

FABULOUS: As a dressing for pasta, couscous, potato, rice, or bulgur salad. As an entree sauce for beef, pork, poultry, seafood, pasta, or rice.

GUACAMOLE

This summer favorite is cholesterol-free.

Yield: about 1½ cups

2 large, ripe avocados, peeled, pitted,
    and chopped

Several canned whole green chiles,
    seeded, deveined, and minced
    (page 20)

1 to 2 cloves garlic, minced, or to
    taste

¼ cup minced cilantro (fresh
    coriander) or to taste

1 to 2 teaspoons ground cumin

Salt, hot pepper sauce, and fresh
    lemon or lime juice to taste

¼ to 1 fresh red jalapeño pepper,
    seeded, deveined, and minced,
    optional

Combine all the ingredients in a food processor fitted with the metal blade or in a blender, or mix together in a mixing bowl. The texture can be smooth or chunky. Taste and adjust the seasonings.

FAST: Can prepare up to 3 days in advance and refrigerate, or freeze for up to 3 months.

FLASHY: As a dunk for Tortilla Chips (page 273), poultry, lamb, pork, beef, fish, and/or seafood. Garnished with minced cilantro, green onions, and/or any nontoxic flower.

FABULOUS: As a dressing for rice or black bean salads or use as a sauce for poultry, pork, seafood, or fish. As an entree sauce for beef, pork, poultry, seafood, pasta, or rice.

MEXICAN CREAM SAUCE

If this is your first encounter with tomatillos, you'll be delighted with their tangy lemonlike flavor. Even kids love this!

Yield: about 2¼ cups

6 medium to large tomatillos, husked and quartered (page 23)

5 canned whole green chiles, seeded and deveined (page 20)

½ to 1 medium-size to large, ripe avocado, peeled and pitted

¾ cup sour cream or plain yogurt

3 to 6 green onions (scallions), white and green parts, cut up

2 cloves garlic

¼ cup minced cilantro (fresh coriander) or more to taste

Salt, ground white pepper, ground cumin, and fresh lemon juice to taste

Combine all the ingredients in a food processor fitted with the metal blade or in a blender and puree. Taste and adjust the seasonings.

FAST: Can prepare up to 3 days in advance and refrigerate, or freeze for up to 3 months.

FLASHY: As a dunk for Tortilla Chips (page 273), poultry, lamb, pork, beef, fish, and/or seafood. Garnished with minced cilantro, green onions, and/or any nontoxic flower.

FABULOUS: As an entree sauce for beef, pork, poultry, seafood, pasta, or rice. With chopped cooked salmon, shrimp, or crabmeat mixed in.

SESAME-FLAVORED SAUCE

Yield: 5 tablespoons

1 tablespoon Chinese sesame oil   *¼ cup soy sauce*

Whisk the ingredients together in a small bowl. Taste and adjust the flavors.

FAST: Can prepare up to 3 months in advance, store in jars, and refrigerate, or freeze up to 1 year.

FLASHY: As a dunk for Chinese Skewered Bites (page 143), Crispy Cocktail Ribs (page 142), Barbecued Pork and Red Cabbage Potstickers (page 254), Chinese Cabbage Sui Mai with Pork and Shrimp (page 251), or any Asian-style hors d'oeuvre. Garnished with toasted sesame seeds (see page 27), minced green onions, and/or cilantro.

FABULOUS: As a seasoning for sauces, vegetables, soups, marinades, and stir-fry dishes, or in place of rich entree sauces on beef, pork, poultry, or seafood.

SOY MUSTARD DUNK

4 parts soy sauce   *2 parts Dijon or hot mustard*

Whisk the ingredients together in a bowl. Taste and adjust the flavors.

FAST: Can prepare up to 3 months in advance, store in jars, and refrigerate, or freeze for up to 1 year.

FLASHY: As a dunk for Chinese Skewered Bites (page 143), Crispy Cocktail Ribs (page 142), Barbecued Pork and Red Cabbage Potstickers (page 254), Chinese Cabbage Sui Mai with Pork and Shrimp (page 251), or any Asian-style hors d'oeuvre. Garnished with toasted sesame seeds (see page 27), minced green onions, and/or cilantro.

FABULOUS: As a seasoning for sauces, vegetables, soups, marinades, and stir-fry dishes, or in place of rich entree sauces on beef, pork, poultry, or seafood.

BALSAMIC CHILI SAUCE

4 parts balsamic vinegar   *4 parts avocado or peanut oil*

1 part Hot Pepper Oil (page 81)

Whisk the ingredients together in a bowl. Taste and adjust the flavors.

FAST: Can prepare up to 3 months in advance, store in jars, and refrigerate, or freeze for up to 1 year.

FLASHY: As a dunk for Chinese Skewered Bites (page 143), Crispy Cocktail Ribs (page 142), Barbecued Pork and Red Cabbage Potstickers (page 254), Chinese Cabbage Sui Mai with Pork and Shrimp (page 251), or any Asian-style hors d'oeuvre. Garnished with toasted sesame seeds (page 27), minced green onions, and/or cilantro.

FABULOUS: As a seasoning for sauces, vegetables, soups, marinades, and stir-fry dishes, or in place of rich entree sauces on beef, pork, poultry or seafood.

SOY SHERRY SAUCE

1 part medium-dry or cream sherry   *1 part soy sauce*

Whisk the ingredients together in a bowl. Taste and adjust the flavors.

FAST: Can prepare up to 3 months in advance, store in jars, and refrigerate or freeze for up to 1 year.

FLASHY: As a dunk for Chinese Skewered Bites (page 143), Crispy Cocktail Ribs (page 142), Barbecued Pork and Red Cabbage Potstickers (page 254), Chinese Cabbage Sui Mai with Pork and Shrimp (page 251), or any Asian-style hors d'oeuvre. Garnished with toasted sesame seeds (page 27), minced green onions, and/or cilantro.

FABULOUS: Used to season sauces, vegetables, soups, marinades, and stir-fry dishes, or in place of rich entree sauces on beef, pork, poultry, or seafood.

COLD HOISIN WINE SAUCE

Yield: about 1¼ cups

¾ cup hoisin sauce (page 17)
⅓ cup Madeira or medium-dry
    sherry
1 tablespoon Chinese sesame oil

2 to 4 green onions (scallions),
    white and green parts, minced
1 tablespoon sesame seeds, toasted
    (page 27)

Whisk the ingredients together in a bowl. Taste and adjust the flavors.

FAST: Can prepare up to 3 months in advance, store in jars, and refrigerate or freeze for up to 1 year.

FLASHY: As a dunk for Chinese Skewered Bites (page 143), Crispy Cocktail Ribs (page 142), Barbecued Pork and Red Cabbage Potstickers (page 254), Chinese Cabbage Sui Mai with Pork and Shrimp (page 251), or any Asian-style hors d'oeuvre. Garnished with more toasted sesame seeds, minced green onions, and/or cilantro.

FABULOUS: Used to season sauces, vegetables, soups, marinades, and stir-fry dishes, or in place of rich entree sauces on beef, pork, poultry, or seafood.

COLD SZECHUAN SAUCE

Yield: about 2¾ cups

1 cup rice wine vinegar
1 cup soy sauce
¼ cup Chinese sesame oil
4 to 6 tablespoons hoisin sauce
    (page 17)
2 to 4 tablespoons Chinese plum
    sauce (page 17)

¼ cup fresh lime juice or to taste
1 to 1½ teaspoons Szechuan
    peppercorns, crushed (page 19)
2 cloves garlic, minced
Ground white pepper to taste

Whisk all the ingredients together in a bowl. Taste and adjust the seasonings.

FAST: Can prepare up to 3 months in advance, store in jars, and refrigerate, or freeze for up to 1 year.

FLASHY: As a dunk for Chinese Skewered Bites (page 143), Crispy Cocktail Ribs (page 142), Barbecued Pork and Red Cabbage Potstickers (page 254), Chinese Cabbage Sui Mai with Pork and Shrimp (page 251), or any Asian-style hors d'oeuvre. Garnished with toasted sesame seeds (see page 27), minced green onions, and/or cilantro.

FABULOUS: As a seasoning sauce for vegetables, soups, marinades, and stir-fry dishes, or in place of rich entree sauces on beef, pork, poultry, or seafood.

PLUM VINEGAR SAUCE

Yield: about 1 cup

½ cup Chinese plum sauce (page 17)   ½ cup Rice Vinegar Sauce (page 80)

Whisk the ingredients together in a bowl. Taste and adjust the flavors.

FAST: Can prepare up to 1 month in advance and refrigerate.

FLASHY: As a dunk for pork, ribs, chicken wings, and/or almost any Asian hors d'oeuvre. Garnished with toasted sesame seeds (page 27), minced green onions, and/or cilantro.

FABULOUS: As a marinade for fish, chicken, seafood, or pork. As an entree sauce on noodles, pork, chicken, fish, or seafood.

MANGO VINEGAR SAUCE

Yield: about 2 cups

1 medium-size to large, ripe mango, peeled and pitted (page 21)
½ cup balsamic vinegar
2 tablespoons minced fresh ginger

½ cup packed fresh basil leaves
½ cup water or orange juice
½ to 1 teaspoon pickled mango (page 18)
Salt to taste

Combine all the ingredients in a food processor fitted with the metal blade or in a blender and process until smooth. Taste and adjust the seasonings.

FAST: Can prepare up to 4 days in advance and refrigerate, or freeze for up to 6 months.

FLASHY: Served at room temperature or hot in a bowl and garnished with a sprinkling of toasted sesame seeds (page 27).

FABULOUS: As a dunk for grilled sausage and/or skewers of seafood, pork, fish, chicken, or beef.

BALSAMIC TONKATSU SAUCE

Yield: about 1 cup

½ cup Madeira
½ cup balsamic vinegar

2 tablespoons tonkatsu sauce (page 19)

Whisk the ingredients together in a bowl. Taste and adjust the flavors.

FAST: Can prepare up to 1 month in advance and refrigerate.

FLASHY: As a dunk for pork, ribs, chicken wings, and/or almost any Asian hors d'oeuvre. Garnished with toasted sesame seeds (page 27), minced green onions, and/or cilantro over the top.

FABULOUS: As a marinade for fish, chicken, seafood, or pork. As an entree sauce on noodles, pork, chicken, fish, or seafood.

VINEGAR MINT SAUCE

Yield: about 1½ cups

1 cup rice wine vinegar
4½ teaspoons Chinese sesame oil
4½ teaspoons minced fresh mint

1 tablespoon minced pickled ginger
(page 18)

Whisk all the ingredients together in a bowl. Taste and adjust the flavors.

FAST: Can prepare up to 1 month in advance and refrigerate.

FLASHY: As a dunk for pork, ribs, chicken wings, or almost any Asian hors d'oeuvre. Garnished with fresh mint leaves and/or any nontoxic flower.

FABULOUS: As a marinade for fish, chicken, seafood, or pork. As an entree sauce on noodles, pork, chicken, fish, or seafood.

MANGO BASIL CHUTNEY

Yield: about 4 cups

1 large, ripe mango, peeled, pitted, and chopped (page 22)
½ to 1 large red onion, chopped
½ cup balsamic vinegar
½ to 1 cup packed fresh basil leaves, chopped

Salt to taste
1 fresh red jalapeño pepper, deveined, seeded, and minced (page 20), or as much as you can handle
1 to 2 tablespoons sugar, optional

Combine all the ingredients in a food processor fitted with the metal blade or in a blender and process using several quick on-and-off motions so as not to destroy all the texture, or combine in a bowl. Taste and adjust the seasonings.

FAST: Can prepare up to 4 days in advance and refrigerate, or freeze for up to 6 months.

FLASHY: Served with Tortilla Chips (page 273), Pita Chips (page 274), any Melba/Crostini (pages 263–273), sourdough bread, and/or sausages. Garnished with fresh basil and/or any nontoxic flower.

FABULOUS: With any kind of fresh or dried chiles added.

RICE VINEGAR SAUCE

Yield: about 1½ cups

1 cup rice wine vinegar

¼ cup Chinese plum sauce (page 17)

1 tablespoon Chinese sesame oil

¼ cup minced cilantro (fresh coriander)

1 clove garlic, minced

1 to 2 green onions (scallions), white and green parts, minced, optional

Combine all the ingredients in a food processor fitted with the metal blade or in a blender and process, or combine in a bowl. Taste and adjust the seasonings.

FAST: Can prepare up to 3 months in advance, store in jars, and refrigerate, or freeze for up to 1 year.

FLASHY: As a dunk for Chinese Skewered Bites (page 143), Crispy Cocktail Ribs (page 142), Barbecued Pork and Red Cabbage Potstickers (page 254), or any Asian-style hors d'oeuvre. Garnished with toasted sesame seeds (page 27), minced green onions, and/or cilantro.

FABULOUS: Used to season sauces, vegetables, soups, marinades, and stir-fry dishes, or in place of rich entree sauces on beef, pork, poultry, or seafood.

CHUTNEY DIPPING SAUCE

Yield: about 1½ cups

¼ cup peach, plum, or mango chutney, homemade (see Index) or purchased

1 cup rice wine vinegar

2 tablespoons soy sauce

1 tablespoon Chinese sesame oil

1 to 2 green onions (scallions), white and green parts, minced

¼ cup minced cilantro (fresh coriander), optional

Combine all the ingredients in a food processor fitted with the metal blade or in a blender and process using several quick on-and-off motions so as not to destroy the texture. Taste and adjust the seasonings.

FAST: Can prepare up to 3 months in advance, store in jars, and refrigerate, or freeze for up to 1 year.

FLASHY: As a dunk for Chinese Skewered Bites (page 143), Crispy Cocktail Ribs (page 142), Barbecued Pork and Red Cabbage Potstickers (page 254), Chinese Cabbage Sui Mai with Pork and Shrimp (page 251), or any Asian-style hors d'oeuvre. Garnished with toasted sesame seeds (page 27), minced green onions, and/or cilantro.

FABULOUS: Used to season sauces, vegetables, soups, marinades, and stir-fry dishes, or in place of rich entree sauces on beef, pork, poultry, or seafood.

HOT PEPPER OIL

For all you hot and spicy fanatics!

Yield: about ½ cup

¼ cup dried red chile peppers
  (page 20)

½ cup peanut oil
Zest of 1 orange, grated

1. Grind the peppers in a food processor fitted with the metal blade until a pastelike consistency is reached.
2. Heat the oil in a skillet or wok over high heat until it begins to smoke. Add the ground peppers and orange zest, remove the skillet from the heat, and let stand for 30 minutes.
3. Strain the oil through a fine strainer into a jar and store in the refrigerator in a tightly covered jar.

FAST: Can prepare up to 3 months in advance, store in jars, and refrigerate, or freeze for up to 1 year.

FLASHY: As a dunk for Chinese Skewered Bites (page 143), Crispy Cocktail Ribs (page 142), Barbecued Pork and Red Cabbage Potstickers (page 254), Chinese Cabbage Sui Mai with Pork and Shrimp (page 251), or any Asian-style hors d'oeuvre. Garnished with toasted sesame seeds (page 27), minced green onions, and/or cilantro.

FABULOUS: For an aromatic variation, add dried tangerine peel, and/or fresh or dried mint leaves. Use to season sauces, vegetables, soups, marinades, and stir-fry dishes, or in place of rich entree sauces on beef, pork, poultry, or seafood.

Sesame Rice Vinegar Sauce

Yield: about 1¼ cups

1 tablespoon tahini (page 23)

2 to 3 cloves garlic, minced

1 to 2 tablespoons minced pickled
  ginger (page 18)

1 cup rice wine vinegar

2 to 4 tablespoons Chinese sesame oil

Combine all the ingredients in a food processor fitted with the metal blade or in a blender and process until smooth, or combine in a bowl. Taste and adjust the seasonings.

FAST: Can prepare up to 1 week in advance and refrigerate, or freeze forever, or up to 1 year, whichever comes first.

FLASHY: As a dunk for Chinese Skewered Bites (page 143), Crispy Cocktail Ribs (page 142), Barbecued Pork and Red Cabbage Potstickers (page 254), Chinese Cabbage Sui Mai with Pork and Shrimp (page 251), or any Asian-style hors d'oeuvre. Garnished with toasted sesame seeds (page 27), minced green onions, and/or cilantro.

FABULOUS: Used to season sauces, vegetables, soups, marinades, and stir-fry dishes, or in place of rich entree sauces on beef, pork, poultry, or seafood.

Gingered Orange Mustard Sauce

Yield: about 1½ cups

2 tablespoons minced pickled ginger
  (page 18)

2 tablespoons orange marmalade

½ cup Dijon or Düsseldorf mustard

1 tablespoon brown sugar

¼ cup cider vinegar

½ cup avocado or peanut oil

Combine all the ingredients in a food processor fitted with the metal blade or in a blender and process until a smooth consistency is reached. Taste and adjust the seasonings.

FAST: Can prepare up to 1 week in advance and refrigerate, or freeze forever, or up to 1 year, whichever comes first.

FLASHY: As a dunk for Chinese Skewered Bites (page 143), Crispy Cocktail Ribs (page 142), Barbecued Pork and Red Cabbage Potstickers (page 254), Chinese Cabbage Sui Mai with Pork and Shrimp (page 251), or any Asian-style hors d'oeuvre. Garnished with toasted sesame seeds (page 27), minced green onions, and/or cilantro.

FABULOUS: Used to season sauces, vegetables, soups, marinades, and stir-fry dishes, or in place of rich entree sauces on beef, pork, poultry, or seafood.

JAPANESE-STYLE DIPPING SAUCE

A teriyaki-style sauce.

Yield: about 1½ cups

1 cup Madeira, medium-dry sherry, or mirin (page 18)

¾ cup soy sauce

¼ cup honey

2 tablespoons sesame seeds, toasted (*page 27*)

¼ teaspoon ground ginger or 1 tablespoon minced fresh ginger

½ to 1 clove garlic, minced

4 green onions (scallions), white and green parts, minced

2 tablespoons Chinese sesame oil

Combine all the ingredients in a saucepan over medium heat and stir until the honey melts and the flavors develop, about 5 minutes. Serve hot or at room temperature.

FAST: Can prepare up to 3 months in advance, place in jars, and refrigerate.

FLASHY: As a dunk for Chinese Skewered Bites (page 143), Crispy Cocktail Ribs (page 142), Barbecued Pork and Red Cabbage Potstickers (page 254), Chinese Cabbage Sui Mai with Pork and Shrimp (page 251), or any Asian-style hors d'oeuvre. Garnished with toasted sesame seeds (page 27), minced green onions, and/or cilantro.

FABULOUS: Used to season sauces, vegetables, soups, marinades, and stir-fry dishes, or in place of rich entree sauces on beef, pork, poultry, or seafood.

2

COVER-UPS—MARINATED & PICKLED ITEMS

Although this chapter sounds as if we are going to change the focus of the book from food to swimsuits and beachwear, it actually refers to marinated or pickled vegetables, seafood, and cheese. Pickling and marinating are wonderful techniques for infusing flavors into food. Both of these techniques enable us to capture the essence of the season and preserve it for future enjoyment. You will be delighted by how inexpensive most of these items are to prepare, especially when you see how costly they are to purchase. As an added bonus, many of these recipes are very low in fat and calories.

Pickled and marinated items are just as appropriate for casual picnics as they are for gala cocktail parties. They provide flavor contrast and balance to menus. One of my favorite winter combinations is a pâté served with Pickled Onions (page 85). In the summer, Roasted and Marinated Peppers (page 88) served with feta or chèvre on Pita Chips (page 274) or French bread make a wonderful hors d'oeuvre. Dress up your next hamburger barbecue with Roasted Red Pepper Chutney (page 88) or Middle-Eastern Vegetable Dunk (page 43). Those hamburgers will be transformed into an exotic treat!

PICKLED MUSHROOMS

Yield: about 3 cups; 12 or more servings

1 cup white wine vinegar

½ cup chicken broth, homemade
(page 11) or canned

½ to 1 cup extra virgin olive oil,
depending on the richness desired

2 to 4 cloves garlic, whole or minced

1 medium-size carrot, thinly sliced

4 to 8 green onions (scallions),
white and green parts, cut into
1-inch pieces

¼ cup minced fresh parsley

Dried marjoram, rosemary, and
oregano to taste

5 black peppercorns

½ bay leaf

1½ teaspoons salt or to taste

1 pound small to medium-size
cultivated white mushrooms, stems
removed

1. Combine all the ingredients, except the mushrooms, in a medium-size saucepan and bring to a boil. Reduce the heat to low and simmer for 5 minutes.
2. Add the mushrooms and simmer for 5 to 10 minutes, until the flavors develop. Taste and adjust the seasonings.
3. Transfer the mixture to a ceramic bowl or glass jar. Cool to room temperature and chill, covered, for at least 8 hours before serving.

FAST: Can prepare up to 2 weeks in advance and refrigerate.

FLASHY: Served at room temperature with toothpicks, sliced baguettes, or any Melba/Crostini (pages 263–273). Garnished with parsley and/or any nontoxic flower.

FABULOUS: With celery, fennel, artichoke hearts, carrots, green beans, zucchini, or bell peppers instead of the mushrooms.

PICKLED ONIONS

Yield: about 4 cups; 12 or more servings

4 cups (about 1½ pounds) tiny white
boiling onions, peeled, washed,
and dried

¼ cup salt

3 cups cider or rice wine vinegar

¼ cup plus 2 tablespoons packed
brown sugar

2 bay leaves

2 teaspoons mustard seed

1 teaspoon dried red pepper flakes

1 teaspoon black peppercorns

1 piece fresh ginger, about the size of
a quarter, peeled and minced

¼ cup minced cilantro (fresh
coriander)

1. Place the onions in a large glass or ceramic bowl and stir in the salt. Let stand, covered, at room temperature overnight to mellow.
2. Rinse the onions off under cold water and drain.
3. Combine all the remaining ingredients except the onion in a medium-size saucepan and boil for 5 minutes. Add the onions and boil for 4 to 5 minutes. The onions should be barely tender.
4. Transfer the mixture to a ceramic bowl or glass jar. Cool to room temperature and chill, covered, for at least 4 hours before serving.

FAST: Can prepare up to 6 months in advance and refrigerate.

FLASHY: With pâtés, cheeses, or cheese fondues. Garnished with cilantro, parsley, and/or any nontoxic flower.

FABULOUS: With balsamic or sherry wine vinegar instead of cider or rice wine vinegar. With 2 tablespoons fresh rosemary instead of cilantro.

PICKLED CAULIFLOWER

Yield: about 7 pints; 50 or more servings

¼ cup salt

1½ cups white wine vinegar or to taste

2 heads cauliflower (about 2 pounds) cut into small florets

1 bay leaf, broken into pieces

1 small dried red chile pepper or to taste, broken into pieces (page 20)

3 cloves garlic, smashed, or to taste

1. To make the brine, in a large pot or bowl combine the salt and vinegar with enough water so that it is not too salty or too sour.
2. Place the cauliflower in plastic or glass jars and cover with the brine. Add a piece of bay leaf, a piece of the red pepper, and a clove of garlic to each container.
3. Cover the containers and leave at room temperature for at least 3 days, or until the flavors develop. (It will probably take about a week in cool weather.)

FAST: Can prepare up to 1 month in advance and refrigerate.

FLASHY: With Dijon Sauce (page 32) and Curry Sauce (page 32).

FABULOUS: With fresh or dried herbs, such as rosemary or fennel, added to the brine. Substitute turnips, celery, green beans, carrots, or jicama for the cauliflower.

Fast & Fabulous
Hors D'Oeuvres

WARM EGGPLANT ANTIPASTO

Rustic exotic!

Yield: about 1 quart; 24 or more servings

2 medium-size eggplants, cut into
  ½-inch-wide strips
2 tablespoons salt
2 tablespoons extra virgin olive oil,
  plus extra for coating
2 medium-size onions, thinly sliced
1 bunch celery, with the leaves, cut
  into 1-inch lengths
4 to 10 cloves garlic, minced
½ cup minced fresh parsley
Two 6-ounce jars marinated artichoke
  hearts, drained and marinade
  reserved
1 cup pitted Greek or Italian olives
2 teaspoons fennel seeds

2 teaspoons mustard seeds
2 bay leaves
¼ cup packed brown sugar
One 6-ounce can tomato paste
1½ cups sherry wine vinegar
2 cups chicken broth, homemade
  (page 11) or canned
Salt and freshly ground white
  and black pepper to taste
Fresh or dried rosemary, oregano,
  marjoram, thyme, and/or basil to
  taste
Crumbled feta cheese to taste
Freshly grated Parmesan to taste

1. Place the eggplant in a colander in the sink. Toss with the salt and allow it to sit for at least 1 hour to draw off any bitter juices. Preheat the oven to 350°F.
2. Heat several tablespoons of olive oil in a large skillet or a wok over medium heat. Add the onions and celery and cook, stirring, until tender and golden, about 10 minutes.
3. Stir in all remaining ingredients, except the reserved artichoke marinade, eggplant, and cheeses. Bring to a boil. Reduce the heat and let simmer for 5 to 10 minutes until the flavors develop.
4. Meanwhile, rinse the eggplant and blot dry with paper towels.
5. Place the eggplant in a bowl and toss with the reserved artichoke marinade, along with enough olive oil to coat the eggplant. Transfer to an aluminum foil-lined baking dish and bake until tender, about 15 to 20 minutes.
6. Add the eggplant to the onion mixture in the skillet and cook over medium heat, for another 5 to 10 minutes. Remove the pan from the heat and stir in the cheeses.

FAST: Can prepare up to 1 week in advance and refrigerate, or freeze for up to 6 months.

FLASHY: Served warm in a chafing dish, chilled, or at room temperature. With crackers, Pita Chips (page 274), thinly sliced baguettes, or any Melba/Crostini (pages 263–273). As a filling in Croustades (page 279), Won Ton Cups (page 246), and/or Tartlets (page 314).

FABULOUS: With fennel bulbs substituted for the celery, zucchini for the eggplant, and sliced mushrooms and carrots. Seasoned with fennel seeds, marjoram, oregano, and/or basil.

ROASTED AND
MARINATED RED PEPPERS

Yield: about 2 cups; 18 or more servings

6 to 8 large green, red, and/or
yellow bell peppers, halved,
seeded, roasted (page 26), peeled,
and sliced into thin strips or
chopped

½ cup extra virgin olive oil or more
to taste

¼ cup minced fresh Italian (flatleaf)
parsley

2 to 4 cloves garlic, minced

Salt, freshly ground black pepper,
and fresh lemon juice to taste

Toss the roasted peppers with the olive oil and mix with the remaining ingredients. Allow the mixture to marinate for at least 1 hour before serving.

FAST: Can prepare up to 5 days in advance and refrigerate, or freeze for up to 6 months.

FLASHY: With the peppers chopped up and served in Croustades (page 279) or on an antipasto platter with French bread. Used to top a chunk of chèvre, feta, teleme, muenster, brie, or mozzarella that is put in a preheated 350°F oven until the cheese just starts to soften, about 15 to 20 minutes. Served with French bread, crackers, and/or any Melba/Crostini (pages 263–273). Garnished with flat-leafed Italian parsley and/or any nontoxic flower.

FABULOUS: As a relish or seasoning ingredient. With fresh basil, rosemary, dill, and/or oregano. Minced and added to dunks or fondues. Instead of a rich entree sauce on fish, pork, poultry, beef, rice, and/or pasta.

ROASTED RED PEPPER CHUTNEY

*Absolutely delicious but not a sweet chutney
as you might expect.*

Yield: about 3 cups; 12 or more servings

1 large yellow or white onion,
chopped

2 to 4 tablespoons extra virgin olive
oil

½ cup calamata olives, pitted and
chopped

1 cup coarsely chopped roasted red
peppers (page 26)

3 to 6 cloves garlic, minced

¼ cup minced fresh Italian (flatleaf)
parsley

Salt, freshly ground black
pepper, and fresh lemon juice
to taste

¼ cup pine nuts, toasted (page 27),
or to taste

¼ to ½ cup crumbled feta cheese

1. Place the onions in a hot wok or black skillet and stir-fry over medium-high heat until tender, without any oil. I call this dry woking. This technique enhances the flavor and caramelizes the sugar in vegetables.
2. Add the olive oil, olives, roasted red peppers, garlic, parsley, and seasonings and stir-fry for about 2 minutes to bring the flavors out.
3. Remove the pan from the heat and stir in the pine nuts and feta.

FAST: Can prepare up to 4 days in advance and refrigerate.

FLASHY: With thinly sliced baguettes, in Won Ton Cups (page 246), Croustades (page 279), Tartlets (page 314), or on Melbas/Crostini (pages 263–273). Garnished with extra crumbled feta and toasted pine nuts.

FABULOUS: With toasted walnuts or almonds instead of pine nuts. With grated Parmesan instead of feta cheese.

COLD SCALLOPS VINAIGRETTE

Yield: 4 to 8 servings

1 clove garlic, minced, or to taste

2 tablespoons minced fresh parsley

3 to 6 green onions (scallions), white and green parts, cut into ½-inch lengths

2 to 4 tablespoons capers, drained and rinsed

½ cup minced softened sun-dried tomatoes (page 23)

¼ cup Chinese sesame oil

1 cup olive oil

Salt, ground white pepper, and fresh lime juice to taste

1 pound bay scallops, washed and soaked in milk for at least 1 hour, refrigerated (to prevent the scallops from being bitter)

8 ounces cubed chèvre (page 20) or mozzarella, optional

1. Bring all the ingredients, except the scallops and cheese, to a boil in a nonreactive saucepan.
2. Add the scallops and cook over medium heat, stirring a few times, until they just turn opaque. Pour the entire contents into a bowl and cool to room temperature.
3. Add the cheese to the bowl and toss well to coat everything with the marinade.
4. Cover the bowl and chill for 12 hours, or overnight, before serving.

FAST: Can prepare up to 2 days in advance and refrigerate.

FLASHY: Served cold or at room temperature with thinly sliced baguettes and toothpicks and/or any Melba/Crostini (pages 263–273). Garnished with parsley and/or any nontoxic flower.

FABULOUS: With shrimp, monkfish, shark, or swordfish cut into bite-size pieces instead of the scallops.

MARINATED SHRIMP

Yield: 4 to 8 servings

1½ pounds cooked, shelled, and
   deveined shrimp (page 24)
¼ cup minced fresh parsley
¼ cup minced green onions
   (scallions), white and green parts
2 tablespoons capers, drained and
   rinsed, or to taste

¼ cup sesame seeds, toasted
   (page 27)
Fresh lemon juice to taste
½ c. Tarragon Caper Vinaigrette
   (page 54)

Combine all the ingredients in a mixing bowl and marinate, covered with plastic wrap, in the refrigerator for at least 4 hours. Taste and adjust the seasonings.

FAST: Can prepare up to 2 days in advance and refrigerate. Can prepare the vinaigrette up to 7 days in advance and refrigerate.

FLASHY: With toothpicks, or Croustades (page 279), and/or with any Melba/Crostini (pages 263–273).

FABULOUS: With cooked crab, mussels, or scallops substituted for the shrimp.

GRAVLAX WITH GINGERED DILL MUSTARD SAUCE

This is cured raw salmon that is absolutely delicious, elegant, and great for the calorie counters!

Yield: up to 12 servings

1 to 2 pounds salmon fillets with
   skin on
2 tablespoons kosher salt
¼ cup packed brown sugar
½ cup minced fresh dill or to taste
½ cup minced pickled ginger or to
   taste (page 18)

Grated zest and juice of 1 to 2 lemons
¼ cup gin
Freshly ground black pepper to
   taste
Gingered Dill Mustard Sauce
   (recipe follows)

1. Slash the skin on each salmon fillet about 4 times with a knife and put in a glass or ceramic pan skin-side up.

2. Pour the salt, sugar, dill, ginger, and lemon zest over the salmon. Pat it in gently over both sides. Add the gin and lemon juice.

3. Cover with plastic wrap and place jars or cans on top to weight it down. Refrigerate for 1 day with the weights. Then remove the weights and place the salmon in a sealed plastic bag with all the ingredients. Return it to the refrigerate for up to 3 days, frequently turning the bag.

4. Slice thinly against grain and serve with the sauce.

FAST: Can prepare through step 3 up to 5 days in advance and refrigerate.

FLASHY: Served on a ceramic, glass, or wooden platter and garnished with fresh dill, watercress leaves, and/or lemon slices. Served with thinly sliced baguettes, pumpernickel squares, and/or any Melba/Crostini (pages 263–273).

FABULOUS: With fresh tarragon instead of, or in addition to, the dill.

FURTHER: The leftovers minced and tossed into a salad or hot or cold pasta.

GINGERED DILL MUSTARD SAUCE

You will find a million uses for this wonderful sauce.

Yield: about 2 cups

½ cup pickled ginger (page 18), drained

½ cup Dijon mustard

2 teaspoons dry mustard

3 to 4 tablespoons packed light or dark brown sugar

4 to 6 tablespoons rice wine vinegar

½ cup minced fresh dill or to taste

⅔ cup grapeseed oil

Combine all the ingredients in a food processor fitted with a metal blade, or in a blender. Taste and adjust the seasonings.

FAST: Can prepare up to 2 weeks in advance and refrigerate, or freeze for up to 6 months. Thaw in the refrigerator for 2 days or at room temperature for about 8 hours.

FABULOUS: With duck, lamb, poultry, or sausages. Used in sauces or marinades. Makes a great gift!

Rosemary Eggplant

This dish will transport you to Greece.

Yield: about 2 cups; 18 or more servings

¼ cup extra virgin olive oil

1 large onion, minced

2 to 4 cloves garlic, minced

Zest of 1 or 2 oranges, grated

1 pound eggplant, chopped or cubed

4 cups chicken broth, homemade (page 11) or purchased

2 tablespoons fresh rosemary leaves or to taste

½ to 1 cup calamata olives, pitted

1 to 2 fresh pasilla chiles, seeded, deveined, and chopped (page 20)

Dash of ground cinnamon

Salt to taste

1. Preheat the oven to 325°F.
2. Heat the olive oil in a large ovenproof skillet over medium heat. Add the onion, garlic, and zest and cook, stirring, until tender.
3. Add the remaining ingredients and bring to a boil. Remove from the heat and place in the oven for about 45 minutes, until the eggplant is tender.

FAST: Can prepare up to 4 days in advance and refrigerate, or freeze for up to 3 months.

FLASHY: With assorted crackers, any Melba/Crostini (pages 263–273), or Pita Chips (page 274). Garnished with a sprig of fresh rosemary, parsley, and/or any nontoxic flower.

FABULOUS: Seasoned with minced sun-dried tomatoes, oregano, and/or fresh basil. As an entree sauce with roast or grilled lamb, chicken, or fish.

Eggplant Caviar

My version of peasant caviar.

Yield: about 4 cups; 24 or more servings

2 large eggplant

4 medium-size red bell peppers, halved, seeded, roasted (page 26), peeled, and minced

1 cup minced fresh Italian (flatleaf) parsley

2 cloves garlic or to taste

¼ cup pine nuts, toasted (page 27) and chopped

½ cup extra virgin olive oil or to taste

½ cup crumbled feta cheese

½ cup calamata olives, pitted and chopped

Salt, freshly ground black pepper, and fresh lemon juice to taste

1. Place the eggplant on an ungreased cookie sheet and pierce with a fork in several places to allow the steam to escape. Bake in a preheated 400°F oven until tender, about 40 minutes. Remove and set aside until cool enough to handle.
2. Scoop out the meat, combine with the remaining ingredients in a food processor fitted with the metal blade, and process, using several quick on-and-off motions so as not to destroy the texture, or combine in a wooden bowl. Taste and adjust the seasonings.

FAST: Can prepare up to 5 days in advance and refrigerate, or freeze up to 3 months.

FLASHY: With assorted crackers, any Melba/Crostini (pages 263–273), or Pita Chips (page 274). Garnished with extra crumbled feta cheese, toasted pine nuts, and/or any nontoxic flower.

FABULOUS: Seasoned with minced sun-dried tomatoes, oregano, and/or fresh basil. As an entree sauce with roast or grilled lamb, chicken, or fish.

ROASTED PEPPERS WITH EGGPLANT, FETA, AND BASIL

Yield: about 4 cups; 12 or more servings

6 to 8 large red and/or yellow bell peppers, halved and seeded

1 large eggplant, cut into ½-inch-thick slices

½ cup extra virgin olive oil, plus extra for brushing

Salt and freshly ground black pepper to taste

¼ pound feta cheese, crumbled

3 to 6 pitted green olives, minced

Minced fresh basil to taste

Fresh lemon or lime juice to taste

1. Preheat the oven to 400°F. Place the peppers on an aluminum-foil-lined cookie sheet, cut-side down.
2. Brush the eggplant slices with the olive oil, place on an aluminum-foil-lined cookie sheet, and season with salt and pepper. Place both sheets in the oven and roast until the skin blackens on the peppers, about 30 to 40 minutes, and the eggplant is tender, about 30 minutes.
3. When the peppers are cool enough, peel them.
4. Place the pepper halves in a bowl along with the eggplant and toss with the remaining ingredients. Taste and adjust the seasonings.

FAST: Can prepare up to 4 days in advance and refrigerate. Can also use two 6-ounce jars roasted red peppers instead of roasting your own.

93

FLASHY: Served chilled, or at room temperature with assorted crackers, any Melba/Crostini (pages 263–273), or Pita Chips (page 274). Placed attractively on a platter. Garnished with more minced basil and crumbled feta cheese.

FABULOUS: With capers, fresh or dried rosemary, and/or calamata olives. With zucchini instead of the eggplant. Used as a salad or vegetable. With the peppers and eggplant cut into bite-size pieces and tossed into any salad, pasta, rice, or bean dish. As a pizza topping.

SOUTHWESTERN JICAMA

Yield: about 4 cups; 8 to 12 servings

1 cup white wine vinegar	Hot pepper sauce to taste
¾ cup water	1 small to medium-size jicama,
1 to 2 cloves garlic, minced	(page 21) peeled and cut into
½ teaspoon salt or to taste	sticks
1 teaspoon ground cumin or to taste	

1. Whisk together the vinegar, water, garlic, salt, cumin, and pepper sauce in a medium-size bowl.
2. Add the jicama sticks and coat well with the marinade. Let marinate for at least 1 hour before serving.

FAST: Can prepare up to 2 weeks in advance and refrigerate.

FLASHY: Served alone or with any Mexican-style dunk (pages 65–74). Garnished with cilantro (fresh coriander) and/or any nontoxic flower.

FABULOUS: With minced cilantro and/or dried oregano added. With ¾ cup minced fresh basil added.

MARINATED HERBED JICAMA

Yield: about 4 cups; 8 to 12 servings

1 cup water	1 to 2 shallots, chopped
1 cup rice wine vinegar	Salt to taste
2 tablespoons chopped fresh rosemary	1 small to medium-size jicama (page
2 tablespoons chopped fresh thyme	22), peeled and cut into sticks

1. Combine all the ingredients in a nonreactive saucepan, except the jicama. Bring to a boil.
2. Place the jicama in a glass, plastic, or ceramic container and cover with the boiling liquid. Cool to room temperature, then refrigerate for a day or so until the flavors are absorbed by the jicama.

FAST: Can prepare up to 2 weeks in advance and refrigerate.

FLASHY: Garnished with fresh rosemary, thyme, and/or any nontoxic flower.

FABULOUS: With garlic and basil instead of the shallots, rosemary, and thyme.

MARINATED FETA WITH PASILLA CHILES AND TOMATOES

Yield: about 4 to 6 servings

½ pound feta cheese
¾ to 1 cup extra virgin olive oil
3 to 4 tablespoons minced fresh
    rosemary
2 to 4 cloves garlic, minced

2 to 3 dried pasilla chiles,
    rehydrated (page 20), stemmed,
    seeded, and minced or pureed
2 to 4 medium-size, ripe tomatoes,
    seeded and minced or chopped

1. Place the feta in an attractive small ovenproof pan or au gratin dish. Cover with the olive oil and scatter in the rosemary and garlic. Mix in the chiles and tomatoes.
2. Let marinate for at least 1 hour at room temperature, or refrigerate for up to 5 days. Warm in a preheated 350°F oven until the cheese begins to melt, about 15 to 20 minutes.

FAST: Can prepare up to 5 days in advance and refrigerate, or freeze for up to 1 month.

FLASHY: Served with thinly sliced baguettes, assorted crackers, any Melba/Crostini (pages 263–273), or Pita Chips (page 274). Garnished with fresh rosemary, whole fresh chiles, and/or any nontoxic flower.

FABULOUS: With toasted (page 27) sesame seeds or nuts scattered over the top. With ½ cup minced sun-dried tomatoes instead of the fresh tomatoes.

MEDITERRANEAN BURIED BRIE

I guarantee you'll love it.

Yield: about 4 to 6 servings

One 8-ounce wheel or wedge of brie

One 6-ounce jar marinated artichoke
hearts, drained and coarsely
chopped

1 to 2 red bell peppers, halved,
seeded, roasted, peeled, and
coarsely chopped (page 26)

Minced fresh rosemary to taste

½ cup garlic cloves, roasted
(page 26)

1. Preheat the oven to 350°F. Place the brie in an attractive ovenproof skillet or low-sided baking pan.
2. Mix together the remaining ingredients and pour over the brie.
3. Place in the oven and bake until the cheese just begins to melt, 10 to 15 minutes.

FAST: Can assemble up to 3 days in advance and refrigerate, or freeze for up to 3 months.

FLASHY: With assorted crackers, any Melba/Crostini (pages 263–273), or Pita Chips (page 274). Garnished with fresh rosemary, extra marinated artichoke hearts, and/or any non-toxic flower.

FABULOUS: With the brie cut into ½-inch pieces and a piece of cheese and a bit of the topping placed on 1-inch squares of uncooked puff pastry (purchased). Place the squares on an ungreased cookie sheet and bake in a preheated 425°F oven until puffed, about 10 minutes. Can prepare ahead and refrigerate for a day, or freeze for up to 1 month on cookie sheets.

BRIE DECADENCE

*This is blissfully wicked, one of those dishes that
fantasies are made of. In fact, it is thought
to possess aphrodisiac powers.*

Yield: 2 to 4 servings

One 8-ounce wheel or wedge of brie

8 ounces fresh or canned whole
tomatoes, peeled, seeded, chopped,
and drained

½ cup Pesto (page 47)

¼ to ½ cup pine nuts or walnuts,
toasted (page 27) and chopped

1. Preheat the oven to 350°F. Place the brie in an au gratin dish or small ovenproof casserole. Mix the remaining ingredients together and pour over the brie.
2. Place in the oven until the cheese just begins to melt, 10 to 15 minutes.

FAST: Can assemble up to 3 days in advance and refrigerate, or freeze for up to 3 months.

FLASHY: With assorted crackers, any Melba/Crostini (pages 263–273), or Pita Chips (page 274). Garnished with fresh basil, more toasted nuts, and/or any nontoxic flower.

FABULOUS: See Fabulous suggestion for Mediterranean Buried Brie on page 96.

STUFFED ROSEMARY BRIE

You could get hooked on this one!

Yield: about 10 to 15 servings

2 ounces dried shiitake mushrooms, rehydrated (page 18), stemmed, and chopped

½ to 1 bunch green onions (scallions), white and green parts, chopped

Freshly ground black pepper to taste

2 to 4 tablespoons minced fresh rosemary

1½ cups almonds, toasted (page 27) and chopped

2 pounds brie (wheel or wedge)

1. Preheat the oven to 350°F. Combine all the ingredients, except the brie, in a food processor fitted with the metal blade and process, or combine in a bowl.
2. Slice the brie in half crosswise to form 2 circles or 2 wedges. Place the bottom half on an ovenproof platter or in an ovenproof pan attractive enough to serve in.
3. Top that piece with half of the shiitake mixture. Place the other piece of brie on top and top with the remaining mixture.
4. Bake until hot and the cheese just starts to melt, about 15 minutes.

FAST: Can prepare through step 3 up to 3 days in advance and refrigerate, or freeze for up to 3 months.

FLASHY: With assorted crackers, any Melba/Crostini (pages 263–273), or Pita Chips (page 274). Garnished with fresh rosemary and/or any nontoxic flower.

FABULOUS: With any fresh herb instead of the rosemary. With minced roasted garlic (page 26) added to the shiitake mixture. Use this mixture in omelets, crepes, lasagna, cannelloni, mushrooms, Garlic Crouton Rounds (page 270), and/or tartlets.

BURIED MONTEREY JACK

Jack never had it so good!

Yield: 15 to 20 servings

One 3- to 4-pound round or wedge jack
    cheese
Two to three 8-ounce jars marinated
    artichoke hearts, chopped

2 bunches fresh chives, minced

1. Preheat the oven to 350°F. Place the cheese in an ovenproof platter or in a pan attractive enough in which to serve.
2. Combine the artichoke hearts and chives in a food processor fitted with the metal blade and process, using several quick on-and-off motions so as not to destroy the texture, or combine in a bowl.
3. Top the cheese with the artichoke mixture.
4. Bake until the cheese just begins to melt, about 20 minutes.

FAST: Can prepare up to 3 days in advance and refrigerate, or freeze for up to 6 months.

FLASHY: With assorted crackers, any Melba/Crostini (pages 263–273), or Pita Chips (page 274).

FABULOUS: With 2 to 4 minced shallots or 1 bunch of green onions, minced, instead of the chives. With brie, muenster, teleme, or feta instead of jack.

Fast & Fabulous
Hors D'Oeuvres

3

TOPS

TOPS starts off with an exploration of spreads—often termed "potted" because they're meant to be served from a crock or bowl—and fillings. Even though these words have a less than enticing sound, they are full of exciting flavors, offering the cook exceptional convenience. You will discover how, in some instances, to create something delicious from dribs and drabs of ingredients in a matter of minutes. To illustrate this point, once when I was faced with a classic case of drop-in-guest panic, I created Potted Camembert. My refrigerator contained butter, a piece of leftover Camembert, and a couple of shallots. Since then, this has become one of my favorites. Necessity is the mother of invention! The real hero involved in these culinary capers is the food processor. I am eternally grateful for this piece of equipment. No matter what the occasion is, you will find a fitting filling.

Seasoned butters are something we often overlook. These mixtures create instant magic and are just the ticket to serve with sliced roast beef, lamb, ham, or turkey instead of the predictable mustard and mayonnaise. Seasoned butters are also good all by themselves, used as a spread for crackers or on thin-sliced baguettes. They are fabulous used in place of a more labor-intensive entree sauce on broiled or grilled chicken, fish, beef, and/or lamb. They can also function as an instant seasoning agent for pasta, rice, or vegetables.

The mere reference to a chafing dish brings to mind refined images of days gone by. This does not mean stuffy or complicated, though. Neither word need apply. Serving hot hors d'oeuvres in this manner is very practical for large groups and even smaller gatherings. It allows you to keep food warm without constantly running back and forth to the kitchen.

There are many beautiful chafing dishes available for purchase, but if your budget demands more creativity and less expense, relax! You can use an inexpensive fondue pot or flame-proof casserole with sterno, or your barbecue for casual outdoor entertaining. If using your grill, make sure your platters and bowls are heat resistant. If you are having a large party, I recommend renting a chafing dish. It will not only look wonderful on your table, but it also will hold enough food to accommodate everyone.

Anything that you want to serve hot and that won't crush or crumble, you can put in a chafing dish. Obviously, hot filled pastry items are out, unless you only put one layer in. Sauced items are ideal.

POTTED SOUTHWESTERN BLACK BEANS

A delicious source of vitamins,
minerals, and fiber.

Yield: about 2½ cups; 18 or more servings

½ pound dried black beans, rinsed, soaked overnight in water to cover, and drained

2 tablespoons extra virgin olive oil

1 medium-size onion, minced

2 cloves garlic, minced

1 bay leaf

3 cups chicken broth, homemade (page 11) or canned

½ cup medium-dry sherry

2 to 4 corn tortillas, torn up

2 to 4 canned whole green chiles, seeded, deveined, and chopped (page 20)

1 tablespoon chili powder

1 tablespoon ground cumin or to taste

1 bunch cilantro (fresh coriander), stemmed and minced

¼ to ½ cup minced green onions (scallions), white and green parts

Salt and hot pepper sauce to taste

½ to 1 cup chopped walnuts, toasted (page 27)

Accompaniments
(amounts are left to your discretion)

Chopped green onions (scallions), white and green parts

Minced cilantro (fresh coriander)

Grated sharp cheddar

Quartered lemons or limes

Deveined, seeded, and chopped canned whole green chiles

Cooked rice

Chopped pitted black olives

Seeded and chopped fresh tomato

Grated jack cheese

Sour cream

Avocado slices, sprinkled with lemon juice to prevent discoloring

1. Heat the olive oil in a large pot over medium heat, then cook the onion and garlic, stirring until tender. Add the bay leaf, broth, sherry, tortillas, and beans and bring it to a boil. Reduce the heat to low and simmer until the beans are tender, about 45 minutes.

2. Preheat the oven to 350°F. Drain the beans and place them in a food processor fitted with the metal blade. Add the chiles, seasonings, cilantro, and green onions. Process until it reaches the consistency you prefer. Taste and adjust the seasonings. Stir in the walnuts.

3. Place in an ovenproof casserole and cook until hot, about 20 minutes. Serve surrounded with small pottery bowls filled with the accompaniments.

FAST: Can prepare up to 2 days in advance and refrigerate, or freeze for up to 3 months.

FLASHY: Served with Tortilla Chips (page 273) or in Tortilla Cups (page 300). Served cold with Guacamole (page 73).

FABULOUS: When combined with generous amounts of sour cream and grated cheese (jack, cheddar, or mozzarella). As a warm dipping sauce to accompany Southwestern Chile Squares (page 224).

HUMMUS

*A bit of Middle-Eastern exotica that can be served
whenever you would serve guacamole.*

Yield: about 2½ cups; 18 or more servings

2 cups (one 16-ounce can) chick-peas, or dried chick-peas prepared according to the package instructions

½ cup extra virgin olive oil or to taste

¼ to ½ cup tahini (page 23)

⅓ cup fresh lemon juice or to taste

2 cloves garlic

¼ cup minced fresh parsley

¼ cup minced cilantro (fresh coriander) or to taste

Salt, hot pepper sauce, and ground white pepper to taste

1. Process all the ingredients in a food processor fitted with the metal blade or in a blender until smooth. Taste and adjust the seasonings.

FAST: Can prepare up to 2 days in advance and refrigerate, or freeze for up to 6 months.

FLASHY: Garnished with minced fresh parsley or cilantro and served with Pita Chips (page 274).

FABULOUS: With ½ cup or more toasted walnuts (page 27) substituted for the tahini.

MEDITERRANEAN CHICKEN

An excellent summer choice.

Yield: about 4 cups; 40 or more servings

3 tablespoons extra virgin olive oil

2½ pounds cultivated white mushrooms, minced

2 cloves garlic, minced

1 shallot, minced

Salt and ground white pepper to taste

1 cooked chicken breast (see note below) or 1 cup leftover chicken meat

2 tablespoons brandy or to taste

¼ pound (1 stick) unsalted butter, cut into 8 pieces

¼ to ½ cup packed fresh basil, minced

¼ cup minced fresh parsley

½ cup water chestnuts, drained and minced

¼ cup minced prosciutto

1. Heat the oil in a skillet over medium-high heat. Cook the mushrooms, garlic, and shallot, stirring, until the liquid released from the mushrooms is evaporated. Season.
2. Combine the chicken, brandy, and butter in a food processor fitted with the metal blade and process until a smooth paste is achieved.
3. Add the mushroom mixture and remaining ingredients to the processor and process, using quick on-and-off motions so as not to destroy the texture. Taste and adjust the seasonings.

FAST: Can prepare up to 3 days in advance and refrigerate.

FLASHY: Served in a crock, pâté terrine, or serving bowl, or spread on top of Beaten Biscuits (page 296) or in Croustades (page 279). For a faster version, serve on thinly sliced baguettes, pumpernickel squares, or crackers.

FABULOUS: With minced jicama (page 21) or fennel bulb instead of the water chestnuts. To stuff cherry tomatoes, raw mushroom caps, or pea pods. With leftover turkey substituted for the chicken.

NOTE: To cook the chicken breast there are several options. Either bake it in a preheated 400°F oven just until no longer pink, about 7 to 10 minutes; cook it gently in a pan of chicken broth over medium-low heat for about 20 minutes; or microwave it, covered, for about 5 minutes.

Roasted Eggplant and Garbanzo Pâté

Yield: about 3½ cups; 24 or more servings

1 pound eggplant, cubed

¼ cup extra virgin olive oil

One 15½-ounce can garbanzo beans (chick-peas), drained and rinsed

¼ cup minced fresh parsley

¼ cup minced fresh mint leaves

2 to 4 cloves garlic

1 large, ripe tomato, seeded and cut up

Salt and hot pepper sauce to taste

1. Preheat the oven to 425°F.
2. In a roasting or baking pan, combine the eggplant and olive oil. Roast until tender, about 45 minutes.
3. Transfer the eggplant to a food processor fitted with the metal blade along with the remaining ingredients and process until pureed. Taste and adjust seasonings.

FAST: Can prepare up to 3 days in advance and refrigerate, or freeze up to 1 month.

FLASHY: Served in a crock, pâté terrine, or a serving bowl. Garnished with minced fresh parsley, basil leaves, and/or any nontoxic flower.

FABULOUS: Seasoned with 1 bunch fresh basil, 2 tablespoons dried or ¼ cup fresh oregano, ¼ cup capers, and/or ½ cup marinated artichoke hearts.

White Bean Pâté with Ham and Jack Cheese

Yield: about 5 cups; 30 or more servings

1 cup grated jack cheese

1 cup cottage or ricotta cheese

4 ounces cream cheese

2 cups (one 16-ounce can) white beans, or use dried beans, drained and rinsed, prepared according to the package instructions

2 teaspoons Dijon mustard or to taste

Salt, ground white pepper, and fresh or dried rosemary to taste

2 to 4 green onions (scallions), white and green parts, minced

1 cup minced ham

½ cup walnuts, toasted (page 27) and chopped

½ cup pimiento-stuffed green olives, minced

1. Puree the cheeses, beans, mustard, and seasonings in a food processor fitted with the metal blade.

2. Add the remaining ingredients and process, using on-and-off motions so as not to destroy the texture. Taste and adjust the seasonings.

FAST: Can prepare up to 2 days in advance and refrigerate, or freeze up to 3 months.

FLASHY: Served in a terrine, crock or bowl with assorted crackers or breads. Garnished with minced green onions, pimiento-stuffed green olives, and/or any nontoxic flower.

FABULOUS: As a filling for Croustades (page 279), cherry tomatoes, raw mushroom caps, pea pods, or celery.

POTTED PORK DEGAN

This pâtélike spread is rustic in feeling, great for picnics,
holiday gatherings, and gifts.

Yield: about 6 cups; 48 or more servings

3 pounds boneless pork roast	2 cups chicken broth, homemade
¼ cup minced fresh parsley	(page 11) or canned
1 medium-size onion, coarsely	Salt, black peppercorns, garlic cloves,
chopped	bay leaves, and fresh or dried
1 medium-size carrot, coarsely	thyme and rosemary to taste
chopped	1 pound unsalted butter or cream
2 cups dry white wine	cheese, at room temperature

1. Place all the ingredients except the butter in a large pot and cover with water. Bring to a boil and let boil for about 5 minutes.
2. Reduce the heat to low and simmer until the pork is tender, about 2 hours.
3. Cool to room temperature and chill, covered, overnight. Skim off the fat, and drain the meat, reserving the liquid for soups and sauces. Discard the bay leaves. Shred the meat by hand or in a food processor fitted with the metal blade.
4. Combine the shreds with the butter in the food processor fitted with the metal blade or in a mixing bowl. Taste and adjust the seasonings.
5. Pack the mixture into crocks, jars, or small serving containers.

FAST: Can prepare up to 3 days in advance and refrigerate, or freeze for up to 4 months.

FLASHY: Served at room temperature with mustard, gherkins, Pickled Onions (page 85), lemon or orange zest; caraway seeds; minced fresh dill; chopped roasted red or green peppers (page 26), chopped green chiles, capers, fresh thyme, green peppercorns, or your favorite seasoning.

FABULOUS: With low-fat cream cheese or just using the cooking liquid instead of butter.

POTTED HAM AND CHEESE

Yield: about 3 cups; 24 or more servings

¾ pound cooked ham, minced

1 cup grated sharp cheddar

¼ cup minced green onions (scallions), white and green parts

2 tablespoons capers, drained and rinsed

1 teaspoon Dijon mustard or to taste

1 tablespoon minced fresh dill or 1 teaspoon dried

¾ cup mayonnaise, homemade (page 13) or purchased

2 tablespoons medium-dry sherry

Ground white pepper and freshly grated nutmeg to taste

1. Combine all the ingredients in a food processor fitted with the metal blade and process until a pleasing consistency is reached, ranging from somewhat chunky to smooth. Taste and adjust the seasonings.
2. Pack the mixture into a crock or mold. Chill for several hours.

FAST: Can prepare up to 2 days in advance and refrigerate, or freeze for up to 3 months.

FLASHY: Served with thinly sliced baguettes or crackers, garnished with minced green onions (scallions), fresh dill, and/or any nontoxic flower.

FABULOUS: With smoked turkey instead of ham and/or with fresh basil instead of fresh dill.

POTTED REUBEN

If you like Reuben sandwiches, you'll love this. Think of it as a Reuben pâté.

Yield: about 7 cups; 58 or more servings

2 tablespoons unsalted butter

2 cups minced onions

¾ pound corned beef, minced

1 cup sauerkraut, drained

¾ cup mayonnaise, homemade (page 13) or purchased

4 ounces cream cheese

1 cup grated Swiss cheese

2 tablespoons Dijon mustard

1 teaspoon caraway seeds or to taste

½ cup minced fresh parsley or to taste

2 to 4 tablespoons minced fresh dill

Ground white pepper to taste

1. Melt the butter in a large skillet over medium heat. When it begins to foam, cook the onions, stirring until golden brown.
2. Combine all the ingredients in a food processor fitted with the metal blade and process until smooth. Taste and adjust the seasonings.
3. Pack the mixture into small crocks or serving containers. Chill for several hours.

FAST: Can prepare up to 3 days in advance and refrigerate, or freeze for up to 3 months.

FLASHY: Served with assorted breads, crackers, and melbas. Garnished with fresh dill and/or any nontoxic flower.

FABULOUS: In Croustades (page 279) made with rye bread, or with small pieces of rye bread.

PICKLED HERRING PÂTÉ

This recipe converts herring-haters every time.

Yield: about 1½ cups; 12 or more servings

6 ounces pickled herring, drained
8 ounces cream cheese

¼ cup minced fresh dill
Zest of 1 lemon, finely grated

1. Combine all the ingredients in a food processor fitted with the metal blade and process until smooth.
2. Pack the mixture into crocks or small soufflé dishes and refrigerate until firm.

FAST: Can prepare up to 4 days in advance and refrigerate, or freeze for up to 3 months.

FLASHY: Garnished with minced fresh dill and served with pumpernickel squares or Bagel Chips (page 272).

FABULOUS: Garnished with grated lemon zest, fresh dill, and/or any nontoxic flower.

TUNA AND ARTICHOKE PÂTÉ

Tuna need not be boring.

Yield: about 2 cups; 18 or more servings

One 6½-ounce can water- or
    oil-packed tuna, drained
½ cup marinated artichoke hearts,
    drained and chopped
4 anchovy fillets
¼ to ½ cup minced green onions
    (scallions), white and green parts

½ cup minced fresh parsley
3 tablespoons capers, drained and
    rinsed
¼ pound (1 stick) unsalted butter
2 tablespoons brandy
Juice of 1 lemon
Ground white pepper to taste

1. Combine all the ingredients in a food processor fitted with the metal blade and process until a pleasing consistency is reached, ranging from somewhat chunky to smooth. Taste and adjust the seasonings.
2. Chill for at least 30 minutes before serving.

FAST: Can prepare up to 3 days in advance and refrigerate.

FLASHY: Spread on assorted crackers, any Melba/Crostini (pages 263–273), or breads. As a filling for Croustades (page 279).

FABULOUS: As a stuffing for raw mushroom caps, cherry tomato halves, or pea pods. Substitute watercress for the parsley and crab or salmon for the tuna. With toasted almonds or walnuts (page 27) added.

CRAB AND EGG SPREAD

Yield: about 4 cups; 24 or more servings

10 ounces crabmeat, picked over
    for cartilage
 4 large eggs, hard-boiled (page 24)
    and cut up
½ cup mayonnaise, homemade (page
    13) or purchased
½ cup sour cream
¼ cup freshly grated Parmesan

1 medium-size to large red bell
    pepper, halved, seeded, roasted,
    and peeled (page 26)
1 tablespoon Dijon mustard
¼ cup minced fresh dill or 1½
    tablespoons dried
1 shallot, minced
Fresh lemon juice to taste

1. Combine all the ingredients in a food processor fitted with the metal blade and process, using on-and-off motions so as not to destroy the texture. Taste and adjust the seasonings.
2. Pack the mixture into a crock or serving bowl. Chill for at least 30 minutes.

FAST: Can prepare up to 2 days in advance and refrigerate.

FLASHY: Served cold with assorted crackers, breads, or raw vegetables. Garnished with chopped fresh dill, a chopped half of a hard-boiled egg, raw bell pepper halves, and/or any nontoxic flower.

FABULOUS: As a filling for raw mushrooms, cherry tomatoes, or Croustades (page 279). As a firmer spread, with cream cheese instead of mayonnaise.

107

Tops

SARDINE SPREAD

Nobody will know what this is, but they will love it!

Yield: about 1½ cups; 12 or more servings

One 3¾-ounce can sardines

8 ounces cream cheese

4 green onions (scallions), white and
green parts, minced, or to taste

1 bunch fresh parsley, stemmed and
minced

Zest of 1 lemon, finely grated

Salt, ground white pepper, and fresh
lemon juice to taste

1. Combine all the ingredients in a food processor fitted with the metal blade and process until a pleasing consistency is reached, ranging from somewhat chunky to smooth. Taste and adjust the seasonings.
2. Chill for at least 30 minutes before serving.

FAST: Can prepare up to 2 days in advance and refrigerate.

FLASHY: Served in cherry tomatoes, Croustades (page 279), or with any Melba/Crostini (pages 263–273), crackers, or Bagel Chips (page 272). Garnished with grated lemon zest, minced parsley, and/or any nontoxic flower.

FABULOUS: With smoked trout, smoked salmon, kippered cod, cooked salmon, cooked shrimp, or crabmeat instead of the sardines.

CURRIED EGG SPREAD

An exotic twist for an old-timer.

Yield: about 3 cups; 24 or more servings

8 large eggs, hard-boiled (page
24) and cut up

2 pears, cored and chopped

⅓ cup minced cilantro (fresh
coriander) or to taste

⅓ cup minced fresh parsley or to
taste

¾ to 1 cup mayonnaise, homemade
(page 13) or purchased

⅓ cup sour cream

2 tablespoons Dijon mustard or to
taste

3 tablespoons mango chutney,
homemade (page 15) or
purchased, optional

4 to 8 green onions (scallions),
white and green parts, minced

1½ teaspoons curry powder or to
taste

Salt and ground white pepper to taste

½ cup salted or unsalted peanuts,
chopped

One 8-ounce can water chestnuts,
drained and minced, or 1 cup
chopped peeled jicama (page 21)

1. Combine all the ingredients, except the peanuts and water chestnuts, in a food processor fitted with the metal blade and process until smooth.
2. Process in the remaining ingredients using on-and-off motions, taking care not to destroy the texture. Taste and adjust the seasonings.
3. Chill for at least 30 minutes.

FAST: Can prepare up to 2 days in advance and refrigerate.

FLASHY: With crackers or as a cold filling for Croustades (page 279), or Tartlets (page 314), or to stuff raw mushroom caps, cucumber cups, or cherry tomatoes.

FABULOUS: With a dash of cardamom. With apples or any other fruit substituted for the pears.

CELERY ROOT PÂTÉ

*We are stretching the limits of a pâté with this recipe, but
even my daughter loves it!*

Yield: about 2 cups; 18 or more servings

½ cup mayonnaise, homemade (page 13) or purchased

4 ounces chèvre (page 20), cut into pieces

1 tablespoon coarse-grained or Dijon mustard

3 to 6 green onions (scallions), white and green parts, minced

¼ cup sesame seeds, toasted (page 27), or to taste

Fresh lemon juice and/or apple cider vinegar to taste

Salt and ground white pepper to taste

1 medium-size celery root, peeled and finely grated

1. Combine all the ingredients, except the celery root, in a food processor fitted with the metal blade and process until smooth.
2. Add the celery root and process with several quick on-and-off motions so as not to destroy the texture.
3. Chill for at least 30 minutes. Pack into a terrine, soufflé dish, or serving bowl.

FAST: Can prepare up to 4 days in advance and refrigerate.

FLASHY: With pumpernickel squares, Pita Chips (page 274), or as a filling for Croustades (page 279), or raw mushroom caps. Garnished with toasted sesame seeds, parsley, and/or any nontoxic flower.

FABULOUS: With ¼ cup fresh dill or 1 to 2 tablespoons fresh tarragon and/or 1 cup fresh crabmeat.

Roasted Garlic Decadence from Heaven

Guaranteed to keep vampires away.

Yield: about 1½ cups; 12 or more servings

3 heads garlic

Olive oil

2 to 4 tablespoons cream sherry

8 ounces chèvre (page 20) or 4 ounces chèvre and 1 stick unsalted butter

Salt and ground white pepper to taste

1. Preheat the oven to 250°F. Cut one third of the garlic off from top of bulb to expose all the cloves.
2. Place the bulbs in a baking dish or heavy skillet and coat with oil to prevent burning. Cover with a lid or aluminum foil. Bake until the cloves are soft and buttery, about 2 hours.
3. Squeeze the garlic cloves out of their wrappers and into a food processor fitted with the metal blade.
4. Combine the garlic with the remaining ingredients in the food processor and process until smooth.
5. Pack into an oiled, plastic wrap-lined bowl or mold. Chill until firm, about 2 hours.

FAST: Can prepare up to 5 days in advance and refrigerate, or freeze for up to 3 months.

FLASHY: Unmolded and topped with toasted pine nuts (page 27) and/or roasted garlic cloves (page 26). Served with thinly sliced baguettes, crackers, or melbas.

FABULOUS: With ½ cup toasted and chopped pecans or blanched or unblanched almonds. On grilled poultry, meats, and/or cooked vegetables. With cream and/or 2 cups chicken broth added and heated to create a marvelous entree sauce.

FURTHER: Toss leftovers into hot pasta or rice.

Roasted Garlic Decadence from Hell

A garlic-lover's fantasy with an X rating.

Yield: about 1½ cups; 12 or more servings

3 or more heads garlic

Olive oil

4 ounces feta cheese

¼ pound (1 stick) unsalted butter

3 to 6 dried pasilla chiles, rehydrated (page 20), stemmed, and seeded

¼ cup minced softened sun-dried tomatoes (page 22)

Fresh or dried rosemary to taste

2 to 4 tablespoons sherry

Salt and ground white pepper to taste

1. Preheat the oven to 250°F. Cut one third of the garlic off from the top of the bulb to expose all of the cloves.
2. Place the bulbs in baking dish or a heavy skillet and coat with oil to prevent burning. Cover with a lid. Bake until the cloves are soft and buttery, about 2 hours.
3. Squeeze the garlic cloves out of their wrappers and into a food processor fitted with the metal blade.
4. Combine the garlic with the remaining ingredients in the food processor and process until smooth.
5. Pack into an oiled, plastic wrap-lined bowl or mold. Chill until firm, about 2 hours.

FAST: Can prepare up to 5 days in advance and refrigerate, or freeze for up to 3 months.

FLASHY: Unmolded and topped with toasted pine nuts (page 27), pink peppercorns, and/or roasted garlic cloves (page 26). Served with thinly sliced baguettes, crackers, or melbas.

FABULOUS: With ½ cup toasted and chopped pecans or blanched or unblanched almonds. On grilled poultry, meats, and/or cooked vegetables. With 2 cups chicken broth added and heated to create a marvelous entree sauce.

FURTHER: Toss leftovers into hot pasta or rice.

DOUBLE PEPPER
AND ONION BRIE PÂTÉ

Yield: about 3 cups; 24 or more servings

1 large red onion, sliced
4 large green bell peppers, halved,
*   seeded, and sliced*

½ cup Roasted Red Pepper Sauce
*   (page 44)*
16 ounces brie, cut up

1. Combine the first 3 ingredients in a roasting pan or heavy cast-iron skillet and roast in a preheated 400°F oven until fully cooked, about 30 minutes.
2. Transfer this mixture to a food processor fitted with the metal blade and process until smooth with the brie.
3. Transfer to a bowl, crock, or pâté terrine and refrigerate until chilled, about 1 hour.

FAST: Can prepare up to 4 days in advance and refrigerate, or freeze for up to 3 months.

FLASHY: Served with thinly sliced baguettes, Bagel Chips (page 272), and/or any Melba/ Crostini (pages 263–273). Garnished with toasted (page 27) walnuts, pine nuts, and/or any nontoxic flower.

FABULOUS: With one large eggplant instead of the bell peppers.

PROSCIUTTO BUTTER

Yield: about 1½ cups; 12 or more servings

¼ pound prosciutto or smoked ham,
   chopped
½ pound (2 sticks) unsalted butter,
   at room temperature, cut into
   small pieces

4 ounces cream cheese
¼ cup minced shallots or to taste
2 tablespoons Madeira
Ground white pepper to taste

1. Combine all the ingredients in a food processor fitted with the metal blade and process until smooth, or use an electric mixer.
2. Pack into a terrine, soufflé dish, or serving bowl.
3. Chill until firm before serving. Unmold if desired.

FAST: Can prepare up to 5 days in advance and refrigerate, or freeze for up to 3 months.

FLASHY: With any Melba/Crostini (pages 263–273), Bagel Chips (page 272), pumpernickel squares, or sliced baguettes. Garnished with a piece of prosciutto rolled around your finger to form a rose and/or any nontoxic flower.

FABULOUS: For Salmon Butter, substitute ¼ pound smoked salmon for the prosciutto and season with ¼ cup minced fresh dill and ¼ cup green onion (scallions), green and white parts. For Hearts of Palm or Artichoke Butter, substitute ½ cup minced drained hearts of palm or drained marinated artichoke hearts for the prosciutto. For Shiitake Mushroom Butter, substitute ½ cup minced, rehydrated (page 18) shiitake mushrooms for the prosciutto. For Roasted Garlic Butter, substitute 2 heads of roasted garlic (page 26) for the prosciutto.

ROASTED RED PEPPER
AND SHALLOT BUTTER

*This compound butter is a delicious spread with lovely
color. It is especially good with any roasted or
grilled pork, lamb, or beef.*

Yield: about 1½ cups; 12 or more servings

3 large red bell peppers, halved,
   seeded, roasted, and peeled (page 26)
6 to 8 shallots, roasted (page 26)
   and squeezed out of their
   wrappings

½ pound (2 sticks) unsalted butter,
   cut up
1 tablespoon green peppercorns,
   dried or in brine and drained
Salt and ground white pepper to taste

1. Combine all the ingredients in a food processor fitted with the metal blade and process until smooth. Taste and adjust the seasonings.
2. Transfer to a bowl and cover with plastic wrap. Chill for at least 1 hour before using.

FAST: Can prepare up to 4 days in advance and refrigerate, or freeze for up to 3 months.

FLASHY: A dollop served on slices of roast tenderloin. Garnished with a piece of roasted red pepper, a roasted shallot, and/or any nontoxic flower.

FABULOUS: With minced sun-dried tomatoes mixed in and seasoned with any fresh or dried herb.

FURTHER: Use leftovers on pasta, fish, lamb, chicken, or vegetables.

CREAMED LEMON FETA

Yield: about 1 cup; 6 or more servings

4 ounces feta cheese	½ to 1 shallot, minced
¼ pound (1 stick) unsalted butter, at room temperature	Ground white pepper to taste
	Zest of 1 lemon, grated

1. Combine all the ingredients in a food processor fitted with the metal blade and process until smooth, or cream together in a bowl.
2. Pack in an oiled crock or serving bowl and chill until firm, about 1 hour. Serve in the crock or unmold.

FAST: Can prepare up to 5 days in advance and refrigerate, or freeze for up to 3 months.

FLASHY: Served with any Melba/Crostini (pages 263–273), Bagel Chips (page 272), thinly sliced baguettes, or crackers. Garnished with grated lemon zest and/or any nontoxic flower.

FABULOUS: With minced fresh or dried rosemary, cilantro, oregano, or dill. Used to stuff mushroom caps, pea pods, Belgian endive, cherry tomatoes, or celery.

POTTED CAMEMBERT

Here's the answer for what to do with leftover pieces of Camembert or brie. This is a caterer's dream!

Yield: about 1½ cups; 12 or more servings

8 ounces Camembert	1 to 2 tablespoons brandy or bourbon
¼ pound (1 stick) unsalted butter, at room temperature	½ to 1 shallot, minced
	Ground white pepper to taste

1. Combine all the ingredients in a food processor fitted with the metal blade and process until smooth, or cream together in a bowl. Taste and adjust the seasonings.
2. Pack in an oiled crock or serving bowl and chill until firm, about 1 hour. Serve in the crock or unmold.

FAST: Can prepare up to 5 days in advance and refrigerate, or freeze for up to 3 months.

FLASHY: Served with any Melba/Crostini (pages 263–273), Bagel Chips (page 272), thinly sliced baguettes, or crackers. Garnished with minced parsley and/or any nontoxic flower.

FABULOUS: Tossed into hot pasta or a dollop placed on grilled steak. With brie instead of Camembert.

MADEIRA CHEESE

Yield: about 2¾ cups; 20 or more servings

½ cup crumbled blue cheese
1½ cups grated sharp cheddar
5 tablespoons Madeira
1 clove garlic, minced

3 green onions (scallions), white and green parts, minced
¼ pound (1 stick) unsalted butter
Ground white pepper to taste

1. Combine all the ingredients in a food processor fitted with the metal blade and process until smooth.
2. Pack into crock, terrine, soufflé dish, or serving bowl and refrigerate for at least 4 hours before serving. To mold, pack the mixture into an oiled plastic wrap-lined container before chilling. To serve, invert mold onto a platter.

FAST: Can prepare up to 2 week in advance and refrigerate, or freeze for up to 3 months.

FLASHY: Excellent with pumpernickel squares or any Melba/Crostini (pages 263–273). Garnished with parsley, green onion fans, and/or any nontoxic flower.

FABULOUS: With 1 to 2 shallots instead of green onions. With port or cream sherry instead of Madeira.

BLUE CHEESE WITH MADEIRA

Yield: about 1½ cups; 12 or more servings

8 ounces blue cheese or Gorgonzola
    at room temperature
¼ pound (1 stick) unsalted butter, at
    room temperature

2 tablespoons Madeira or to taste
Salt and ground white pepper to taste

1. Cream all the ingredients in a food processor fitted with the metal blade or in a bowl. Taste and adjust the seasonings.
2. To mold, pack the mixture into an oiled plastic wrap-lined container before chilling. Refrigerate until firm, about 4 hours. To serve, invert the mold onto a platter.

FAST: Can prepare up to 1 week in advance and refrigerate, or freeze for up to 3 months.

FLASHY: Garnished with grapes and/or sliced nectarines in the summer. Served with crackers, sliced baguettes, and apple slices.

FABULOUS: Seasoned with chopped nuts and/or fresh herbs.

GORGONZOLA WITH WALNUTS

Abbondanza!

Yield: about 1½ cups; 12 or more servings

2 ounces Gorgonzola
2 tablespoons sour cream
¼ cup cream cheese, at room
    temperature
½ to 1 shallot, minced

1 to 2 tablespoons brandy
Ground white pepper to taste
½ cup walnuts, toasted (page 27) and
    chopped

1. Combine all the ingredients, except the walnuts, in a food processor fitted with the metal blade and process until smooth.
2. Add the nuts and process with quick on-and-off motions so as not to destroy the texture. To mold, pack the mixture into an oiled plastic wrap-lined container before chilling. To serve, invert mold into a platter.

FAST: Can prepare up to 4 days in advance and refrigerate, or freeze for up to 3 months.

FLASHY: Served in a small bowl. Spread on Beaten Biscuits (page 296), Croustades (page 279), any Melba/Crostini (pages 263–273), or crackers. Garnished with extra toasted walnuts, parsley, and/or any nontoxic flower.

FABULOUS: In cherry tomatoes.

PEPERONCINI CHEESE

*Peperoncini are pickled Greek-style peppers that are full of
personality. You can find them in the pickle section
of most supermarkets.*

Yield: about 1 cup; 6 or more servings

8 ounces cream cheese, at room
temperature

¾ to 1 cup imported peperoncini,
stemmed and chopped

¼ cup freshly grated Parmesan

1. Combine all the ingredients in a food processor fitted with the metal blade and process until smooth, or combine in a bowl.
2. Pack into a serving container and refrigerate for at least 1 hour before serving. To mold, pack the mixture into an oiled and plastic wrap-lined container before chilling. To serve, invert mold onto a platter.

FAST: Can prepare up to 1 week in advance and refrigerate, or freeze for up to 3 months.

FLASHY: Served with any Melba/Crostini (pages 263–273), assorted breads, and/or crackers.

FABULOUS: With marinated artichoke hearts or imported or domestic olives substituted for the peperoncini. As a filling for pea pods or cherry tomatoes. Spread on thinly sliced baguettes or pumpernickel squares and baked in a preheated 350°F oven until hot.

BASIC CHEESE MIXTURES

Yield: about 4 cups; 24 or more servings

One 8-ounce package cream cheese,
at room temperature

3 cups grated sharp cheddar

¼ cup Madeira

2 teaspoons Dijon mustard

1 to 3 cloves garlic, minced

Salt, ground white pepper, and sweet
Hungarian paprika to taste

1. Combine all the ingredients in a food processor fitted with the metal blade and process until smooth or mix together in a bowl. Taste and adjust the seasonings.
2. Chill for at least 1 hour before serving to allow the flavors to develop. To mold, pack the mixture into an oiled and plastic wrap-lined container before chilling. To serve, invert mold onto a platter.

FAST: Can prepare up to 1 week in advance and refrigerate, or freeze for up to 3 months.

FLASHY: Served with assorted crackers, thinly sliced baguettes, or any Melba/Crostini (pages 263–273). Used as a filling for raw mushroom caps, puffs, crepes, Croustades (page 279), lavosh (cracker bread), or pita bread. For a wonderful sauce, add some of the cheese mixture to a white sauce or to chicken broth. Garnished with minced green onions and/or parsley and/or any nontoxic flower.

FABULOUS: With any of these variations:

PLUM CHEDDAR SPREAD: Add Chinese plum sauce (page 17) to taste.

APRICOT CHEDDAR SPREAD: Add 6 ounces minced dried apricots and ¼ cup toasted sesame seeds (page 27).

ALMOND CHEDDAR SPREAD: Add 1 cup chopped toasted almonds (page 27).

SALAMI AND CHEDDAR SPREAD: Add 1 cup minced Italian salami and ½ cup minced green onions (scallions), white and green parts, to the basic spread.

CRAB AND CHEESE FILLING

Yield: about 4 cups; 24 or more servings; fills about 30 tartlets, croustades, or won ton cups

1 to 2 cups grated Swiss, Gruyère, cheddar, or jack cheese, plus extra for topping

11 ounces cream cheese, at room temperature

4½ teaspoons dry to medium-dry sherry

1 tablespoon Dijon mustard

¼ to ½ cup minced green onions (scallions), white and green parts

2 tablespoons minced fresh parsley

1 tablespoon capers, drained and rinsed

½ teaspoon Worcestershire sauce or to taste

½ teaspoon prepared horseradish

Salt, ground white pepper, and fresh lemon juice to taste

12 ounces cooked fresh or frozen crabmeat, picked over for cartilage

1. Combine all the ingredients, except the crabmeat, in a food processor fitted with the metal blade and process until smooth, or cream together in a bowl.

2. Add the crabmeat, using several quick on-and-off motions so as not to destroy the texture. Taste and adjust the seasonings.

FAST: Can prepare the filling up to 1 day in advance and refrigerate or freeze for up to 3 months. Pastries can be filled up to 3 hours in advance and left at room temperature. Can also be completely assembled and flash frozen (page 24) for up to 3 months. Do not thaw before heating.

FLASHY: As a filling for Croustades (page 279), Tartlets (page 314), Phyllo Cups (page 294), or Flo Braker's Magic Puff Pastry (page 309). Top each with more grated cheese before baking if desired. Place on a cookie sheet and bake in a preheated 350°F oven until golden and set, about 15 minutes.

FABULOUS: As a hot dunk. As a sauce, thinned with heavy cream, broth, or white wine and served over fish, chicken breasts, broccoli, asparagus, or pasta. With drained tuna or shrimp substituted for the crab for a less expensive alternative. With fresh or dried dill.

SALMON MANGO FILLING

Yield: about 2½ cups; 20 or more servings; fills about 30 tartlets, croustades, or won ton cups

12 ounces canned salmon, picked
  over for bones and skin
½ cup Tarragon Mayonnaise (page
  35)
¼ to ½ teaspoon dried tarragon
1 small, ripe mango, peeled, pitted,
  and chopped (page 21)

2 shallots, minced
Salt and fresh lemon or lime juice to
  taste
1 tablespoon white wine
  Worcestershire sauce
1 cup coarsely chopped peeled jicama
  (page 21)

Combine all the ingredients in a mixing bowl by hand. Taste and adjust the seasonings.

FAST: Can prepare up to 4 days in advance and refrigerate, or freeze for up to 3 months.

FLASHY: Served chilled as a pâté in a bowl or crock. As a filling for cherry tomatoes, raw mushroom caps, Croustades (page 279), and/or Won Ton Cups (page 246). Garnished with fresh sprigs of tarragon, parsley, and/or any nontoxic flower.

FABULOUS: With minced fresh dill instead of the tarragon. With ¼ to ½ cup toasted (page 27) slivered blanched almonds added.

SPINACH AND HAM FILLING

Yield: about 3 cups; 24 or more servings; fills about 40 tartlets, croustades, or won ton cups

2 tablespoons unsalted butter
2 to 3 cloves garlic, minced
1 small onion, minced
2 tablespoons all-purpose flour
½ cup heavy cream
3 tablespoons brandy
¼ cup grated Swiss cheese

One 10-ounce package frozen chopped
  spinach, thawed and drained
¼ to ½ cup chopped ham
½ to 1 teaspoon Dijon mustard
¼ cup minced fresh parsley
Freshly grated nutmeg to taste
Ground white pepper to taste

1. Melt the butter in a saucepan over medium heat. When it begins to foam, add the garlic and onions and cook, stirring, until tender.
2. Whisk in the flour and cook for 1 minute. Remove the pan from the burner and whisk in the cream and brandy. Return to the burner and cook, stirring, until thickened.
3. Stir in the remaining ingredients, reduce the heat to low, and stir until the flavors develop and the cheese melts, about 10 minutes.
4. Taste and adjust the seasonings.

FAST: Can prepare the filling up to 2 days in advance and refrigerate, or freeze for up to 3 months. Tartlets or Croustades can be filled up to 3 hours in advance and left at room temperature. They can also be assembled completely and flash frozen (see page 24) for up to 3 months. Do not thaw before heating.

FLASHY: As a filling for Croustades (page 279), Flo Braker's Magic Puff Pastry (page 309), or Tartlets (page 314). Top with grated Parmesan, and place under a hot broiler for a few minutes, until the Parmesan turns a golden color.

FABULOUS: For a faster version, spread the mixture on thinly sliced baguettes or pumpernickel squares. With minced Swiss chard, broccoli, bok choy, or asparagus instead of the spinach.

ONION AND HAM TARTLET FILLING

A rich and heavenly winter recipe that works as well at a casual après-ski party as at a Christmas gala.

Yield: about 6 cups; 60 or more servings; fills about 80 tartlets, croustades, or won ton cups

4 tablespoons (½ stick) unsalted butter	2 tablespoons brandy
6 large onions (about 2 pounds), minced	1 cup heavy cream
2 to 4 cloves garlic, minced	¼ cup minced fresh parsley
½ pound smoked ham, minced	1 cup grated jack cheese
2 tablespoons all-purpose flour	½ teaspoon dried thyme
2 teaspoons Dijon mustard	Salt, ground white pepper, and freshly grated nutmeg to taste
½ cup sherry	2 large eggs, lightly beaten

1. Melt the butter in a large skillet over medium heat. When it begins to foam, cook the onion, garlic, and ham, stirring until the onions are tender.
2. Stir in the flour and mustard and cook for 1 minute.
3. Add the sherry and brandy and cook for several minutes until they are absorbed.
4. Stir in the cream, parsley, cheese, thyme, salt, pepper, and nutmeg, and simmer over low heat until the flavors develop and the mixture is nicely thickened, about 5 minutes. Taste and adjust the seasonings.
5. Cool the mixture and stir in the eggs.

FAST: Can prepare the filling up to 2 days in advance and refrigerate, or freeze for up to 3 months. Tartlets or Croustades can be filled up to 3 hours in advance and left at room temperature. Can also be assembled completely and flash frozen (page 24) for up to 3 months. Do not thaw but cook frozen, adding about 5 minutes to the baking time.

FLASHY: As a filling for Croustades (page 279), Tartlets (page 314), Phyllo Cups (page 294), or Flo Braker's Magic Puff Pastry (page 309). Top each one with more cheese before baking, if desired. Place on an ungreased cookie sheet and bake in a preheated 350°F oven until golden and set, about 15 minutes.

FABULOUS: For a faster version, spread the mixture on thinly sliced baguettes or pumpernickel squares.

MEXICAN CRAB AND CHEESE FILLING

Yield: about 2½ cups; 20 or more servings; fills about 30 tartlets, croustades, or won ton cups

1 cup fresh or frozen crabmeat, picked over for cartilage

2 to 4 green onions (scallions), white and green parts, minced

¼ to ½ cup minced cilantro (fresh coriander)

½ cup sour cream or to taste

2 cups grated jack cheese

¼ teaspoon chili powder

¼ to ½ teaspoon ground cumin

Salt, ground white pepper, and fresh lemon or lime juice to taste

Combine all the ingredients in a mixing bowl or in a food processor fitted with the metal blade, using several quick on-and-off motions so as not to destroy the texture.

FAST: Can prepare the filling up to 2 days in advance and refrigerate, or freeze for up to 3 months. Tortilla Cups or Croustades can be filled up to 3 hours in advance and left at room temperature. Can also be completely assembled and flash frozen (page 24) for up to 3 months. Do not thaw but cook frozen, adding about 5 minutes to the baking time.

FLASHY: As a filling for Tortilla Cups (page 300) or Croustades (page 279). Place on an ungreased cookie sheet and bake in a preheated 425°F oven until the cheese melts, 8 to 10 minutes.

FABULOUS: For a faster version, spread the mixture on tortilla chips (page 273).

CHILI CHEESE FILLING

Yield: about 4½ cups; 30 or more servings; fills about 60 tartlets, croustades, or won ton cups

⅔ cup canned whole green chiles, drained, seeded, deveined, and chopped (page 20)

2 cups grated jack cheese

1 teaspoon dried oregano

½ cup green onions (scallions), white and green parts, minced

½ cup pitted black olives, drained and chopped

1 cup refried beans (page 14) or 1 cup freshly cooked pinto beans	1 tablespoon ground cumin
	½ cup minced cilantro (fresh coriander)
½ cup sour cream or plain yogurt	2 cloves garlic, minced

Combine all the ingredients in a mixing bowl or in a food processor fitted with the metal blade, using several quick on-and-off motions so as not to destroy the texture. Taste and adjust the seasonings.

FAST: Can prepare the filling up to 2 days in advance and refrigerate, or freeze for up to 3 months. Tortilla Cups, puff pastry, or Croustades can be filled up to 3 hours in advance and left at room temperature. Can also be completely assembled and flash frozen (page 24) for up to 3 months. Do not thaw but cook frozen, adding about 5 minutes to the baking time.

FLASHY: As a filling for Croustades (page 279), Tartlets (page 314), tortilla chips (see recipe for Heritage Nachos page 273), or Flo Braker's Magic Puff Pastry (page 309). Place on an ungreased cookie sheet and bake in a preheated 350°F oven until hot, about 10 minutes.

FABULOUS: For a faster version, spread the mixture on tortilla chips. With black beans instead of pinto beans.

CURRIED OLIVE AND CHEESE FILLING

*Keep olives on hand and you will be able to whip this up
at a moment's notice.*

Yield: about 3 cups; 24 or more servings; fills about 40 tartlets, croustades, or won ton cups

1½ cups pitted black olives, drained and minced	½ cup minced fresh parsley
½ cup mayonnaise, homemade (page 13) or purchased	¼ cup minced green onions (scallions), white and green parts, or to taste
1 cup grated sharp cheddar	¼ to ½ teaspoon curry powder or to taste

Mix all the ingredients together in a bowl or in a food processor fitted with the metal blade, using quick on-and-off motions so as not to destroy the texture. Taste and adjust the seasonings.

FAST: Can prepare up to 4 days in advance and refrigerate.

FLASHY: As a stuffing for raw mushroom caps, to top Garlic Crouton Rounds (page 270), or to fill Flo Braker's Magic Puff Pastry (page 309), Tartlets (page 314), or Croustades (page 279). Bake in a 350°F oven until bubbly, about 10 to 15 minutes. For a faster version, spread the mixture on thinly sliced baguettes or pumpernickel squares.

FABULOUS: For a southwestern variation, substitute minced cilantro for the parsley and ground cumin for the curry powder.

MEXICAN ALMOND PORK

A great way to use up leftovers.

Yield: about 2½ cups; 20 or more servings; fills about 30 tortilla cups, tartlets, croustades, or won ton cups

4½ teaspoons extra virgin olive oil
1 large red onion, minced
1 to 2 cloves garlic, minced
¼ to ½ cup minced cilantro (fresh coriander)
One 7-ounce can whole green chiles, stemmed, seeded, and deveined (page 20)

1 cup minced cooked pork
1 large, ripe tomato, peeled and seeded
Ground cumin to taste
½ cup raw or blanched almonds, toasted (page 27) and chopped

1. Heat the oil in a skillet over medium heat, then add the onion and cook, stirring, until tender.
2. Add the garlic, cilantro, chiles, pork, tomato, and seasonings. Cook, stirring occasionally, until the flavors develop. Stir in the almonds.

FAST: Can prepare the filling up to 2 days in advance and refrigerate, or freeze for up to 3 months. Tortilla Cups can be filled up to 3 hours in advance and left at room temperature. Can also be completely assembled and flash frozen (page 24) for up to 3 months. Do not thaw but cook frozen, adding about 5 minutes to the baking time.

FLASHY: As a filling for Tortilla Cups (page 300) or Croustades (page 279), place on an ungreased cookie sheet and bake in a preheated 350°F oven until hot, about 10 minutes.

FABULOUS: Add sour cream, chopped green onions, chopped olives, and/or grated jack cheese to taste. Serve on English muffins, black beans, or rice; in crepes, enchiladas, tacos, pita bread, or raw mushroom caps. Also as a filling for Won Ton Cups (page 246). With cooked chicken or beef instead of pork.

LEMON MUSTARD SHRIMP AND MUSHROOMS

Yield: about 5 cups; 10 or more servings

1 cup Lemon Mustard Vinaigrette (page 59)

½ to 1 pound small, cultivated white mushrooms or large mushrooms, quartered

½ to 1 cup dry to medium-dry sherry

1 pound medium-size or large raw shrimp, shelled (tails left on) and deveined

1. Add the first 3 ingredients to a large skillet and cook, stirring, over high heat until the mushrooms are cooked to your liking, about 5 minutes.
2. Add the shrimp and continue to cook over high heat, stirring, until the shrimp just turn pink, about 5 minutes.

FAST: Can prepare up to 3 days in advance and serve chilled. Can prepare through step 1 up to 4 days in advance and refrigerate. Complete right before serving.

FLASHY: Served hot in an attractive skillet or ceramic bowl, or chafing dish, fondue pot, or over an alcohol burner with toothpicks and thinly sliced baguettes.

FABULOUS: With ¼ cup drained and rinsed capers added, or with cooked chicken breast meat (cut into bite-size pieces) instead of the shrimp.

MUSHROOM MELANGE

If you are a mushroom maniac, this dish will put you into a state of ecstasy!

Yield: about 5 cups; 30 or more servings

4 tablespoons (½ stick) unsalted butter

⅔ cup minced shallots

3 to 4 ounces dried shiitake mushrooms, rehydrated (page 18), stemmed, and thinly sliced

1½ to 2 pounds cultivated white mushrooms, thinly sliced

¼ cup minced fresh parsley

Salt, ground white pepper, and fresh or dried rosemary and thyme to taste

3 cups dry red wine

3 cups beef broth, homemade (page 12) or canned

2 teaspoons tomato paste

½ cup heavy cream

2 teaspoons cornstarch dissolved in 2 teaspoons water

123

Tops

1. Melt the butter in a large skillet over medium heat. When it begins to foam, cook the shallots, stirring, until tender but not brown.
2. Stir in the mushrooms and parsley and cook, stirring, until the cultivated mushrooms are cooked and the liquid they release is cooked away, about 10 to 15 minutes. Season.
3. Increase the heat to high and add the wine, broth, and tomato paste. Bring this to a boil. Reduce the heat to medium and cook until the mixture is reduced by about half, stirring from time to time.
4. Stir in the cream and bring to a boil again. While boiling, stir in the dissolved cornstarch. Continue to simmer for a few minutes until the flavors are pleasing and the liquid has thickened to a saucelike consistency.

FAST: Can prepare up to 2 days in advance and refrigerate, or freeze for up to 3 months.

FLASHY: Served in Croustades (page 279), on Grilled Polenta (page 227), with any Melba/Crostini (pages 263–273), in a chafing dish, fondue pot, or over an alcohol burner.

FABULOUS: With ½ pound crisp-cooked chopped pancetta mixed in. This can be done in a microwave for about 5 minutes or in a sauté pan over medium heat for about 15 minutes.

FURTHER: Use leftovers in risotto, pilaf, pasta, or in soups.

DOUBLE MUSHROOM NIRVANA

For devout mushroom lovers.

Yield: about 3 cups; 24 or more servings

2 tablespoons unsalted butter

1 tablespoon extra virgin olive oil

¼ cup minced shallots or to taste

1 pound cultivated white mushrooms, minced

1 ounce dried shiitake mushrooms, rehydrated (page 18), stemmed, and chopped

½ cup Madeira

¼ cup minced fresh parsley

Salt, ground white pepper, dried thyme, and freshly grated nutmeg to taste

1 cup heavy cream

1. Melt the butter with the oil in a skillet over medium heat. When the butter begins to foam, cook the shallots, stirring, until tender but not brown.
2. Add the mushrooms and cook, stirring, until the liquid from the mushrooms evaporates.
3. Add the Madeira, parsley, and seasonings and cook until the liquid reduces by half, about 5 minutes, stirring from time to time.
4. Stir in the cream and cook until thickened, for about 10 minutes. Check the seasonings.

FAST: Can prepare the filling up to 2 days in advance and refrigerate, or freeze for up to 3 months. Phyllo Cups, Phyllo Triangles, Croustades, Flo Braker's Magic Puff Pastry, or Tartlets can be filled up to 3 hours in advance and left at room temperature. Can also be assembled completely and flash frozen (page 24) for up to 3 months. Do not thaw, but add about 5 minutes to the baking time.

FLASHY: Served in a chafing dish, fondue pot or over an alcohol burner. Use to fill Phyllo Cups (page 294), Croustades (page 279), Flo Braker's Magic Puff Pastry (page 309), or Tartlets (page 314). Place on an ungreased cookie sheet and bake in a preheated 350°F oven until hot, about 10 minutes.

FABULOUS: With minced, cooked seafood, prosciutto, poultry, or veal added. Delicious served in a chafing dish for large groups. A wonderful sauce for veal, pork, poultry, or pasta.

CAULIFLOWER MORNAY

Well received at winter cocktail parties and an excellent prelude to formal dinners.

Yield: about 1¾ cups; 12 or more servings

1 cup fresh cauliflower florets, minced
½ cup Mornay Sauce (recipe follows)
Salt, ground white pepper, and freshly grated nutmeg to taste

1. Bring a medium-size saucepan of water to a boil. Add the cauliflower and cook until just tender, about 1 to 2 minutes.
2. Combine the mornay sauce and cauliflower in a bowl and season to taste.

FAST: Can prepare the filling up to 2 days in advance and refrigerate, or freeze for up to 3 months. Flo Braker's Magic Puff Pastry or Croustades can be filled up to 3 hours in advance and left at room temperature. Can also be assembled completely and flash frozen (page 24) for up to 3 months. Do not thaw before heating, but add about 5 minutes to the baking time.

FLASHY: Served in a chafing dish, fondue pot, or over an alcohol burner. Spread on Beaten Biscuits (page 296), any Melba/Crostini (pages 263–273), or Pita Chips (page 274), or pour into Flo Braker's Magic Puff Pastry (page 309) or Croustades (page 279). Top with 3 ounces grated Swiss cheese and brown under a hot broiler. (May be kept warm in a low oven.)

FABULOUS: For a faster version, spread the mixture on thinly sliced baguettes or pumpernickel squares. With minced broccoli, hearts of palm, spinach, mushrooms, eggplant, etc., instead of the cauliflower.

MORNAY SAUCE

Yield: about ½ cup

1 tablespoon unsalted butter	*3 tablespoons dry to medium-dry*
1 shallot, minced	*sherry*
1 to 2 teaspoons Dijon mustard or to taste	*Salt, ground white pepper, and freshly grated nutmeg to taste*
2 tablespoons all-purpose flour	*¼ cup freshly grated Parmesan or*
5 tablespoons hot milk	*Gruyère or to taste*

1. Melt the butter in a saucepan over low heat. When the butter starts to foam, cook the shallot, stirring, until tender but not brown.
2. Blend in the mustard and flour and cook, stirring, for 2 minutes, being careful not to brown.
3. Slowly stir in the milk and sherry. Whisk while bringing the mixture to a boil. Reduce the heat to medium, season, then cook until thickened, whisking constantly, about 3 to 5 minutes.
4. Reduce the heat to low, stir in the cheese, and cook until melted.

FAST: Can prepare up to 4 days in advance and refrigerate, or freeze for up to 3 months.

FABULOUS: With dry vermouth, Madeira, or Marsala instead of sherry.

Fast & Fabulous
Hors D'Oeuvres

WARM CRAB AND ROASTED PEPPERS

Yield: about 2½ cups; 20 or more servings; fills about 30 tartlets, croustades, or won ton cups

6½ ounces fresh or frozen crabmeat, picked over for cartilage

¼ to ½ cup minced roasted red bell peppers (page 26)

2 to 4 tablespoons minced green onions (scallions), white and green parts

½ cup mayonnaise, homemade (page 13) or purchased

¼ cup cream cheese, at room temperature

¼ to ½ cup grated jack cheese

2 to 4 tablespoons capers, drained and rinsed

¼ cup minced fresh parsley

2 tablespoons minced fresh dill

Salt and ground white pepper to taste

Blend all the ingredients together in a food processor fitted with the metal blade, using several quick on-and-off motions so as not to destroy the texture, or combine in a mixing bowl. Taste and adjust the seasonings.

FAST: Can prepare the filling up to 1 day in advance and refrigerate or freeze for up to 3 months.

FLASHY: Served in a chafing dish, fondue pot, or over an alcohol burner. As a filling for Croustades (page 279), Won Ton Cups (page 246), Flo Braker's Magic Puff Pastry (page 309), or Tartlets (page 314). Bake in a preheated 350°F oven or until puffy and golden, about 10 minutes. On pita bread, and/or flour tortillas baked in a preheated 350°F oven until puffy and golden, 8 to 10 minutes. Serve warm.

FABULOUS: In raw mushroom caps or spread on thin slices of baguette. Substitute cooked chicken, shrimp, or tuna for the crab.

SPRING MORNAY

Prepare and freeze large batches during
the asparagus season.

Yield: about 2½ cups; 20 or more servings; fills about 30 croustades, phyllo cups, or won ton cups

3 large eggs, hard-boiled (page 24)
   and coarsely chopped
1 clove garlic, minced
One 6-ounce jar marinated artichoke
   hearts, drained and coarsely
   chopped
3 tablespoons capers, drained,
   rinsed, and coarsely chopped

¼ cup Mornay Sauce (page 126)
½ cup asparagus tips, chopped and
   blanched (page 23) for about 3
   minutes
Salt and ground white pepper to taste
3 ounces sharp cheddar cheese,
   grated

Combine all the ingredients and mix well.

FAST: Can prepare the filling up to 2 days in advance and refrigerate, or freeze for up to 3 months. Phyllo Cups, Beaten Biscuits, Won Ton Cups or Croustades can be filled up to 3 hours in advance and left at room temperature. Can also be assembled completely and flash frozen (page 24) for up to 3 months. Do not thaw before heating, but add about 5 minutes to the baking time.

FLASHY: Served in a chafing dish, fondue pot, or over an alcohol burner. Spread on Beaten Biscuits (page 296) or poured into Croustades (page 279), Won Ton Cups (page 246), or Phyllo Cups (page 294) and browned under a hot broiler or in a preheated 350°F oven for about 5 to 10 minutes.

FABULOUS: For a faster version, spread the mixture on thinly sliced baguettes or pumpernickel squares. In crepes or on English muffins for brunches or luncheons. On pasta or rice for entrees. With crab added to the filling.

MUSHROOMS IN
MADEIRA BLUE CHEESE SAUCE

Sheer bliss!

Yield: about **8** or more servings

Sauce

¾ cup Madeira

2 tablespoons minced shallots

1 cup heavy cream

½ cup beef broth, homemade (page 12) or canned

4 tablespoons (½ stick) unsalted butter

2 ounces blue cheese, crumbled

2 teaspoons Dijon mustard, or more

Salt, ground white pepper, dried thyme, and freshly grated nutmeg to taste

Mushroom mixture

2 tablespoons unsalted butter

2 tablespoons extra virgin olive oil

1 pound cultivated white mushrooms

3 to 4 dried shiitake mushrooms, rehydrated (page 18), stemmed, and thinly sliced

1 to 2 cloves garlic, minced

3 tablespoons minced fresh parsley

Salt and ground white pepper to taste

1. Bring the Madeira and shallots to a boil in a saucepan and continue to boil until the liquid reduces to 2 tablespoons.
2. Add the cream and broth and let boil until reduced to 1 cup, for about 10 minutes.
3. Meanwhile, combine the butter, cheese, and mustard in a food processor fitted with the metal blade and process until smooth, or cream together in a bowl. Reduce the heat to low and whisk this mixture a tablespoon at a time into the sauce until it reaches a thickened sauce consistency and the flavor is pleasing. You may not wish to use all of the cheese-and-butter mixture.
4. Simmer for a few minutes over low heat.
5. Meanwhile, melt the butter with the olive oil in a skillet. When it begins to foam, add all the mushroom mixture ingredients and cook, stirring, until the liquid that the white mushrooms release evaporates.
6. Place the sauce in a fondue pot, chafing dish, or burner-proof casserole and add the mushroom mixture. Serve with toothpicks and French bread.

FAST: Can prepare any or all elements up to 4 days in advance and refrigerate, or freeze for up to 3 months. Reheat in a preheated 350°F oven for about 30 minutes.

FABULOUS: With the cheese-and-butter mixture served as a spread for French bread, pumpernickel squares, or crackers. Used to season cooked vegetables.

129

Tops

MUSHROOMS ESCARGOT

Mushrooms prepared with an escargot-style butter.

Yield: 10 or more servings

½ pound (2 sticks) unsalted butter

4 cloves garlic, minced, or to taste

½ to 1 cup minced fresh parsley

1 pound cultivated white mushrooms

Finely grated zest and juice of 1
  lemon

2 tablespoons brandy

Salt and ground white pepper to taste

Melt the butter in a large skillet over medium-high heat. When it begins to foam, add the garlic, parsley, and mushrooms and stir. Cook until the liquid that the mushrooms release cooks away. Add the lemon zest and juice, brandy, salt, and white pepper and cook, stirring, until flavors are pleasing. Taste and adjust the seasonings.

FAST: Can prepare up to 2 days in advance and refrigerate. It's best to slightly undercook the mushrooms and finish cooking before serving.

FLASHY: Served in a chafing dish, fondue pot, or over an alcohol burner with toothpicks, any Melba/Crostini (pages 263–273), sliced baguettes, or Garlic Crouton Rounds (page 270).

FABULOUS: As a side dish with roast beef, pork, veal, or poultry.

MUSHROOMS MICHELE

The Ultimate, in all modesty!

Yield: 10 or more servings

4 tablespoons (½ stick) unsalted
  butter

2 tablespoons extra virgin olive oil

2 cloves garlic, minced

1 pound cultivated white mushrooms

⅔ cup minced ham

1 to 3 shallots, minced

¼ cup bourbon

¼ cup minced fresh parsley

½ teaspoon dried thyme

1 cup beef broth, homemade (page
  12) or canned

3 tablespoons heavy cream

Salt and ground white pepper to taste

1. Melt butter with the olive oil in a large, heavy skillet over high heat. When the butter begins to foam, add the garlic and mushrooms and cook, stirring, until the mushrooms are browned. Transfer to a bowl.

2. Add the ham, shallots, and bourbon and cook, stirring, until the bourbon is reduced to a glaze, about 5 minutes.

3. Add the remaining ingredients and cook, stirring, until the liquid is reduced to a nice thickness and the flavors are developed, about 5 to 10 minutes. Taste and adjust the seasonings.
4. Add the mushroom mixture and cook over low heat until the mushrooms are hot. Transfer to a chafing dish, fondue pot, or set over an alcohol burner.

FAST: Can prepare up to 2 days in advance and refrigerate, or freeze for up to 3 months.

FLASHY: Served with toothpicks. As a dunk for any Melba/Crostini (pages 263–273) or thinly sliced baguettes.

FABULOUS: As a vegetable dish for dinner.

BEST-EVER CHILE VERDE SAUCE

Yield: about 3 cups; 24 or more servings

One 12-ounce can green chile enchilada sauce
1 cup chicken broth, homemade (page 11) or canned
2 to 4 green onions (scallions), white and green parts, minced

½ cup cream sherry
½ to 1 bunch cilantro (fresh coriander), stemmed and minced
Salt to taste

1. Combine all the ingredients, except the cilantro and salt, in a saucepan and bring to a boil. Let simmer over medium heat until the flavors are pleasing, about 10 minutes.
2. Stir in the cilantro and salt.

FAST: Can prepare up to 4 days in advance and refrigerate, or freeze for up to 6 months.

FLASHY: Served in a chafing dish, fondue pot, or over an alcohol burner as a warm dunk for chicken wings, shrimp, or skewers of pork.

FABULOUS: With ½ cup sour cream mixed in. As an entree sauce for fish, chicken, pork, vegetables, pasta, or rice. On a baked potato.

Mexican Tomato Sauce

An intriguing sauce with a mild, yet complex flavor.

Yield: about 3 cups; 24 or more servings

2 tablespoons extra virgin olive oil

½ cup chopped onions

2 cloves garlic, minced

1 cup peeled, seeded, and chopped tomatoes (fresh or canned)

1½ cups chicken broth, homemade (page 11) or canned

2 tablespoons tomato paste

2 teaspoons sugar

½ teaspoon salt

½ teaspoon ground cumin

Ground white pepper to taste

1 tablespoon cornstarch dissolved in 2 tablespoons water

1. Heat the oil in a medium-size skillet over medium heat. Add the onions and garlic and cook, stirring, until tender.
2. Add the remaining ingredients, except the dissolved cornstarch, and simmer over medium heat until the tomatoes disintegrate.
3. Puree the sauce in a blender or a food processor fitted with the metal blade. (You may need to do this in two batches. Also, remember to leave a vent at the top so you won't cause an explosion because of the built-up steam.)
4. Return the sauce to the burner and bring to a boil. Stir in the dissolved cornstarch and cook, stirring over high heat, until thickened, about 3 minutes.

FAST: Can prepare up to 1 week in advance and refrigerate, or freeze for up to 6 months.

FLASHY: Served in a chafing dish, fondue pot, or over an alcohol burner as a warm dunk for Tortilla Chips (page 273), Albondigas (page 164), or cooked pieces of seafood, pork, or poultry.

FABULOUS: As an entree sauce for pasta, rice, chicken, pork, fish, or lamb dishes.

Fast & Flashy Marinara

Here's my version of a sauce I discovered at Modesto Lanzone's in San Francisco.

Yield: about 2 cups; 18 or more servings

2 tablespoons olive oil

2 to 4 cloves garlic, minced

1 large onion, minced

1 pound canned or fresh, ripe tomatoes, peeled, seeded, and pureed

¼ cup Madeira

1 bunch fresh parsley, stemmed and minced

1 bay leaf

Salt, ground white pepper, and freshly grated nutmeg to taste

1. Heat the olive oil in a large skillet over medium heat. Add the garlic and onion and cook, stirring, until tender.
2. Add the tomatoes and Madeira and bring to a simmer. Reduce the heat to low, and add the parsley, bay leaf, and seasonings.
3. Simmer until the flavors develop to your taste, about 30 minutes. Remove the bay leaf.

FAST: Can prepare up to 4 days in advance and refrigerate, or freeze for up to 6 months.

FLASHY: Served in a chafing dish, fondue pot, or over an alcohol burner as a warm dunk for sliced Italian sausages, chicken wings, or any Melba/Crostini (pages 263–273), or sliced baguettes.

FABULOUS: As a sauce for everything from pasta to veal. Varied with touches of minced fresh rosemary, basil, oregano, fennel, or marjoram.

CREAMED TOMATO SAUCE

*A rich, elegant alternative to the standard tomato sauce
with a French flair.*

Yield: about 2 cups; 18 or more servings

One 2-pound, 30-ounce can peeled
   Italian tomatoes, drained and
   pureed
1/4 cup medium-dry sherry or
   Madeira
1 to 2 shallots, minced

2 to 4 tablespoons minced fresh
   parsley
1/4 to 1/2 teaspoon dried thyme
1 bay leaf
Salt and ground white pepper to taste
1/2 cup heavy cream

1. Combine all the ingredients, except the cream, in a saucepan and bring to a boil over medium-high heat.
2. Cook until the mixture thickens, about 15 to 20 minutes. Stir in the heavy cream and continue cooking until the sauce coats the back of a spoon, about 5 to 10 minutes. Taste and adjust the seasonings.
3. Strain to remove the bay leaf, parsley, and tomato seeds.

FAST: Can prepare up to 4 days in advance and refrigerate, or freeze for up to 6 months.

FLASHY: Served in a chafing dish, fondue pot, or over an alcohol burner as a warm dunk for Italian Sausage and Mushroom Calzette (page 261), Artichoke Heart and Goat Cheese Calzette (page 260), or Leek and Goat Cheese Calzette (page 262), or any Melba/Crostini (pages 263–273), or Italian Veal, Mozzarella, and Anchovy Sausages (page 167).

FABULOUS: With touches of minced fresh rosemary, basil, oregano, fennel, or marjoram.

TOMATO SAUSAGE SAUCE

An intensely aromatic and robust sauce. Great cold weather choice.

Yield: about 2½ cups; 20 or more servings

2 Italian sweet sausages, about ½ pound, casings removed

4 to 6 cloves garlic, minced

2 large onions, minced

1 pound canned or fresh, ripe tomatoes, peeled, seeded, and pureed

¼ cup dry white or red wine

1 bunch fresh parsley, stemmed and minced

1 bay leaf

1 teaspoon fennel seeds

Salt and ground white pepper to taste

1. Place the sausage, garlic, and onions in a skillet over medium heat. Break the sausages up using a wooden spatula and brown. Pour out the excess fat.
2. Add the remaining ingredients and bring to a boil. Reduce the heat and simmer until it reaches a thick, chunky consistency, about 15 to 30 minutes. Remove the bay leaf. Taste and adjust the seasonings.

FAST: Can prepare up to 4 days in advance and refrigerate, or freeze for up to 6 months.

FLASHY: In a chafing dish, fondue pot, or over an alcohol burner with meatballs. As a warm dunk for fried zucchini or eggplant, or Garlic Crouton Rounds (page 270), or any Melba/ Crostini (pages 263–273).

ROASTED GARLIC CHUTNEY SAUCE

Yield: about 2½ cups; 20 or more servings

1 cup beef broth, homemade (page 12) or canned

½ to ¾ cup cream sherry

¼ to ½ cup mango chutney, home-made (page 15) or purchased

½ cup garlic cloves, roasted (page 26)

2 teaspoons cornstarch dissolved in 2 tablespoons water or white wine

1. Place all the ingredients, except for the dissolved cornstarch, in a small saucepan and bring to a boil.
2. Stir the dissolved cornstarch into the boiling sauce, adding only as much as is needed to reach the desired thickness.

FAST: Can prepare up to 5 days in advance and refrigerate, or freeze for up to 6 months.

Fast & Fabulous
Hors D'Oeuvres

FLASHY: Served in a chafing dish, fondue pot, or over an alcohol burner as a dunk for sliced baguettes, crackers, or any Melba/Crostini (pages 263–273). At room temperature on fish, pork, chicken, rice and/or vegetables.

FABULOUS: With 2 tablespoons toasted sesame seeds (page 27) and/or with 2 to 4 tablespoons minced cilantro mixed in. As a seasoning agent for soups, sauces, and marinades.

Coconut Basil Sauce

Wild and exotic flavors.

Yield: about 3 cups; 24 or more servings

2 tablespoons peanut or extra virgin olive oil

2 shallots, minced

2 to 3 cloves garlic, minced

1 cup shrimp stock (page 13) or 1 cup clam juice

1 cup chicken broth, homemade (page 11) or canned

½ cup dry white wine

2 to 4 dried pasilla chiles stemmed, rinsed, seeded, and torn into pieces (page 20)

½ cup frozen coconut milk

2 to 4 tablespoons minced fresh basil

Salt, ground white pepper, and fresh lemon or lime juice to taste

2 tablespoons cornstarch dissolved in 2 tablespoons water

1. Heat the oil in a medium-size saucepan over medium heat. Cook the shallots and garlic, stirring, until tender.
2. Place shrimp stock, chicken broth, and wine in a saucepan and bring to a boil.
3. Add the chiles and return to a boil. Reduce the heat to medium and cook until the liquid is flavorful, about 20 minutes.
4. Add the coconut milk and basil. Bring the mixture to a boil again over medium-high heat and season to taste.
5. Stir as much of the dissolved cornstarch into the boiling sauce as you need to thicken it.

FAST: Can prepare up to 1 day in advance and refrigerate, or freeze for up to 6 months.

FLASHY: Served in a chafing dish, fondue pot, or over an alcohol burner as a dunk for skewers of seafood, pork, beef, or chicken.

FABULOUS: As an entree sauce for pasta, rice, seafood, pork, beef, or chicken dishes.

YUCATÁN SAUCE

Yield: about 2½ cups; 20 or more servings

1 large, ripe tomato, peeled, seeded, and chopped

2 medium-size bell peppers, preferably red, chopped

½ bunch cilantro (fresh coriander), stemmed and chopped

1 cup tomato juice

¼ to ½ large Bermuda onion, minced

6 to 8 green onions (scallions), white and green parts, minced

2 tablespoons vinegar

¾ cup beer

1. Place all the ingredients in a food processor fitted with the metal blade, or in a blender, or combine in a bowl. The texture can be smooth or chunky.
2. Place in a saucepan and warm gently over medium-low heat; do not boil. Taste and adjust the flavors.

FAST: Can prepare up to 1 week in advance and refrigerate, or freeze for up to 6 months.

FLASHY: Served in a chafing dish, fondue pot, or over an alcohol burner as a dunk for Tortilla Chips (page 273), Albondigas (page 164), cooked seafood, pork, or poultry.

FABULOUS: As an entree sauce for beef, pork, poultry, seafood, pasta, or rice.

CILANTRO, ROASTED GARLIC, AND ALMOND SAUCE

Yield: about 2 cups; 18 or more servings

¼ cups medium-dry sherry

1 cup chicken broth, homemade (page 11) or canned

1 head garlic, roasted (page 26), cloves squeezed out of their wrappers

Juice of 1 lemon

¼ cup slivered blanched almonds, toasted (page 27) and chopped

1 bunch cilantro (fresh coriander), stemmed and chopped or pureed

Salt and ground white pepper to taste

½ cup heavy cream, optional

1. Place the first 5 ingredients in a saucepan over high heat and bring to a boil. Reduce the heat to medium-low and simmer for several minutes, until the flavors develop.
2. Stir in the cilantro, season, and add the cream. Continue to simmer over medium-low heat for about 5 minutes until the flavors are pleasing.

FAST: Can prepare up to 3 days in advance and refrigerate, or freeze for up to 3 months.

FLASHY: Served in a chafing dish, fondue pot, or over an alcohol burner as a warm dunk for Tortilla Chips (page 273), cooked seafood, chicken, pork, and/or lamb.

FABULOUS: As a marinade or sauce for vegetables, seafood, beef, lamb, poultry, and/or pork. On any salad.

CILANTRO CUMIN SAUCE

Another winner!

Yield: about 3 cups; 24 or more servings

1 tablespoon unsalted butter

½ to 1 carrot, minced

1 large onion, minced

1 to 2 cloves garlic, minced

1 teaspoon Dijon mustard

2 tablespoons all-purpose flour

2 cups chicken broth, homemade (page 11) or canned, reduced to 1 cup over high heat

½ cup dry white wine, reduced to ¼ cup over high heat

½ teaspoon ground cumin or to taste

Salt and ground white pepper to taste

½ cup minced cilantro (fresh coriander)

1. Melt the butter in a saucepan over medium-low heat. When it starts to foam, add the carrots and onions and cook, stirring, until golden, about 20 to 30 minutes.

2. Whisk in the garlic, mustard, and flour, and cook over low heat for 1 minute.

3. Increase the heat to medium-high, add the remaining ingredients, except the cilantro, and stir until the mixture comes to a boil. Reduce the heat to medium-low and simmer until the sauce thickens and the flavors develop, about 10 minutes, stirring frequently.

4. Taste and adjust the seasonings. Strain through a fine metal sieve and stir in the cilantro.

FAST: Can prepare up to 3 days in advance and refrigerate, or freeze for up to 6 months.

FLASHY: Served hot or at room tmeperature in a chafing dish, fondue pot, or over an alcohol burner with any Asian-style hors d'oeuvre in this book, from Crispy Cocktail Ribs (page 142) to Barbecued Pork and Red Cabbage Potstickers (page 254).

FABULOUS: As a seasoning sauce to enhance other sauces, marinades, vegetables, soups, and stir-fry dishes. As an entree sauce for pasta, rice, seafood, pork, or chicken.

SATE SAUCE

A variation of an Indonesian classic.

Yield: about 3 cups; 24 or more servings

4 shallots, peeled

2 to 4 cloves garlic, peeled

4 canned whole green chiles, seeded
   and deveined (page 20)

4 to 8 Brazil nuts

½ cup minced cilantro (fresh
   coriander)

¼ cup peanut oil

¼ cup soy sauce or to taste

¼ cup Chinese plum sauce (page 17)

1 cup chicken broth, homemade
   (page 11) or canned

¾ cup medium-dry sherry

¼ cup fresh lemon juice

Salt, ground white pepper, and sugar
   to taste

1. Puree the shallots, garlic, chiles, nuts, and cilantro in a food processor fitted with
   the metal blade.
2. Heat the oil in a saucepan over medium-high heat and cook the mixture, stirring
   frequently.
3. Add the remaining ingredients, continuing to cook over medium-high heat, stirring
   frequently until it thickens, about 5 to 10 minutes. If the sauce is too thick, add
   more chicken broth.

FAST: Can prepare up to 1 week in advance and refrigerate.

FLASHY: Served hot or at room temperature in a chafing dish, fondue pot, or over an alcohol
   burner with any Asian-style hors d'oeuvre in this book, from Crispy Cocktail Ribs (page
   142) to Barbecued Pork and Red Cabbage Potstickers (page 254).

FABULOUS: As a seasoning sauce to enhance other sauces, marinades, vegetables, soups,
   and stir-fry dishes. As an entree sauce for pasta, rice, seafood, pork, or chicken.

GARLIC ANCHOVY SAUCE

Yield: about 1½ cups; 12 or more servings

2 tablespoons unsalted butter

2 cloves garlic, minced, or to
   taste

½ to 1 shallot, minced

2 tablespoons all-purpose flour

2 cups chicken broth, homemade
   (page 11) or canned

¼ cup dry vermouth

2 anchovy fillets, rinsed and
   mashed, or to taste

1 to 2 tablespoons minced fresh
   basil or 1 teaspoon dried

1 to 2 tablespoons minced fresh
   parsley

Salt, ground white pepper, and fresh
   lemon juice to taste

1. Melt the butter in a saucepan over medium-low heat. When the butter starts to foam, cook the garlic and shallots, stirring briefly, until tender; do not brown them.
2. Stir in the flour and cook over low heat for a minute more, without browning.
3. Remove the pan from the burner and stir in the broth and vermouth. Return to the burner and cook until it thickens, while stirring over medium heat.
4. Stir in the remaining ingredients and cook over medium heat for about 5 minutes. Taste and adjust the seasonings.

FAST: Can prepare up to 4 days in advance and refrigerate, or freeze for up to 3 months.

FLASHY: Served in a chafing dish, fondue pot, or over an alcohol burner with cooked seafood, bite-size pieces of poultry, veal, or mushroom.

FABULOUS: Over pork, poultry, beef, or veal as an entree sauce.

BAGNA CAUDA

Here's one more Italian garlic-and-anchovy sauce. This is my interpretation of the Italian classic, which translates literally to "a hot bath."

Yield: about 1½ cups; 12 or more servings

4 cloves garlic, finely chopped, or to taste

4 to 6 rinsed anchovy fillets, finely chopped

¼ cup minced fresh parsley

Finely grated zest and juice of 1 to 2 lemons

1 cup unsalted butter

¼ cup extra virgin olive oil

Freshly ground coarse black pepper to taste

1. Puree the garlic, anchovies, parsley, and zest in a food processor fitted with the metal blade, or combine in a bowl.
2. Heat the butter and oil together in a skillet over medium-low heat. When the butter begins to foam, add the garlic mixture, lemon juice, and pepper and cook, stirring, over low heat until the flavors are pleasing, 3 to 5 minutes. Taste and adjust the seasonings.

FAST: Can prepare up to 3 days in advance and refrigerate, or freeze for up to 3 months.

FLASHY: Served in a chafing dish, fondue pot, or over an alcohol burner with raw or cooked vegetables or sliced baguettes.

FABULOUS: As a warm dunk for cooked artichoke leaves. As an entree sauce drizzled over pasta, any cooked vegetable, chicken, veal, or seafood.

MUSHROOMS, HEARTS OF PALM, AND SHRIMP IN A TARRAGON CREAM SAUCE

Yield: about 8 servings

5 tablespoons unsalted butter

1 pound cultivated white mushrooms

Salt and ground white pepper to taste

2 to 4 shallots, minced

1 pound medium-size raw shrimp, shelled and deveined

⅓ to ½ cup minced softened sun-dried tomatoes (page 22)

1 teaspoon dried tarragon

¾ cup dry white wine

Fresh lemon or lime juice and finely grated zest to taste

⅔ cup clam juice

1⅓ cups heavy cream

1 tablespoon cornstarch dissolved in 1 tablespoon white wine or water

One 14-ounce can hearts of palm, drained and cut into ¾-inch lengths

1. Melt 2 tablespoons of the butter in a heavy skillet over medium-high heat. When the butter starts to foam, cook the mushrooms, stirring. Season with salt and pepper, and add the shallots. Cook until mushrooms are just tender and transfer them to an ovenproof dish and keep warm in a low oven.

2. Melt the remaining butter in a saucepan over medium heat. When it starts to foam, cook the shrimp briefly, stirring, until almost fully opaque, about 3 to 5 minutes. Transfer them to the dish with the mushrooms.

3. Add the tomatoes, tarragon, wine, lemon juice and zest, and clam juice to the empty saucepan. Bring to a boil and cook until it reduces by one-third, about 5 minutes.

4. Add the cream and cook until it reduces by half, about 5 to 10 minutes. Taste and adjust the seasonings.

5. Return the sauce to a boil and slowly stir in the cornstarch mixture. Cook while stirring until the sauce is thick enough to coat the back of a spoon, about 3 to 5 minutes. (This will stabilize the sauce and prevent it from separating.)

6. Place the hearts of palm, shrimp, and mushrooms in the sauce. Cook over medium heat until the shrimp are fully cooked, being careful not to overcook them. This will only take about 3 to 5 minutes.

7. Transfer this to an ovenproof serving dish or chafing dish and serve.

FAST: Can prepare the sauce up to 3 days in advance and refrigerate, or freeze for up to 3 months. Or can prepare the complete dish up to 1 day in advance, bring to room temperature, and warm in a 350°F oven.

FLASHY: Served in a chafing dish, fondue pot, or over an alcohol burner with toothpicks or on small hors d'oeuvre plates with forks.

FABULOUS: Cut ingredients into smaller pieces and fill Flo Braker's Magic Puff Pastry (page 309), Tartlets (page 314), or Croustades (page 279).

PORK AND MUSHROOMS MERLOT

A robust cold-weather dish. For added flavor, marinate
the pork.

Yield: about 2 quarts; 10 or more servings

Pork marinade

2 tablespoons extra virgin olive oil

⅓ cup Merlot

2 cloves garlic, minced

2 tablespoons minced fresh parsley

¼ cup fresh rosemary leaves, minced

½ to 1 teaspoon dried thyme, crushed

2 whole green onions (scallions), white and green parts, minced

1 large egg

Pork mixture

1 pound boneless pork tenderloin, cut into ½-inch cubes

4 tablespoons (½ stick) unsalted butter, plus extra

2 tablespoons olive oil

1 pound cultivated white mushrooms

2 cups beef broth, homemade (page 12) or canned

⅔ cup plus 1 tablespoon Merlot

2 tablespoons minced fresh parsley

1 tablespoon Dijon mustard

2 to 4 shallots, minced

2 to 4 cloves garlic, minced

2 to 4 tablespoons fresh rosemary leaves, minced

½ teaspoon dried thyme, crushed

1 tablespoon cornstarch

¼ to ½ cup heavy cream, optional

1. Combine all the marinade ingredients with the pork cubes. Allow them to sit at room temperature for up to 1 hour, or refrigerate for up to 48 hours.
2. Remove the pork from the marinade, drain, and pat dry with paper towels.
3. In a skillet or wok, melt the butter with the olive oil over medium-high heat. When the butter begins to foam, brown the pork in batches. Do not fully cook! Add more butter and oil as needed. Remove the browned pork and set aside.
4. Add the mushrooms and more butter if necessary to the skillet and quickly brown them.
5. Add the broth, ⅔ cup of the Merlot, the parsley, mustard, shallots, garlic, and herbs. Bring this to a boil and cook, stirring, until the flavors develop fully.
6. Dissolve the cornstarch in the remaining Merlot.
7. Slowly stir this mixture into the boiling sauce. Stir in the cream, if desired. Cook stirring frequently until the sauce is thick enough to coat the back of a spoon.
8. Return the pork to the sauce. Cook over low heat until the pork is still a bit pink, about 5 to 10 minutes. Taste and adjust the seasonings.

FAST: Can prepare up to 2 days in advance through step 7 and refrigerate, or freeze for up to 3 months.

FLASHY: Served in a chafing dish, fondue pot, or over an alcohol burner with toothpicks, skewers, and/or cocktail forks and plates.

FABULOUS: With different varieties of mushrooms and/or with 2 to 3 rehydrated, stemmed, and seeded dried pasilla chiles (page 20). With ½ pound crisp cooked pancetta added at step 5. Over rice or pasta as an entree.

Crispy Cocktail Ribs

Make plenty—they will disappear like popcorn!

Yield: about 10 to 15 servings

3 pounds lean pork spareribs (have butcher cut them into 2-inch lengths) or use baby back ribs	Salt and freshly ground black pepper to taste Cornstarch

1. Preheat the oven to 425°F.
2. Wash and trim the ribs. Blot off the excess moisture with paper towels.
3. Place the ribs in a large bowl and season them with salt and pepper. Then coat them lightly with cornstarch, shaking off the excess. This will create a crisp crust.
4. Place the ribs on an ungreased aluminum foil-lined cookie sheet and bake until fully cooked and crisp, about 20 minutes.

FAST: Can prepare through step 3 up to 1 hour before serving and leave at room temperature.

FLASHY: Served in a chafing dish or on a warming tray with any combination of hot or cold Asian sauces on pages 75–83, and especially the sweet-and-sour-style sauces on pages 149–153.

FABULOUS: With ribs first marinated up to 2 days ahead with your choice of sauce or with Asian Merlot Marinade (recipe follows) for added flavor. With chicken wings prepared in the same manner.

Fast & Fabulous
Hors D'Oeuvres

ASIAN MERLOT MARINADE

Yield: about 7 cups

4 cups Merlot or any dry full-bodied red wine

2 cups soy sauce

½ cup Chinese plum sauce (page 17) or to taste

1 to 2 cups minced green onions (scallions), white and green parts

½ cup fresh mint leaves, minced

2 teaspoons dried thyme

6 to 12 cloves garlic, minced

2 to 4 tablespoons fermented black beans (page 17), optional

1. Combine all the ingredients in a large saucepan and bring to a boil over high heat, stirring frequently.
2. Reduce the heat to medium-low and simmer for 5 to 10 minutes. Cool this mixture before marinating with it.

FAST: Can prepare up to 3 months in advance and refrigerate, or freeze for up to 6 months.

FLASHY: As a marinade for 5 to 7 pounds of pork, beef, chicken, and/or lamb.

FABULOUS: With ½ cup Chinese sesame oil and/or with 1 cup mirin mixed in.

CHINESE SKEWERED BITES

Let your guest get into the act by cooking their own on the barbecue while having cocktails outside.

Yield: 4 to 6 servings

Marinade

1 cup dry red wine

½ cup soy sauce

3 tablespoons Chinese plum sauce or to taste (page 17)

2 tablespoons Chinese sesame oil

1 to 3 cloves garlic, minced

½ cup minced green onions (scallions), white and green parts

¼ to ½ teaspoon dried thyme

2 tablespoons sesame seeds, toasted (page 27)

To complete the dish

1 pound pork, beef, chicken, or turkey, cut into bite-size pieces

1 package bamboo skewers, soaked in water for about 1 hour to prevent them from burning

1. Place all the ingredients for the marinade in a saucepan, and bring to a boil. Reduce the heat to medium and simmer until the flavors develop, about 5 minutes. Let this cool to room temperature.
2. Place the meat in a nonreactive bowl and pour the marinade over it. Let sit for 1 hour at room temperature or refrigerate for up to 2 days.
3. Skewer the meat and broil or barbecue. While the meat cooks, place the marinade in a saucepan and bring it to a boil and let boil for about 10 minutes. The reduced marinade will be used as a sauce. Test the meat by cutting into a piece after 5 minutes to see if it is done to your liking.

FAST: Can marinate up to 2 days in advance and refrigerate, or freeze for up to 1 month. The marinade can be prepared up to 3 months in advance and refrigerated or frozen for up to 6 months.

FLASHY: Placed in a chafing dish with the reduced marinade and serve, or with the skewers stuck in a cabbage, melon, or pineapple and served with the marinade in a chafing dish.

FABULOUS: With ½ to 1 cup chopped dried prunes or apricots added to the marinade for a flavor surprise. The sauce made from the marinade embellished with 1 teaspoon Dijon mustard and ¼ to ½ cup heavy cream added at step 3.

RATATOUILLE NIÇOISE

This is a perfect hors d'oeuvre for gardeners who have a bounty of summer vegetables. It's a good idea to make several batches and freeze them for the winter.

Yield: about 2½ quarts; 50 or more servings

½ cup extra virgin olive oil

3 cups minced or thinly sliced onions

¼ to ½ pound pancetta, sliced ¼-inch thick and cut into ¼-inch-wide strips

3 to 6 heads garlic, roasted (page 26), cloves squeezed from their wrappers

3 to 4 medium-size zucchini, chopped or cubed

1 large eggplant, chopped or cubed

3 medium-size red bell peppers, halved, seeded, roasted (page 26), and chopped

3 yellow bell peppers, halved, seeded, roasted (page 26), and chopped

½ cup Italian or Greek olives, pitted, or to taste

Two 6-ounce jars marinated artichoke hearts, drained and minced

1 bunch fresh parsley, stemmed and minced

1 bunch fresh basil, stemmed and minced

1 bay leaf

½ cup grated mizithera cheese or to taste (page 22)

1 cup grated mozzarella

Salt and ground white pepper to taste

1. Heat 3 tablespoons of the oil over medium-low heat in a large skillet. Cook the onions and pancetta, stirring until the pancetta is browned and the onions are soft and golden.
2. Add remaining ingredients, along with more olive oil, if needed. Simmer, covered, until the vegetables are tender, about 30 minutes. This can also be done in a preheated 350°F oven.
3. Taste and adjust the seasonings.

FAST: Can prepare up to 3 days in advance and refrigerate, or freeze for up to 6 months.

FLASHY: Served hot in a chafing dish, fondue pot, or over an alcohol burner or at room temperature. With Garlic Crouton Rounds (page 270) or any Melba/Crostini (pages 263–273). Can also be served in Croustades (page 279).

FABULOUS: With leeks instead of the onions and ham instead of the pancetta. With fresh or about 1 to 2 tablespoons dried rosemary, oregano, and/or thyme instead of the basil. Served on pasta, beans, or rice as an entree.

FURTHER: Add 6 cups chicken broth to create a soup. Mixed with 1 cup ricotta and ½ cup grated Parmesan and used to fill crepes or egg-roll skins and served with a marinara sauce.

CHILEQUILES APPETIZERS

Fun and casual—perfectly suited for large groups.

Yield: about 2½ quarts; 50 or more servings

One 3-pound chicken
2 tablespoons extra virgin olive oil
Salt to taste
3 cloves garlic, minced
1 medium-size onion, quartered
1 teaspoon ground cumin or to taste
½ teaspoon chili powder or to taste
One 7-ounce can whole green chiles,
   seeded, deveined, and minced
   (page 20)

20 ounces tomatillos, husked and
   minced (page 23)
1½ cups sour cream
1½ cups grated sharp cheddar
One 6-ounce can pitted black olives
3 to 6 green onions (scallions),
   white and green parts, minced
1 bunch cilantro (fresh coriander),
   stemmed and minced, or to taste
Freshly ground black pepper to taste

1. Preheat the oven to 400°F. Place the chicken in a roasting pan and rub it with the oil, salt, and garlic. Sprinkle the inside of the chicken with salt and the cumin and stuff with the onion. Bake for 45 minutes to 1 hour, until the meat is no longer pink.
2. Remove the chicken and let cool. Pull the meat from the bones and shred it; discard the bones and skin.
3. Combine the chicken with all the remaining ingredients. Taste and adjust the seasonings.
4. Place this mixture in an ovenproof casserole or chafing dish and bake in a preheated 350°F oven until hot and bubbly, about 20 to 30 minutes.

FAST: Can prepare up to 2 days in advance and refrigerate, or freeze for up to 6 months.

FLASHY: Served in a chafing dish, fondue pot, or over an alcohol burner with tortilla chips for dunking.

FABULOUS: With salsa. With pork substituted for the chicken or use your leftover turkey. As a filling for Tortilla Cups (page 300), Croustades (page 279), and/or Won Ton Cups (page 246). As a filling for crepes, burritos, or a Southwestern lasagna. Prepared with a variety of chiles.

ALMOND MUSTARD DUNK

A creamy, crunchy delight.

Yield: about 2 cups; 18 or more servings

2 tablespoons unsalted butter	½ cup heavy cream
2 to 3 shallots, minced	2 tablespoons Dijon mustard or to
6 tablespoons dry white wine or dry	taste
vermouth	3 ounces blanched almonds, slivered
2 tablespoons medium-dry sherry	and lightly toasted (page 27),
2 cups chicken broth, homemade	about ⅔ cup
(page 11) or canned	Salt and ground white pepper to taste

1. Melt the butter in a saucepan over medium-low heat. When it begins to foam, cook the shallots, stirring until tender.
2. Stir in the wine and sherry, increase the heat to high, and reduce until it forms a glaze, about 2 minutes.
3. Add the broth and reduce it by half over medium-high heat for about 10 to 15 minutes, stirring frequently.
4. Stir in the remaining ingredients and return to a boil. Taste and adjust the seasonings.

FAST: Can prepare up to 1 week in advance and refrigerate, or freeze for up to 3 months.

FLASHY: Served in a chafing dish, fondue pot, or over an alcohol burner as a dunk for cooked asparagus, cauliflower, pork, poultry, or seafood.

FABULOUS: As an entree sauce for pork, poultry, beef, seafood, or veal.

CHINESE BLACK BEAN DUNK

A pungent oriental delicacy.

Yield: about 2 cups; 18 or more servings

2 to 4 tablespoons minced fresh
  ginger
2 cloves garlic, chopped, or to taste
2 tablespoons fermented black beans
  (page 17)
½ pound ground pork
2 tablespoons peanut oil
1 cup chicken broth, homemade
  (page 11) or canned

2 tablespoons sherry
1 large egg, slightly beaten
2 to 4 green onions (scallions),
  white and green parts, cut into
  1-inch lengths
½ bunch cilantro (fresh coriander),
  stemmed and minced
1 tablespoon cornstarch dissolved in
  2 tablespoons broth, wine, or
  water

1. Combine the ginger, garlic, and beans together in a food processor fitted with the metal blade, or mash together into a paste.
2. Fry the pork in a wok over high heat. Remove and drain on paper towels.
3. Reduce the heat to medium-low and add the peanut oil to the wok and cook the bean mixture, stirring, being careful not to burn it. Add the pork, broth, and sherry and bring it to a boil.
4. Stir in the egg, then add the green onions and cilantro.
5. Add the cornstarch mixture to the wok, and cook until thickened over medium-high heat. Taste and adjust the seasonings.

FAST: Can prepare up to 3 days in advance and refrigerate, or freeze for up to 3 months.

FLASHY: Served in a chafing dish, fondue pot, or over an alcohol burner as a dunk for small pieces of cooked pork, chicken, or shrimp or for Crispy Cocktail Ribs (page 142).

FABULOUS: With 1 tablespoon Szechuan peppercorns added (page 19). As an entree sauce for pork, chicken, seafood, pasta, and/or rice.

FRIJOLES CALIENTES

*A hot and spicy bean dunk that makes you wonder why
you ever bought the canned prepared stuff.*

Yield: about 5 cups; 30 or more servings

3 cups refried beans (*page 14*) or 3
   cups pureed fresh cooked pinto
   beans

2 cups grated jack cheese

1 cup sour cream or to taste

1 bunch whole green onions
   (*scallions*), white and green parts,
   minced

3 cloves garlic, minced

1 bunch cilantro (*fresh coriander*),
   stemmed and minced

4 to 10 canned whole green chiles,
   seeded, deveined, and chopped
   (*page 20*)

Ground cumin, salt, and chili powder
   to taste

1. Combine all the ingredients in an ovenproof casserole or chafing dish. Taste and adjust the seasonings.
2. Bake in a preheated 350°F oven until hot and bubbly, about 15 to 20 minutes.

FAST: Can prepare up to 2 days in advance and refrigerate, or freeze for up to 6 months.

FLASHY: Served in a chafing dish, fondue pot, or over an alcohol burner with Tortilla Chips (page 273).

FABULOUS: As a filling for Won Ton Cups (page 246), Croustades (page 279), or Tortilla Cups (page 300). As an entree used to fill burritos, pita bread, omelets, etc.

SWEET-AND-SOUR-STYLE SAUCES

SWEET AND SOUR SAUCE

Yield: about 1 cup; 6 or more servings

¼ cup catsup

¼ cup soy sauce

¼ cup white or packed brown sugar

¼ cup rice wine vinegar

2 tablespoons medium-dry sherry or
   port

1 tablespoon cornstarch

1 clove garlic, minced

4 green onions (*scallions*), white
   and green parts, cut into 1-inch
   lengths

1 quarter-size piece fresh ginger,
   peeled and minced

Salt and ground white pepper to taste

1. Combine all the ingredients in a food processor fitted with the metal blade or in a blender and process until smooth, or combine in a bowl. Taste and adjust the flavors.
2. Pour this mixture into a saucepan over medium-low heat and cook, stirring, until thickened, about 10 to 15 minutes. Serve warm.

FAST: Can prepare up to 1 week in advance and refrigerate, or freeze for up to 1 year.

FLASHY: Served hot in a fondue pot or over an alcohol burner or at room temperature with any Asian-style hors d'oeuvre in this book, from Crispy Cocktail Ribs (page 142), to Barbecued Pork and Red Cabbage Potstickers (page 254).

FABULOUS: As a seasoning sauce to enhance other sauces, marinades, vegetables, soups, and stir-fry dishes. As an entree sauce for pasta, rice, seafood, pork, or chicken.

HOT AND SOUR SAUCE

Yield: about 2½ cups; 20 or more servings

½ medium-size green bell pepper, seeded and slivered

½ medium-size red bell pepper, seeded and slivered

2 dried small red chile peppers, seeded (page 20)

2 to 4 green onions (scallions), white and green parts, cut into 1-inch lengths

2 tablespoons slivered fresh ginger

¼ cup catsup

1 tablespoon soy sauce

¼ cup sugar

¼ cup rice wine vinegar

1 cup chicken broth, homemade (page 11) or canned

Salt and ground white pepper to taste

2 tablespoons cornstarch dissolved in 4 tablespoons medium-dry sherry

1. Combine all the ingredients, except the cornstarch mixture, in a medium-size saucepan and bring to a boil.
2. Add the cornstarch mixture and cook until thickened, about 1 minute, stirring continuously. Taste and adjust the flavors. Remove the chile peppers before serving.

FAST: Can prepare up to 1 week in advance and refrigerate, or freeze for up to 1 year.

FLASHY: Served hot in a chafing dish, fondue pot, or over an alcohol burner or at room temperature with any Asian-style hors d'oeuvre in this book, from Crispy Cocktail Ribs (page 142), to Barbecued Pork and Red Cabbage Potstickers (page 254).

FABULOUS: As a seasoning sauce to enhance other sauces, marinades, vegetables, soups, and stir-fry dishes. As an entree sauce for pasta, rice, seafood, pork, or chicken.

PLUM MUSTARD SAUCE

Yield: about 1¾ cups; 12 or more servings

1 to 2 tablespoons Dijon mustard
¼ cup port
¼ cup rice wine vinegar
¼ cup Chinese plum sauce (page 17)
1 cup chicken broth, homemade (page 11) or canned
1 tablespoon Chinese sesame oil

1 tablespoon sugar
1 to 2 tablespoons minced cilantro (fresh coriander)
Salt and ground white pepper to taste
1 tablespoon cornstarch, dissolved in 2 tablespoons water

1. Combine all the ingredients, except the cornstarch mixture, in a medium-size saucepan and bring to a boil.
2. Whisk in the cornstarch and cook until thickened, about 1 minute, stirring continuously. Taste and adjust the flavors.

FAST: Can prepare up to 1 week in advance and refrigerate, or freeze for up to 1 year.

FLASHY: Served hot in a chafing dish, fondue pot, or over an alcohol burner or at room temperature with any Asian-style hors d'oeuvre in this book, from Crispy Cocktail Ribs (page 142), to Barbecued Pork and Red Cabbage Potstickers (page 254).

FABULOUS: As a seasoning sauce to enhance other sauces, marinades, vegetables, soups, and stir-fry dishes. As an entree sauce for pasta, rice, seafood, pork, or chicken.

HOISIN SWEET AND SOUR SAUCE

Yield: about 1 cup; 6 or more servings

¼ cup hoisin sauce (page 17)
¼ cup port
¼ cup rice wine vinegar
1 tablespoon Chinese sesame oil
2 tablespoons soy sauce
2 tablespoons sugar

1 to 3 tablespoons minced cilantro (fresh coriander)
1 clove garlic, minced
1 quarter-size piece fresh ginger, peeled and minced
1 tablespoon cornstarch, dissolved in 2 tablespoons water

1. Combine all the ingredients, except the cornstarch mixture, in a medium-size saucepan and bring to a boil.
2. Add the cornstarch and cook until thickened, about 1 minute, stirring continuously. Taste and adjust the flavors.

FAST: Can prepare up to 1 week in advance and refrigerate, or freeze for up to 1 year.

FLASHY: Served hot in a chafing dish, fondue pot, or over an alcohol burner or at room temperature with any Asian-style hors d'oeuvre in this book, from Crispy Cocktail Ribs (page 142), to Barbecued Pork and Red Cabbage Potstickers (page 254).

FABULOUS: As a seasoning sauce to enhance other sauces, marinades, vegetables, soups, and stir-fry dishes. As an entree sauce for pasta, rice, seafood, pork, or chicken.

APRICOT AND SESAME SAUCE

Yield: about 1½ cups; 12 or more servings

½ cup apricot preserves

¼ cup bourbon

1 tablespoon Dijon mustard

1 clove garlic, minced

2 to 4 tablespoons minced fresh ginger

¼ cup rice wine vinegar

¼ cup soy sauce

2 tablespoons sugar

1 to 3 tablespoons minced cilantro (fresh coriander)

1 tablespoon tahini (page 23)

1 to 2 tablespoons sesame seeds, toasted (page 27)

Pinch of Chinese five spice powder (page 17)

Salt and ground white pepper to taste

1 tablespoon cornstarch, dissolved in 2 tablespoons water

1. Combine all the ingredients, except the cornstarch mixture, in a medium-size saucepan and bring to a boil over high heat.
2. Stir the cornstarch mixture into the boiling sauce. Cook until thickened, about 5 minutes, over medium heat, stirring continuously. Taste and adjust the seasonings.

FAST: Can prepare up to 1 week in advance and refrigerate, or freeze for up to 1 year.

FLASHY: Served hot in a chafing dish, fondue pot, or over an alcohol burner or at room temperature with any Asian-style hors d'oeuvre in this book, from Crispy Cocktail Ribs (page 142), to Barbecued Pork and Red Cabbage Potstickers (page 254).

FABULOUS: As a seasoning sauce to enhance other sauces, marinades, vegetables, soups, and stir-fry dishes. As an entree sauce for pasta, rice, seafood, pork, or chicken.

CHINESE LEMON SAUCE

Yield: about 2 cups; 18 or more servings

3 tablespoons fresh lemon juice or to
  taste
Zest of 1 lemon, finely grated
1 to 2 cloves garlic, minced, or to
  taste
2 tablespoons minced fresh ginger
2 tablespoons sesame seeds, toasted
  (page 27)

1 cup chicken broth, homemade
  (page 11) or canned
¼ cup medium-dry sherry
⅓ cup Chinese plum sauce (page 17)
1 tablespoon soy sauce
1 tablespoon sugar or to taste
Salt and ground white pepper to taste
1 tablespoon cornstarch dissolved in
  2 tablespoons medium-dry sherry

1. Combine all the ingredients, except the cornstarch mixture, in a saucepan and bring
   to a boil.
2. Stir the cornstarch mixture into the boiling sauce. Cook, stirring, until thickened,
   about 5 minutes over medium heat. Taste and adjust the flavors.

FAST: Can prepare up to 1 week in advance and refrigerate, or freeze for up to 1 year.

FLASHY: Served hot in a chafing dish, fondue pot, or over an alcohol burner or at room
temperature with any Asian-style hors d'oeuvre in this book, from Crispy Cocktail Ribs
(page 142), to Barbecued Pork and Red Cabbage Potstickers (page 254).

FABULOUS: As a seasoning sauce to enhance other sauces, marinades, vegetables, soups,
and stir-fry dishes. As an entree sauce for pasta, rice, seafood, pork, or chicken.

GINGER MERLOT SAUCE

Fabulous with barbecued anything!

Yield: about 2 cups; 18 or more servings

2 tablespoons unsalted butter
2 to 4 cloves garlic, minced
¼ cup minced fresh ginger or to
  taste
4 green onions (scallions), white
  and green parts, minced
1 cup Merlot or any dry, full-bodied
  red wine

1½ cups chicken broth, homemade
  (page 11) or canned
¼ cup soy sauce
¼ cup packed brown sugar or to
  taste
Salt and ground white pepper to taste
1 tablespoon cornstarch dissolved in
  2 tablespoons water

1. Melt the butter in a saucepan over medium heat. When it begins to foam, briefly cook the garlic, ginger, and green onions, stirring.
2. Add the remaining ingredients, except the dissolved cornstarch, and bring to a boil over high heat. Reduce the heat to medium and cook until the flavors develop to your liking, about 10 minutes.
3. Return the sauce to a boil and stir in the dissolved cornstarch. Continue cooking, stirring frequently until thickened, about 30 seconds. Taste and adjust the flavors.

FAST: Can prepare up to 1 week in advance and refrigerate, or freeze for up to 1 year.

FLASHY: Served hot in a chafing dish, fondue pot, or over an alcohol burner or at room temperature with any Asian-style hors d'oeuvre in this book, from Crispy Cocktail Ribs (page 142), to Barbecued Pork and Red Cabbage Potstickers (page 254).

FABULOUS: The sauce strained through a fine wire mesh strainer before serving for a more elegant look.

FONDUES

MADEIRA JACK FONDUE

Yield: about 3 cups; 24 or more servings

1 tablespoon cornstarch
1 pound jack cheese, grated
2 cups dry white wine
1 to 2 cloves garlic, minced

3 to 4 tablespoons Madeira
Ground white pepper and freshly
grated nutmeg to taste

1. Toss the cornstarch and cheese together in a bowl. This will prevent the oil from separating from the cheese.
2. Place the white wine in a heavy saucepan along with the garlic. Let this boil for about 5 minutes, then reduce the heat to medium-low and stir in the cheese. Stir constantly until the cheese melts; *do not* let it boil.
3. Stir in the remaining ingredients.
4. When a smooth and thick consistency is reached, transfer the fondue to a heavy, heatproof casserole or fondue dish. Keep warm over an alcohol lamp or fondue warmer.

FAST: Can prepare up to 3 days in advance and refrigerate, or freeze for up to 3 months. Reheat in a double boiler over medium heat before serving.

FLASHY: As a warm dunk for French, rye, black, or sourdough bread cubes, or blanched vegetables, especially boiled baby potatoes or baby artichokes.

FABULOUS: With half jack and half shallot jack, jack and/or cheddar and one 7-ounce can minced green chiles (page 20), or cheddar and 1 large minced browned onion. With any fresh or dried herb. As an entree sauce for chicken, fish, seafood, or pasta.

SWISS HAM FONDUE

Have this ready and waiting for the gang when they come in from the slopes.

Yield: about 3½ cups; 24 or more servings

1 tablespoon cornstarch

1 pound Swiss, Gruyère, or Emmenthaler cheese, shredded

⅔ cup heavy cream

1 to 2 tablespoons minced shallots

1 teaspoon Dijon mustard or to taste

⅓ to ⅔ cup dry white wine

⅓ pound ham, cut into bite-size pieces

Salt, ground white pepper, and freshly grated nutmeg to taste

1. Combine the cornstarch and cheese together in a bowl. This will prevent the oil from separating from the cheese.
2. Bring the cream, shallots, mustard, and wine to a boil in a heavy saucepan. Continue to cook over high heat for about 5 minutes.
3. Reduce the heat to medium-low and slowly stir in the cheese and ham. Continue to cook, stirring constantly, until the cheese mixture melts; *do not* let it boil. Taste and adjust the flavors.
4. When thickened, transfer to a heavy, heatproof casserole or fondue dish. Keep warm over an alcohol lamp or fondue warmer.

FAST: Can prepare up to 3 days in advance and refrigerate, or freeze for up to 3 months. Reheat in a double boiler before serving.

FLASHY: As a warm dunk for French bread cubes, blanched asparagus, cauliflower or broccoli florets, cooked artichoke leaves, or cooked shrimp.

FABULOUS: As a sauce for vegetable dishes, pasta, chicken, or veal.

CHILE CHEESE FONDUE

A Mexican twist to a classic Swiss dish.

Yield: about 4 cups; 24 or more servings

1 tablespoon cornstarch	*½ cup pitted minced green olives*
2 cups grated jack cheese	*½ cup pitted minced black olives*
⅔ cup canned whole green chiles, seeded, deveined, and chopped (page 20)	*1 tablespoon ground cumin*
	½ cup minced cilantro (fresh coriander)
1 cup heavy cream	*2 cloves garlic, minced*
⅓ cup dry sherry	*Salt and ground white pepper to taste*
1 teaspoon dried oregano	

1. Combine the cornstarch and cheese together in a bowl. This will prevent the oil from separating from the cheese.
2. Add all the ingredients, except for the cheese, to a saucepan and bring to a boil.
3. Reduce the heat to medium-low and slowly stir in the cheese, stirring constantly until the cheese melts; *do not* let boil. Taste and adjust the seasonings.
4. When thickened, transfer to a heavy, heatproof casserole or fondue dish. Keep warm over an alcohol lamp or fondue warmer.

FAST: Can prepare up to 3 days in advance and refrigerate, or freeze for up to 3 months. Reheat in a double boiler before serving.

FLASHY: Served with warm Tortilla Chips (page 273) and/or boiled baby potatoes.

FABULOUS: As an entree sauce for pasta, rice, beans, vegetables, pork, poultry, and/or fish.

FAST & FABULOUS BAKED CHEESE

*If you can slice cheese, you can prepare this. A great
choice for casual fun.*

Yield: **8 or more servings**

*12 to 18 ounces sharp or medium
cheddar or jack cheese, thinly
sliced*

Toppings

*Canned whole green chiles, seeded,
deveined, and minced (page 20)*

Minced cilantro (fresh coriander)

*Minced green onions (scallions),
white and green parts*

Sliced pitted black olives

Minced ham

Chopped seeded fresh tomatoes

*Raw or blanched almonds, toasted
(page 27) and chopped*

*Salsa, homemade (see Index) or
purchased*

Cooked baby shrimp (page 24)

1. Preheat the oven to 450°F.
2. Place the cheese slices in two layers in a shallow, attractive ovenproof dish or cast-iron skillet.
3. Bake until melted, about 10 minutes. Watch carefully.
4. Serve in the container in which it is baked. Don't worry about keeping it warm; it won't last that long. Can be kept warm over a chafing dish warmer or on a warming tray.

FAST: Can prepare the toppings up to 1 day in advance and refrigerate.

FLASHY: The topping served in separate bowls and let guests make their own. Served with warm tortillas, tortilla chips, or Tortilla Cups (page 300). For summer barbecues, cooked in a skillet on the grill instead of in the oven.

FABULOUS: Mozzarella substituted for the jack or cheddar cheese and serve with minced anchovies, pesto (page 47), walnuts and garlic sautéed in olive oil over medium heat for about 10 minutes, roasted red or green peppers (page 26), marinated artichoke hearts, and minced sun-dried tomatoes for an Italian version.

HERBED CREAM FONDUE

Yield: about 3 cups; 24 or more servings

4 tablespoons (½ stick) unsalted
   butter
1 cup cultivated white mushrooms,
   minced
¼ cup minced shallots
1 to 2 cloves garlic, minced
2 teaspoons all-purpose flour
¼ teaspoon dried oregano
¼ teaspoon dried basil

Pinch dried thyme
2 tablespoons capers, drained and
   rinsed
Zest of 1 lemon, finely grated
2 tablespoons minced fresh parsley
Salt, ground white pepper, and fresh
   lemon juice to taste
2 cups grated jack cheese

1. Melt the butter in a saucepan over medium heat. When it begins to foam, cook the
   mushrooms, shallots, and garlic, stirring, until the ingredients are tender, about 2
   to 3 minutes.
2. Blend in the flour, then stir in the remaining ingredients, except the cheese. Stir
   until the sauce thickens and the flavors develop. If it is too thick, thin with some
   heavy cream, wine, or chicken broth.
3. Reduce the heat to medium-low and stir in the cheese. Cook, stirring constantly,
   until the cheese melts.
4. Transfer to a heavy, heatproof casserole or fondue dish. Keep warm over an alcohol
   lamp or fondue warmer.

FAST: Can prepare up to 3 days in advance and refrigerate, or freeze for up to 3 months.
Reheat in a double boiler.

FLASHY: As a dunk for cubes of French bread, cooked vegetables, or cooked seafood.

FABULOUS: As a sauce for grilled or poached fish or poultry.

Fast & Fabulous
Hors D'Oeuvres

SHRIMP AND BOURSIN FONDUE

Quick, with a French accent!

Yield: about 3 cups; 24 or more servings

2   tablespoons unsalted butter
½   shallot, minced
2   tablespoons all-purpose flour
½   cup dry vermouth
½   cup heavy cream
1   pound raw medium-size shrimp,
      shelled, deveined, and coarsely
      chopped

One 4-ounce container Boursin or
      other soft herbed cheese, cut into
      pieces
Salt and ground white pepper to taste

1. Melt the butter in a saucepan over medium heat. When it begins to foam, cook the shallots, stirring, until tender, 2 or 3 minutes.
2. Remove the saucepan from the burner and whisk in the flour. Return it to the burner and cook for 1 minute over medium heat.
3. Whisk in the vermouth and cream and cook until the sauce thickens, whisking continuously over medium to medium-high heat.
4. Reduce the heat to medium-low and stir in the shrimp and cheese. Cook until the cheese melts and the shrimp cooks, about 5 minutes. *Do not* allow it to boil. Taste and season.
5. Transfer to a heavy, heatproof casserole or fondue dish. Keep warm over an alcohol lamp or fondue warmer.

FAST: Can prepare up to 2 days in advance and refrigerate, or freeze for up to 3 months. Reheat in a double boiler before serving.

FLASHY: Served with sourdough bread cubes, Bagel Chips (page 272), or Pita Chips (page 274).

FABULOUS: As an entree sauce for pasta, fish, veal, or poultry. With crabmeat substituted for the shrimp.

CRAB AND BRIE FONDUE

Unscaled heaven!

Yield: about 4 cups; 24 or more servings

1 pound brie, rind removed and cut
   into small chunks
2 tablespoons cornstarch
½ cup chicken broth, homemade
   (page 11) or canned
½ cup bottled clam juice
1 cup dry white wine

1 teaspoon Dijon mustard
2 shallots, minced
8 ounces fresh or frozen crabmeat,
   picked over for cartilage
Salt, ground white pepper, and freshly
   grated nutmeg to taste

1. Combine the brie and cornstarch together in a bowl. This will prevent the oil from separating from the cheese.
2. Bring the chicken broth, clam juice, wine, mustard, and shallots to a boil in a saucepan. Allow it to boil until the liquid reduces by half, about 10 minutes.
3. Reduce the heat to medium-low and slowly stir in the cheese and crab. Stir until the flavors develop and the alcohol cooks away, about 10 minutes.
4. Taste and season.
5. Transfer to a heavy, heatproof casserole or fondue dish. Keep warm over an alcohol lamp or fondue warmer.

FAST: Can prepare up to 2 days in advance and refrigerate, or freeze for up to 3 months. Reheat in a double boiler before serving.

FLASHY: As a warm dunk for sourdough bread cubes, raw or cooked broccoli florets, and/or cooked artichoke leaves.

FABULOUS: As an entree sauce over cooked broccoli, asparagus, chicken breasts, or fish. Season with either ½ teaspoon dried tarragon, crushed, or 2 to 4 minced, seeded, and deveined canned green chiles (page 20).

PARMESAN BÉCHAMEL FONDUE

Yield: about 3 cups; 24 or more servings

2 tablespoons unsalted butter	½ to 1 bay leaf
½ to 1 shallot, minced	½ cup Madeira or sherry
3 tablespoons all-purpose flour	¼ cup dry white wine or vermouth
1½ cups milk	Salt, ground white pepper, and freshly
¼ teaspoon dried thyme	grated nutmeg to taste
5 sprigs fresh parsley	½ cup freshly grated Parmesan

1. Melt the butter in a saucepan over medium-low heat. When it begins to foam, cook the shallots, stirring, until tender. Whisk in the flour and cook for 1 minute.
2. Remove the saucepan from the burner and whisk in the milk gradually. Return it to the burner and add the thyme, parsley, and bay leaf, then bring to a boil over high heat while whisking.
3. Add the Madeira, white wine, and seasonings and cook until the flavors develop, about 10 minutes. Remove the parsley and bay leaf.
4. Reduce the heat to medium-low and stir in the cheese. Stir constantly until melted. Taste and adjust the seasonings.
5. Transfer to a heavy, heatproof casserole or fondue dish. Keep warm over an alcohol lamp or fondue warmer.

FAST: Can prepare up to 3 days in advance and refrigerate, or freeze for up to 3 months. Reheat in a double boiler before serving.

FLASHY: As a warm dunk for cooked vegetables, French bread cubes, seafood, or poultry.

FABULOUS: With 8 ounces cooked, minced clams or mussels added, or mixed with 8 ounces cooked, minced spinach, eggplant, artichoke hearts, seafood, chicken, or ham and used to fill Tartlets (page 314), Flo Braker's Magic Puff Pastry (page 309), Croustades (page 279), crepes, or raw mushroom caps.

4

FORMS

Despite the fact that this title sounds as if we are going to discuss design concepts, it refers to interestingly seasoned mixtures that are shaped or formed. Meatballs and sausages, pâtés and terrines, mousses and cold soufflés, tortas, puffs, fried hors d'oeuvres, frittatas, and flans will all be explored. Most are extremely well-suited to large parties, but can be made in smaller amounts or sizes just as easily. They range in character from sublimely elegant to warm and unpretentious.

Meatballs/sausages are the first variety of hors d'oeuvres to be investigated in this chapter. I prefer to use the term "sausages" in place of "meatballs." My aversion to meatballs stems from their shabby reputation. This was acquired as a result of all those unimaginatively catered parties that served meatballs consisting primarily of fillers, floating in sugary, catsup-based sauces. I came face-to-face with this version of a mediocre meatball when I did a TV show in a viewer's kitchen. She was selected to prepare her favorite hors d'oeuvre. You guessed it, it was a bland meatball in a sauce of catsup, grape jelly, and dehydrated parsley. Need I say more? This does not mean that all meatballs/sausages must be tacky. I feel confident that as soon as you try any one of the recipes that follow, you will see that the meatball has been a victim of a bum rap.

Pâtés and terrines are the next form to be explored. Whether you are planning a picnic with panache or a more elegant cocktail party, they will fit the occasion. Too often, this is an area of intimidation. Relax, pâtés and terrines are simple mixtures of well-seasoned ground meats. Think of them as glamorous, upscale meat loaves. Pâtés and terrines offer the cook a great deal of convenience, as they can be refrigerated for several days or prepared up to six months in advance and frozen. They can be made in huge quantities to serve an army or made up in very small batches. You will be thrilled by how economical it is to prepare your own, rather than purchasing them.

Please allow me to put another fear to rest: All pâtés and terrines do not contain liver. They can be made with vegetables, pork, veal, poultry, liver, or seafood.

The difference between a pâté and terrine is fuzzy. Traditionally, a terrine is cooked in an earthenware mold. The word "terrine" comes from *terre*, the French word for earth. It is loaf-shaped and consists of chopped or pureed meat, seafood, and/or vegetables bound together with eggs, heavy cream, and/or fat and seasonings. It may also consist of some strips or chunks of ingredients to provide a contrast in texture.

Technically, pâtés are meant to be enclosed in pastry and baked. However, pâtés have come to stand for any well-seasoned, minced or pureed mixture. It can either be baked or cooked by another means and served in a container or unmolded.

I have included a wide variety of recipes for pâtés and terrines, ranging from very simple spreads to more complex mixtures. None of the recipes are difficult or overly rich. Often, you'll see pâté recipes calling for huge amounts of fat. This produces fabulous results, but I cannot do that in good conscience. Feel free to splurge and increase the amount of fat on your own.

Mousses and cold soufflés are divine, delicate, and decadent. Because of this, I find them the perfect prelude to a formal dinner. For large groups, mousses are a fabulous choice, as they can be prepared quickly and easily doubled or tripled and frozen. This is another area where your food processor will be invaluable. If you plan to serve a mousse outdoors, remember not to let it sit in the direct sun. Place the mousse on a plate in a bowl of ice or on blue ice to prevent an embarrassing meltdown.

Tortas can be described accurately as rich, cheese-based pâtés, layered with interesting ingredients. As far as I am concerned, it's enough to say that they are pure ambrosia! I first tasted a torta at my friend's home—a pesto and a smoked salmon torta, and instantly began to get ideas for exciting variations. Terrifically versatile, they offer opportunities for experimentation in any size or shape. Most of you have probably seen this type of hors d'oeuvre at gourmet food stores. I guarantee that these are far superior in flavor and, as an added bonus, less expensive.

All puffs are not created equal. Hors d'oeuvre puffs need not be overly fussy, bland-tasting little cream puffs. I'm not very fond of pâte a choux (the classic cream puff batter). I find it tasteless and uninteresting, which led me to create the Gougère Puffs. For the most part, I've interpreted puffs to mean small, individual tidbits that rise when baked. You'll see a variety of recipes, ranging from well-seasoned, mayonnaise-based mixtures that top French bread or even tortilla chips to small cubes of French bread that have been drenched in a cheese-based sauce, frozen, and then baked until fluffed. All puff recipes are extremely Fast & Fabulous and offer you a chance to prepare individual hors d'oeuvres with the greatest of ease.

On to the "F" word. When I was younger, I didn't think twice about filling my wok with oil and frying up a batch of hors d'oeuvres. Now, it takes a lot to motivate me to deep-fat fry; so you can be sure that the fried hors d'oeuvres I've included are worth it.

In case you are worried about this technique being greasy, it simply isn't, if done correctly. Have your oil hot and fry in small batches. Overcrowding lowers the temperature of the oil; when the temperature isn't hot enough, the food absorbs the oil and becomes greasy. To determine whether the oil is at the right temperature, drop a piece of green onion in; when it fries, the oil is hot enough to use.

For added convenience, use the Chinese technique of twice-frying. Fry the first time until the item is only partially cooked (this can be done in advance). The messy part is done before your guests arrive. The final frying is done right before serving and requires only half the amount of time.

Last but not least, we venture on to frittatas and flans, more "F"'s. Think of frittatas and flans as crustless quiches that can be whipped up at a moment's notice for brunches, picnics, luncheons, or light suppers, as well as for cocktail parties. This type of hors d'oeuvre provides the quickest way to prepare individual hors d'oeuvres.

MEATBALLS/SAUSAGES

ALBONDIGAS

Mexican meatballs.

Yield: about 20 meatballs; 10 or more servings

Sauce

2 tablespoons unsalted butter

1 large onion, chopped

1 medium-size carrot, chopped

2 cloves garlic, chopped

2 cups chopped fresh or canned tomatoes

1 cup salsa, homemade (see Index) or purchased, or to taste

1/4 cup dry vermouth

2 cups chicken broth, homemade (page 11) or canned

2 teaspoons ground cumin

1/4 cup chopped cilantro (fresh coriander) or to taste

Juice of 1 lemon

1/2 to 1 teaspoon chili powder and dried oregano to taste

Salt and ground white pepper to taste

Meatballs

1/2 cup cooked white rice

1 pound lean ground pork

4 green onions (scallions), white and green parts, minced

1/2 onion, chopped

1/2 cup minced cilantro (fresh coriander)

3 teaspoons dried oregano

1/2 to 1 teaspoon ground cumin

1/2 to 1 teaspoon chili powder

Salt to taste

1. Melt the butter in a skillet. When it begins to foam, cook the onions and carrots, stirring, over medium heat until tender.
2. Add the remaining sauce ingredients. Bring to a boil and simmer for at least 30 minutes. Taste and adjust the seasonings.
3. Meanwhile, combine all the meatball ingredients by hand in a mixing bowl and mix

well. Shape the mixture into small meatballs and brown them on all sides in a large skillet. Cook until they are brown but not fully cooked.

4. Puree the sauce in a blender or food processor fitted with the metal blade.
5. Add the sauce to the skillet and simmer for about 20 minutes over medium to medium-low heat.

FAST: Can assemble, but do not simmer the meatballs, up to 2 days in advance and refrigerate, or freeze for up to 4 months. Thaw and simmer before serving.

FLASHY: The meatballs and sauce served in a chafing dish, and garnished with a sprinkling of minced cilantro and/or green onions.

FABULOUS: As an entree served over rice, pasta, seafood, pork, or poultry. With 1 cup of sour cream added to the finished sauce.

SPICY PORK SAUSAGE IN GRAPE LEAVES

Unusual and exotic, but simple!

Yield: about 20 sausages; 10 or more servings

1 pound lean ground pork
2 tablespoons pickled mango (page 18) or to taste
¼ cup minced fresh mint

2 to 4 tablespoons Chinese plum sauce (page 17)
About 20 preserved grape leaves
Olive oil

1. Mix together all the ingredients, except the grape leaves and olive oil, in a bowl using a wooden spoon or your hands. Fry 1 teaspoon of the mixture until cooked all the way through to check the seasonings.
2. Form the mixture into small sausage shapes about 1½ inches long.
3. Wrap each sausage in a grape leaf, placing the shiny side of each leaf toward the work surface. Roll the sausages up as tightly as possible.
4. Brush the wrapped sausages with olive oil and grill over a medium-hot fire or place in a baking dish or on a baking sheet and bake in a preheated 350°F oven until the mixture is no longer pink, about 15 minutes.

FAST: Can prepare through step 3 up to 2 days in advance and refrigerate, or freeze for up to 6 months. Thaw in the refrigerator overnight.

FLASHY: Served hot on a platter and garnished with fresh herbs and/or nontoxic flowers or leaves.

FABULOUS: With minced cilantro (fresh coriander) mixed in.

CRISPY LAMB
AND ARTICHOKE SAUSAGES

Yield: about 25 sausages; 10 or more servings

¼ cup uncooked bulgur (page 20)

½ cup dry white wine

1 pound ground lamb

1 large egg

One 6-ounce jar marinated artichoke
    hearts, drained and minced

2 cloves garlic, minced

Freshly ground black pepper to taste

2 tablespoons Dijon mustard

About 25 egg roll wrappers
    (page 17)

Olive oil for brushing

1. Place the bulgur and wine in a bowl and let it sit until the wine is absorbed. Preheat the oven to 350°F.
2. Combine all the ingredients, except the egg roll wrappers and olive oil, in a food processor fitted with the metal blade and process until smooth, or combine in a bowl. Fry 1 teaspoon of the mixture until cooked through to check the seasonings.
3. Form the mixture into 1½- to 2-inch-long sausages and wrap each one in an egg roll wrapper. Brush with olive oil and place seam side down on an oiled cookie sheet.
4. Place in the oven and cook until medium-rare, 10 to 15 minutes. Serve on a platter and keep warm on a warming tray or over an alcohol lamp or fondue warmer.

FAST: Can prepare through step 3 up to 2 days in advance and refrigerate, or flash freeze (page 24) for up to 6 months. Cook frozen, adding about 5 minutes to the cooking time.

FLASHY: Served hot on a platter and garnished with fresh herbs and/or nontoxic flowers or leaves.

FABULOUS: Wrapped in moistened rice paper, phyllo dough, or moo shoo wrappers.

Italian Veal, Mozzarella, and Anchovy Sausages

Yield: about 30 sausages; 15 or more servings

1 slice sourdough bread, torn into
   pieces

¼ cup milk

1½ pounds ground lean veal

6 canned pear-shaped Italian
   tomatoes, drained, halved, and
   seeded

½ to 1 cup grated mozzarella

3 to 4 anchovy fillets, mashed

½ cup minced fresh parsley

2 cloves garlic, minced, or to taste

1 large egg

1 teaspoon dried oregano or to
   taste

Zest of 2 lemons, grated

Salt and ground white pepper

1 cup fine cracker crumbs, spread
   on a dinner plate

Olive oil

1. Preheat the oven to 400°F.
2. Soak the bread in the milk in a small bowl until softened, about 10 to 20 minutes. Place in a strainer to remove the excess moisture. Squeeze out the excess moisture.
3. Place the meat in a food processor fitted with the metal blade and add the remaining ingredients, except for the cracker crumbs, and process until smooth, or mix together by hand in a bowl.
4. Shape the mixture into 2-inch-long sausages or balls.
5. Roll the sausages or balls in the cracker crumbs to coat them.
6. Place them on an oiled cookie sheet and liberally drizzle olive oil over them. Bake until golden, about 10 to 15 minutes. Avoid overcooking; they should still be slightly pink inside. Serve on a platter and keep warm on a warming tray or over an alcohol lamp or fondue warmer.

FAST: Can prepare through step 5 up to 1 day in advance and refrigerate, or flash freeze (page 24) for up to 3 months. It is not necessary to defrost before cooking.

FLASHY: Served alone or with any Italian-style dunk in Chapter 1 or 3. Garnished with a sprinkling of minced fresh parsley.

FABULOUS: With ground beef, turkey, or pork substituted for the veal. With 1 cup packed fresh basil leaves, minced, mixed in. As an entree served on pasta or rice.

Turkey Ham Sausages

Yield: about 60 meatballs; 30 or more servings

1½ pounds ground turkey

1½ pounds lean ground pork

½ pound ham, ground

1½ cups soft sourdough bread
    crumbs

¾ cup heavy cream

1 large onion, minced

2 tablespoons unsalted butter

6 tablespoons minced fresh parsley

2 to 4 cloves garlic, minced

1 tablespoon Dijon mustard or to
    taste

Zest of 1 lemon, grated

Salt, ground white pepper, and dried
    thyme to taste

Flour for dusting

1. Preheat the broiler or the oven to 400°F. Combine all the ingredients, except the flour, in a food processor fitted with the metal blade, or by hand in a mixing bowl. Fry 1 teaspoon of the mixture until cooked all the way through to check the seasonings.
2. Form the mixture into 2-inch-long sausages and coat lightly with the flour, tapping off any excess.
3. Place them on an oiled cookie sheet. Broil or bake until no longer pink in the middle, 15 to 25 minutes.

FAST: Can prepare through step 2 up to 1 day in advance and refrigerate, or flash freeze (page 24) for up to 3 months. Cook frozen, adding about 5 minutes to the baking time.

FLASHY: Serve in a chafing dish on a platter, on a warming tray, or over an alcohol lamp or fondue warmer. Served with any of the following dunks: Cold Lemon Tarragon Sauce (page 30), Dill Cream Sauce (page 31), Dijon Sauce (page 32), or in a chafing dish with Almond Mustard Dunk (page 147), Madeira Jack Fondue (page 154), and/or Herbed Cream Fondue (page 158). Garnished with a sprinkling of minced fresh parsley and/or lemon zest.

FABULOUS: With leftover rice substituted for the bread crumbs. Seasoned with 1 cup packed fresh basil leaves, minced, or 3 tablespoons minced fresh rosemary.

HAM SAUSAGES

Yield: about 32 meatballs; 15 or more servings

1 cup soft sourdough bread crumbs

3 tablespoons milk

1 pound lean ground pork

½ pound smoked ham, ground

3 to 4 tablespoons minced fresh dill
   or to taste

½ teaspoon caraway seeds

¼ to ½ cup minced green onions
   (scallions), white and green parts

¼ cup minced fresh parsley

2 cloves garlic, minced

1 tablespoon Dijon mustard

1 large egg, lightly beaten

2 tablespoons unsalted butter

2 tablespoons peanut oil

½ cup dry red wine

¼ cup brandy

1. Soak the bread crumbs in the milk for 5 minutes. Drain them in a fine wire mesh strainer to remove the excess milk.

2. Combine the ground meats with the soaked crumbs in a food processor fitted with the metal blade, or by hand in a mixing bowl. Add the dill, caraway, green onions, parsley, garlic, mustard, and egg, and mix well.

3. Fry 1 teaspoon of the mixture until cooked all the way through to check the seasonings. Form into 2-inch-long sausages and chill for at least 30 minutes.

4. Preheat the oven to 400°F. Melt the butter with the oil in a skillet over high heat. When the butter begins to foam, add the sausages to the skillet, and toss them in the butter mixture until well coated.

5. Transfer the sausages to a baking dish or jelly-roll pan. Bake until well browned, about 10 minutes. Shake the pan periodically to rotate the sausages.

6. Pour out the remaining oil and butter and heat the wine and brandy in the skillet. Cook over medium-high heat until it reduces by half. Pour this liquid over the sausages. Cover the dish tightly with aluminum foil, lower the oven temperature to 350°F, and bake for about 20 minutes, until they are firm to the touch.

FAST: Can prepare through step 6 up to 2 days in advance and refrigerate, or flash freeze (page 24) for up to 3 months. Bring to room temperature before finishing.

FLASHY: Served in a chafing dish with toothpicks. Garnished with a sprinkling of minced green onions, fresh parsley, and/or dill.

FABULOUS: With 1 teaspoon Dijon mustard and ¼ cup heavy cream added and reduced with the wine and brandy.

PEARL CHUTNEY BALLS

*This is a take-off on a Chinese classic. I have given it a
slight Indian flavor.*

Yield: about 36 meatballs; 18 or more servings

1 cup uncooked sweet rice
(page 18)

1½ pounds lean ground pork

¼ cup soy sauce

⅔ cup mango chutney, homemade
(page 15) or purchased

2 tablespoons medium-dry or
cream sherry

1 large egg

2 to 4 green onions (scallions),
white and green parts, minced

¼ cup minced cilantro (fresh
coriander)

2 tablespoons minced fresh ginger
or ¼ teaspoon ground or to taste

Salt and ground white pepper to taste

1. Cover the rice with cold water and soak it for 7 hours. Drain.
2. Combine all the ingredients, except the sweet rice, in a food processor fitted with the
   metal blade, or by hand in a mixing bowl. Fry 1 teaspoon of the mixture until cooked
   all the way through to check the seasonings.
3. Shape the mixture into 1-inch balls and roll them in the drained rice to coat them.
4. Place the balls in a steamer and steam for 30 minutes. To steam fill the lower part
   of a steamer with water to a level of one inch below the steamer tray. Bring this to
   a boil over high heat. Place the balls on the tray and cover with a lid. For a steamer
   substitute use a heavy large pot with a lid. Fill with several inches of water and place
   an empty can or a heatproof bowl in the center. Top this with a heatproof plate. Add
   the balls to the plate and cover with the lid. It is important for the plate to be several
   inches smaller than the pot so the steam can circulate.

FAST: Can prepare through step 3 up to 3 days in advance, or flash freeze (page 24) for up
to 3 months. Cook frozen, adding about 5 minutes to the steaming time.

FLASHY: Served with any Asian-style dunk from Chapter 1 or 3 in a chafing dish. Garnished with a sprinkling of minced green onions and/or cilantro.

FABULOUS: As an entree served over rice or pasta.

Fast & Fabulous
Hors D'Oeuvres

Skewered Ground Lamb Sausages

Let guests grill their own.

Yield: about 30 sausages; 15 or more servings

1 large onion, chopped

2 to 4 cloves garlic, chopped

2 pounds ground lamb

2 large eggs, lightly beaten

¼ cup minced fresh parsley

½ cup minced cilantro (fresh coriander)

¼ cup packed fresh mint leaves, minced, or to taste

1 tablespoon Dijon mustard

Zest of 2 lemons, grated

½ cup extra virgin olive oil

1 tablespoon sweet Hungarian paprika

Bamboo skewers, soaked in water for about 1 hour to prevent burning

Cold Yogurt Sauce (recipe follows)

1. Combine all the ingredients, except the olive oil, paprika, and yogurt sauce, in a food processor fitted with the metal blade and process until smooth, or combine in a bowl.
2. Fry 1 teaspoon of the mixture until cooked all the way through to check the seasonings.
3. Shape the mixture into 2-inch-long sausages. Let them stand at room temperature for 1 hour or refrigerate overnight.
4. Preheat the broiler or start the grill. Skewer the sausages. Combine the olive oil with the paprika and brush on the sausages.
5. Broil or barbecue the sausages until they are just firm to the touch. Be careful not to overcook. Cut into one to test. Serve in a chafing dish or fondue pot or on a platter over a warming tray. Serve with the yogurt sauce on the side.

FAST: Can prepare through step 5 up to 2 days in advance and refrigerate, or flash freeze (page 24) for up to 3 months. Can cook frozen, adding about 5 minutes to the broiling time.

FLASHY: With quartered pita breads or with Pita Chips (page 274) surrounded by bowls of the yogurt sauce, chopped fresh tomato, chopped imported olives, crumbled feta cheese, lemon wedges, minced green onions, minced fresh mint, and minced cilantro. Garnished with sprigs of minced cilantro, parsley, and/or mint.

FABULOUS: With ground beef, turkey, or pork substituted for all or part of the lamb.

COLD YOGURT SAUCE

2 cups plain yogurt

2 cloves garlic, minced

2 tablespoons minced fresh mint or
1½ teaspoons dried

2 to 4 whole green onions
(scallions), minced

¼ cup minced fresh parsley

¼ to ½ teaspoon fenugreek
(page 21)

1 teaspoon salt or to taste

Ground white pepper and fresh lemon
juice to taste

Combine all the ingredients in a food processor fitted with the metal blade or in a blender and process until smooth, or combine by hand in a mixing bowl. Taste and adjust the seasonings.

FAST: Prepare up to 4 days in advance and refrigerate.

FLASHY: Garnished with a fresh mint and/or any nontoxic flower.

FABULOUS: Seasoned with 1 tablespoon of pickled mango (page 18) or 1 teaspoon of Jamaican jerk seasoning paste (page 21).

EASTERN-STYLE GARBANZO BALLS

Unusual, delicious, and healthy!

Yield: about 20 balls; 10 or more servings

1 cup uncooked bulgur (page 20)

¼ cup plus 2 tablespoons peanut or
canola oil

1 large onion, minced

2 to 4 cloves garlic, minced

1 to 2 medium-size carrots, minced

1 large egg, slightly beaten

¼ cup minced pickled ginger or to
taste (page 18)

½ cup minced green onions
(scallions), white and green parts

¼ cup Chinese plum sauce or to taste
(page 17)

½ cup minced cilantro (fresh
coriander)

¼ to ½ cup minced fresh parsley

1½ cups canned garbanzo beans
(chick-peas), drained and rinsed

1 cup walnuts, toasted (page 27)

½ cup minced Chinese barbecued
pork, smoked ham, or cooked
Chinese sausages (page 17)

Cornmeal, spread over a sheet of
aluminum foil

1. Soak the bulgur in hot water to cover until softened, about 20 minutes. Drain in a fine mesh strainer or in a clean kitchen towel, squeezing out any excess moisture.

2. Heat 2 tablespoons of the oil in a skillet over medium heat. Add the onion, garlic, and carrots and cook, stirring, until golden. Set aside.

3. Combine the bulgur, egg, ginger, green onions, plum sauce, cilantro, parsley, beans, and walnuts in a food processor fitted with the metal blade and process until well blended.

4. Process in the pork and the onion mixture, using several quick on-and-off motions, so as not to destroy the texture. For added texture, add more walnuts. Fry a teaspoon of this mixture until cooked through to check the seasonings.

5. Place the mixture in the freezer until well chilled, about 30 minutes. Shape into small balls and roll in cornmeal to coat them.

6. Can be oven or pan fried. To oven fry, place the balls on an oiled baking sheet and drizzle with oil. Bake in a preheated 425°F oven until crisp, about 15 to 20 minutes, shaking the pan frequently. To pan fry, heat ¼ cup oil in a skillet over medium heat and fry until crisp, also shaking the pan frequently to cook completely, about 10 minutes. Do this in several batches so as not to overcrowd the pan.

FAST: Can prepare through step 4 up to 1 day in advance and refrigerate, or shape into balls and flash freeze (page 24) for up to 3 months. Thaw before cooking.

FLASHY: Served with Asian Mayonnaise (page 36). Garnished with minced green onions and/or cilantro. Keep warm on a platter set on a warming tray. Can also be served at room temperature.

FABULOUS: Made hot and spicy by seasoning it with several tablespoons of Tabasco sauce, pickled mango (page 18), any Asian chile sauce, and/or Jamaican jerk seasoning paste (page 21).

CURRIED GROUND LAMB SAUSAGES

Yield: about 20 sausages; 10 or more servings

½ cup blanched almonds, toasted (page 27)

¼ cup all-purpose flour

1 pound ground lamb

1 cup minced onions

2 tablespoons minced pickled ginger (page 18)

2 teaspoons curry powder or to taste

¼ cup minced cilantro (fresh coriander)

¼ cup minced fresh parsley

¼ cup fresh lemon juice

2 tablespoons plain yogurt

Zest of 1 to 2 oranges, finely grated

2 teaspoons salt

Freshly ground pepper to taste

Bamboo skewers, soaked in water for 1 hour to prevent burning

1. Grind the almonds with the flour in a food processor fitted with the metal blade, using several quick on-and-off motions so as not to destroy the texture, or chop by

hand in a mixing bowl. Combine all the ingredients together in a mixing bowl. Allow the mixture to set for 30 minutes at room temperature.

2. Preheat the broiler or start the grill. Form the mixture into 2-inch-long sausages and skewer them.

3. Broil or grill over white-hot coals until browned on the outside and slightly pink on the inside.

FAST: Can prepare through step 2 up to 2 days in advance and refrigerate, or flash freeze (page 24) for up to 3 months.

FLASHY: Served in a chafing dish or on a platter, and garnished with a sprinkling of minced cilantro or parsley. Dunked in Curry Sauce (page 32), Pickled Mango Sauce (page 33), or Cold Papaya Cream Sauce (page 38).

FABULOUS: With ground lean pork or turkey substituted for all or part of the lamb.

PECAN CHICKEN BALLS

A great way to use up leftover chicken.

Yield: about 24 balls; 12 or more servings

1 cup ground and cooked chicken

8 ounces cream cheese or chèvre, at room temperature

1/4 to 1/2 teaspoon curry powder

2 to 4 tablespoons chutney, homemade (see Index) or purchased

2 to 4 tablespoons drained and rinsed capers

1/4 cup minced green onions (scallions), white and green parts, and/or cilantro (fresh coriander)

1 teaspoon Dijon mustard

Salt and white pepper to taste

1 cup finely chopped toasted pecans

1. Combine all the ingredients, except the pecans, in a food processor fitted with the metal blade and process until well blended, or combine in a mixing bowl. Taste and adjust the seasonings. Chill for about 1 hour.

2. Form into 1-inch balls and roll in the pecans to coat them. Serve chilled.

FAST: Can prepare up to 3 days in advance and refrigerate.

FLASHY: Served on a platter and garnished with minced cilantro, parsley, and/or any nontoxic flower.

FABULOUS: With minced green onions, cilantro, or unsweetened shredded coconut substituted for the pecans. With any cooked leftovers, especially fish or pork, substituted for the chicken.

SKEWERED BARBECUED CHEESE

This isn't a meatball, but it just seemed to belong here!
A great summer choice.

Yield: about 8 servings

2 to 4 cloves garlic, minced

1 cup extra virgin olive oil

¼ cup packed fresh basil leaves or
other herb of your choice, minced,
or 1 tablespoon dried

4 to 8 peperoncini (page 116),
stemmed, or to taste

One 12- to 14-inch-long loaf
sourdough bread, crusts removed
and cut into 1-inch cubes

12 to 14 ounces jack cheese, cut into
1- to 1½-inch chunks

Bamboo skewers, soaked in water for
1 hour to prevent burning

1. Combine the garlic, olive oil, basil and peppers in a food processor fitted with the metal blade or in a blender until pureed.
2. Transfer to a shallow bowl or a glass baking dish. Add the cheese cubes and coat with the seasoned oil. Let this marinate for at least 1 hour at room temperature or for up to 5 days refrigerated.
3. Preheat the broiler or start the grill. Skewer the bread and cheese, stringing them close together, beginning and ending with bread.
4. Brush the bread with the oil.
5. Broil or barbecue until the bread toasts and the cheese softens, about 1 to 2 minutes. Serve on cocktail plates.

FAST: Can prepare through step 2 up to 7 days in advance and refrigerate.

FLASHY: Served on cocktail plates and garnished with a sprig of fresh herbs and/or any nontoxic flower or leaves.

FABULOUS: With mozzarella, cheddar, or Gruyère instead of the jack. With slices of salami, Canadian bacon, or prosciutto added to the skewers. The seasoned olive oil used to marinate lamb, pork, poultry, beef, and/or seafood. It will keep refrigerated for about 3 months.

SAUSAGE AND WHITE BEAN PÂTÉ WITH COLD TOMATO SAUCE

I created this when I was featured in Bon Appetit
magazine. It is a dish that says "summer" loud and clear.

Yield: about 4 cups; 30 or more servings

2 cups (16 ounces) dried white
  beans, rinsed and soaked
  overnight in water to cover
1 ham hock
10 black peppercorns
1 medium-size yellow onion,
  quartered
1 celery stalk
1 bay leaf
4 sprigs fresh parsley
2 cloves garlic, peeled and smashed
1 teaspoon salt
One 1-pound eggplant (approximately),
  peeled and coarsely grated
3 envelopes unflavored gelatin
  dissolved in 6 to 8 tablespoons dry
  vermouth
⅔ cup dry sourdough bread crumbs
½ cup freshly grated Parmesan or
  Romano, plus extra for topping

¼ cup capers, drained and rinsed
2 to 4 cloves garlic, minced
Freshly grated nutmeg to taste
Ground white pepper to taste
1 pound sweet Italian sausage, casings removed
2 cups minced onion
1 cup packed fresh basil leaves,
  minced, or 2 tablespoons dried,
  crumbled
⅔ cup walnuts, toasted (page 27)
  and finely ground
Fresh lemon juice to taste
4 large red bell peppers, roasted,
  seeded, deveined, and peeled
  (page 26)
Cold Tomato Cucumber Sauce (recipe
  follows)

1. Discard any beans that float to the surface, then drain and place in a large saucepan
   with the ham hock, peppercorns, quartered onion, celery, bay leaf, parsley, smashed
   garlic, and salt. Cover with water and simmer over low heat until the beans are
   tender, about 1 hour.
2. While the beans are cooking, place the eggplant in a colander, sprinkle with salt,
   and let drain for 30 minutes. Rinse the eggplant lightly, and blot dry with paper
   towels. Set aside.
3. Drain the beans well. Transfer them to a food processor fitted with the metal blade

and puree in batches, being careful to leave an air vent so the steam doesn't cause an explosion. Measure 3 cups of the puree and reserve any extra for another use. Return the measured amount to the food processor. Process in the dissolved gelatin. Then add the bread crumbs, cheese, capers, minced garlic, nutmeg, pepper, and more salt and blend thoroughly.

4. Meanwhile, heat a large skillet over medium heat, then add the sausage meat and cook until well-browned, breaking it up with a fork as it cooks. Remove the sausage from the skillet using a slotted spoon and drain on paper towels. Break the sausage up into small pieces using a fork.

5. Preheat the oven to 350°F. Discard all but 2 tablespoons of the fat from the skillet. Heat over medium-low, then add the minced onion and cook, stirring, until it is well-browned. Stir in the eggplant and basil. Place the skillet in the oven and bake until fully cooked, about 20 minutes.

6. Stir in the sausage and ground walnuts and season with lemon juice, salt, and pepper.

7. Cut the roasted red peppers into strips and line the bottom of an oiled and plastic wrap-lined 1½-quart terrine, or use several smaller ones. Layer the bean puree on top of the peppers, then add a layer of the eggplant mixture. Continue alternating mixtures until the dish is filled. Sprinkle with Parmesan cheese, if desired. Cover tightly with plastic wrap or a lid and refrigerate until set, at least 6 hours.

8. To serve, invert the pâté onto a platter and serve with the tomato cucumber sauce on the side.

FAST: Can prepare up to 3 days in advance and refrigerate, or freeze for up to 3 months.

FLASHY: Served with thinly sliced baguettes, crackers, or pumpernickel squares. Garnished with olives, fresh basil leaves, lemon zest, roasted red peppers, paprika, and/or any nontoxic flower. Surrounded with lemon slices.

FABULOUS: With canned beans, drained and rinsed, when pressed for time.

COLD TOMATO CUCUMBER SAUCE

Yield: 6 cups

4 cups pureed, peeled fresh tomatoes, strained through a fine mesh strainer to remove seeds

¾ cup minced green onions (scallions), green and white parts

¼ cup minced fresh parsley

½ cup packed fresh basil leaves, minced, or 2 tablespoons dried, crumbled

½ cup minced, seeded, and peeled cucumber

2 to 4 cloves

Salt, ground white pepper, and fresh lemon juice to taste

Combine all the ingredients in a food processor fitted with the metal blade and process using several quick on-and-off motions so as not to destroy the texture, or combine in a bowl. Taste and adjust the seasonings. Refrigerate until ready to use.

FAST: Can prepare up to 4 days in advance and refrigerate or freeze for up to 3 months.

FLASHY: As a dunk for any Melba/Crostini (pages 263–273) and/or Pita Chips (page 274).

FABULOUS: With ½ cup fresh cilantro instead of fresh basil.

ITALIAN CHICKEN VEGETABLE TERRINE

Tastes best when prepared several days in advance.

Yield: about 7 cups; 50 or more servings

Minced whole green onions (scallions)
  and fresh parsley to taste
½ pound eggplant, cut into
  ¼-inch-thick slices
Olive oil for brushing
1 pound raw boneless chicken or
  turkey breast meat, coarsely cut up
2 large eggs
1 tablespoon Dijon mustard
1 cup ricotta cheese
¼ to ½ cup freshly grated Parmesan

2 cloves garlic
3 shallots, minced
¾ cup heavy cream
2 large peperoncini (page 116)
Salt, ground white pepper, and freshly
  grated nutmeg to taste
1 cup softened sun-dried tomatoes
  (page 22) or roasted red peppers
  (page 26), minced
Two 6-ounce jars marinated artichoke
  hearts, drained and chopped

1. Oil an 8-cup terrine or mold of your choice. Line the bottom with minced green onions and parsley.
2. Sprinkle the eggplant slices with salt and drain in a colander for 30 minutes. Rinse lightly and blot dry with paper towels. Brush both sides of the eggplant slices with olive oil and place them on a cookie sheet. Bake in a preheated 400°F oven until just tender, about 10 minutes. Turn the heat down to 300°F.
3. Meanwhile, combine the meat, eggs, mustard, cheeses, garlic, shallots, cream, peperoncini, and seasonings in a food processor fitted with the metal blade until a smooth paste is formed.
4. Fry 1 teaspoon of the mixture until cooked all the way through to check the seasonings.
5. Place a layer of the filling in the terrine, top with several of the eggplant slices and then a layer of sun-dried tomatoes and artichoke hearts, alternating layers until all the vegetables and filling are used up, ending with a layer of green onions and parsley.

6. Cover tightly with parchment and top with aluminum foil. Pierce a small hole in the foil for steam to escape.
7. Place the mold in a pan of hot water that reaches halfway up the sides of the mold.
8. Bake until a meat thermometer inserted in the middle registers 150°F, about 1½ hours. Remove from the water bath, uncover, and cool to room temperature.
9. Refrigerate for at least 4 hours topped with a 2-pound weight. Drain off any accumulated juices and remove the aluminum foil.
10. When chilled, unmold onto a serving platter and slice.

FAST: Can prepare up to 3 days in advance and refrigerate.

FLASHY: Served with thinly sliced baguettes and assorted mustards. Garnished with sprigs of fresh parsley, whole peperoncini, and/or marinated artichoke hearts, and/or nontoxic flowers or leaves.

FABULOUS: With your favorite vegetables substituted for the eggplant and/or chopped imported olives added. With each vegetable layer dusted with extra Parmesan for added flavor.

ROLLED VEAL LOAF

This will be equally well received at a picnic as at a cocktail party.

Yield: 8 or more servings

½ pound ground veal

⅓ cup minced fresh parsley and/or basil

1 to 2 cloves garlic

⅓ cup fresh sourdough bread crumbs

1 large egg, slightly beaten

Salt and ground white pepper to taste

2 to 3 ounces peperoncini (page 116), stemmed and thinly sliced

¼ cup any type freshly grated cheese or to taste

⅓ cup minced whole green onions (scallions), white and green parts

Dijon mustard to taste

All-purpose flour or cornmeal for dusting

½ cup chicken broth, homemade (page 11) or canned

1 bay leaf

1 cup dry white wine

Sprig of fresh parsley

Dried thyme to taste

1. Combine the veal, 2 tablespoons of the parsley, the garlic, bread crumbs, 1 tablespoon of the egg, the salt, and pepper in a food processor fitted with the metal blade, or mix together in a bowl. Place the mixture on a piece of aluminum foil and cover it with a second piece of foil. Shape it into a rectangle about 6 inches wide by 9 inches long and ¼ inch thick and remove the top piece of foil.

2. Place ½ of the peperoncini on top of the veal.
3. Combine the remaining parsley and egg, cheese, green onion, and the mustard. Spread this over the veal and peperoncini, leaving a border of 1-inch all the way around.
4. Place the remaining peperoncini on top in a row running down the center. Roll up the log jelly-roll fashion. Pinch the seams together and chill for 1 hour.
5. Dust the log lightly with flour.
6. Heat the oil over medium-high heat in a Dutch oven or large skillet and brown the roll. Add the broth, bay leaf, wine, sprig of parsley, and thyme and bring to a boil. Cook, partially covered, over medium-low heat for 30 minutes.
7. Remove the meat, cool to room temperature, and refrigerate overnight. Slice before serving.

FAST: Can prepare up to 4 days in advance and refrigerate, or freeze for up to 3 months.

FLASHY: Served with thinly sliced baguettes and Anchovy Basil Mayonnaise Sauce (page 34), Roasted Red Pepper Sauce (page 44), or any mayonnaise-based sauce from Chapter 1. Excellent served with watercress sprigs, cucumber slices, mustards, and gherkins. Garnished with minced fresh parsley, basil, and/or any nontoxic flower or leaves.

FABULOUS: Seasoned with a variety of fresh herbs. With ground pork or lamb substituted for the ground veal.

BAKED SAUSAGE AND NUT TERRINE

Yield: about 2 cups; 10 or more servings

2 tablespoons unsalted butter	¼ pound ham, minced
1 large onion, minced	¼ cup minced fresh parsley
2 cloves garlic, minced	⅓ cup dry sourdough bread crumbs
¼ pound frozen spinach, thawed and squeezed dry	½ cup walnuts, toasted (page 27) and coarsely chopped
¼ pound sweet or hot Italian sausage, casings removed	1 pound sliced bacon
	1 bay leaf

1. Preheat the oven to 350°F.
2. Melt the butter in a skillet over medium heat. When it begins to foam, cook the onion and garlic, stirring, until golden.
3. Combine the spinach with the onion-garlic mixture, then puree in a food processor fitted with the metal blade or in a blender.
4. Blend the sausage, ham, parsley, and bread crumbs into the puree. Fry 1 teaspoon until cooked all the way through to test the seasonings. Stir in the walnuts.

5. Line a 2- to 4-cup terrine with the bacon strips, overlapping the strips slightly.
6. Fill the terrine with the mixture, place the bay leaf on top, and cover with the overlapping bacon strips.
7. Top with a sheet of aluminum foil and a lid, or three layers of foil.
8. Place the terrine in a pan of hot water that reaches halfway up the sides of the terrine and bake for 1 hour. Cool to room temperature, then refrigerate until chilled, at least 6 hours before serving. Drain off any accumulated juices and remove the lid or foil. Unmold onto a platter and remove and discard the slices of bacon.

FAST: Can prepare up to 4 days in advance and refrigerate, or freeze for up to 3 months.

FLASHY: Served with thinly sliced cucumbers, baguettes, or pumpernickel squares, gherkins, and assorted mustards. Garnished with minced fresh parsley and/or any nontoxic flower or leaves.

FABULOUS: With ground lean pork and liver instead of the sausage and ham.

CHICKEN AND HAM TERRINE

Yield: 20 or more servings

One 3-pound chicken
½ cup hot milk
2 cups cubed sourdough bread
2 cups chicken broth, homemade (page 11) or canned
1 tablespoon Dijon mustard or to taste
¼ to ½ pound smoked ham, minced
6 large eggs, beaten

3 tablespoons capers, drained and rinsed, or to taste
½ cup minced green onions (scallions), white and green parts
½ teaspoon dried thyme
½ cup minced fresh parsley
1 cup walnuts, toasted (page 27) and coarsely chopped
Salt and ground white pepper to taste

1. Place the chicken in an ovenproof pan and bake in a preheated 425°F oven for about 1 hour.
2. Pour the milk over the bread cubes and allow them to absorb the liquid, about 20 minutes. Squeeze the excess liquid from the bread.
3. Reduce the oven temperature to 350°F.
4. When the chicken is cool enough to handle, remove the meat from the skin and bones and chop in a food processor fitted with the metal blade or by hand.
5. Add all the ingredients to the food processor, or put in a bowl and mix well using an electric mixer.
6. Pour the mixture into a buttered 4- to 12-cup terrine or loaf pan(s). Set in a larger pan of hot water that reaches halfway up the sides of the terrine and bake for 1 hour.
7. Let the terrine sit at room temperature for about 15 to 20 minutes before unmolding and serve hot or cold.

181

Forms

FAST: Can prepare up to 4 days in advance and refrigerate, or freeze for up to 3 months.

FLASHY: Served with Cold Tomato Cucumber Sauce (page 177), or any mayonnaise-based sauce from Chapter 1. Garnished with minced fresh parsley, watercress, and/or any non-toxic flower or leaves.

FABULOUS: With leftover turkey substituted for the chicken.

CHICKEN AND VEAL PÂTÉ WITH SHIITAKE MUSHROOMS

A French-style pâté with a Greek touch!

Yield: about 5 cups; 40 or more servings

Olive, peanut, or canola oil
Grape leaves and/or thinly sliced
   lemon
½ pound ground veal
2 shallots, cut up
2 tablespoons Dijon mustard
1½ pounds raw boneless chicken
   breasts or thighs, skinned, cut
   into chunks, and chilled

2 cups heavy cream
2 large egg whites
Dried thyme to taste
Salt, ground white pepper, and freshly
   grated nutmeg to taste
1 ounce dried shiitake mushrooms,
   rehydrated (page 18), stemmed,
   and minced

1. Preheat the oven to 350°F.
2. Oil a 6- to 8-cup terrine, oval mold, or loaf pan and line the bottom with parchment or aluminum foil.
3. Use the grape leaves or lemon slices to line the bottom and sides of the terrine.
4. Process the veal, shallots, mustard, and chicken in a food processor fitted with the metal blade until pureed. Then add the cream, egg whites, and seasonings.
5. Fry 1 teaspoon of the mixture until cooked all the way through to check the seasonings.
6. Stir the mushrooms into the chicken mixture and transfer to the prepared terrine.
7. Place the terrine in a pan filled with hot water that reaches halfway up the sides of the terrine and bake for 1 hour. Chill for at least 6 hours before unmolding and serving. Invert onto a serving platter.

FAST: Can prepare up to 3 days in advance and refrigerate, or freeze for up to 3 months.

FLASHY: Served with assorted mustards and thinly sliced breads. Garnished with fresh grape leaves, minced fresh parsley, and/or any nontoxic flower or leaves.

FABULOUS: With ½ to 1 cup chopped pistachios added when mixing in the mushrooms.

POACHED CHICKEN AND PISTACHIO PÂTÉ

Another recipe created for Bon Appetit

Yield: about 2½ cups; 10 or more servings

Pâté mixture

1 medium-size potato, boiled in water to cover until tender (peeled or unpeeled)

½ cup crumbled goat cheese (*chèvre* or *feta*) or to taste

1 large egg

1 to 2 cloves garlic

14 ounces raw boneless chicken breasts

3 tablespoons minced fresh parsley

1 teaspoon dried basil

Salt and ground white pepper to taste

10 imported pitted green olives

½ cup minced smoked ham

¼ cup pistachios or to taste

1 cup softened sun-dried tomatoes or to taste, optional

Flavored poaching liquid

1 cup dry white wine or vermouth

1 medium-size carrot, cut up

Celery leaves, plus 1 stalk, cut up

6 parsley stems

1 large onion, chopped

Salt and ground white pepper to taste

1. Combine the cooked potato, cheese, egg, garlic, chicken, parsley, basil, salt, and pepper in a food processor fitted with the metal blade and puree.
2. Fry 1 teaspoon of the mixture until cooked all the way through to check the seasonings.
3. Moisten a piece of cheesecloth and squeeze out the excess moisture. Lay it out flat and place the chicken mixture, flattened, on it.
4. In the center of the mixture sprinkle the olives, ham, pistachios, and tomatoes and roll it up jelly-roll fashion in the cheesecloth. Shape the mixture into a log about 2½ inches in diameter. Wrap in a second layer of cheesecloth; twist the ends and place them under the log.
5. Place the log in a saucepan or casserole and add all the ingredients for the flavored poaching liquid plus enough water to cover the log by 1 inch.
6. Bring it to a boil, then reduce the heat to low and allow it to simmer gently for 45 minutes.
7. Remove the pâté and cool it to room temperature. Unwrap and serve chilled or at room temperature.

FAST: Can prepare the pâté up to 3 days in advance and refrigerate, or freeze for up to 3 months.

FLASHY: With Dill and Chive Mayonnaise (page 37) and thinly sliced baguettes. Garnished with cucumber slices, minced fresh parsley, and/or any nontoxic flower or leaves.

FABULOUS: With prosciutto or Italian salami substituted for the smoked ham. With uncooked turkey, tuna, shrimp, or salmon instead of the chicken.

PÂTÉ DE NICOLE

*Named for my daughter, who wouldn't even consider
tasting it!*

Yield: about 5 cups; 40 or more servings

1½ pounds chicken livers, trimmed of
    fat and cut into pieces, soaked in
    dry sherry to cover for 1 hour or
    overnight in the refrigerator, and
    drained
1½ pounds ground veal
  1 medium-size onion
  2 to 4 cloves garlic
  ½ cup minced fresh parsley

  2 large eggs
  2 tablespoons all-purpose flour
  ¼ teaspoon dried thyme
  1 tablespoon salt
  2 teaspoons ground white pepper
  1 tablespoon poultry seasoning
  ¼ cup brandy
  1 pound sliced bacon
  4 bay leaves

1. Preheat the oven to 350°F.
2. Process the liver, veal, onion, garlic, and parsley in a food processor fitted with the metal blade to a smooth consistency.
3. Add the remaining ingredients, except the bacon and bay leaves, and process until combined. Fry 1 teaspoon of the mixture until cooked all the way through to check the seasonings.
4. Line a 6- to 8-cup loaf pan or terrine with the bacon and pack in the mixture. Place the bay leaves on top and cover with the flaps of bacon.
5. Set the loaf pan or terrine in a pan with hot water that reaches halfway up the sides of the loaf pan. Bake, covered with aluminum foil, for 1¾ hours.
6. Cool to room temperature; then place a light weight on top and refrigerate until chilled, about 4 hours. Drain off any accumulated juices before removing the aluminum foil. Invert onto serving platter.

FAST: Can prepare up to 4 days in advance and refrigerate, or freeze for up to 3 months.

FLASHY: With the bacon removed and discarded and garnished with sprigs of watercress, parsley, and/or any nontoxic flower. Served with cornichons, assorted mustards, and thinly sliced baguettes, and/or pumpernickel squares.

FABULOUS: With ground pork instead of ground veal.

PÂTÉ SPREAD WITH
FIGS AND WALNUTS

*An exotic pâté with rich, contrasting textures and unusual
flavors, that is a great choice for fall.*

Yield: about 4 cups; 30 or more servings

½ pound (2 sticks) unsalted butter

1 onion, sliced

4 shallots, minced

8 ounces dried figs, cut up and
   soaked in Marsala or port for at
   least 1 hour to soften, drained

1 pound chicken livers, trimmed of
   fat, soaked in milk to cover for
   one hour or overnight and
   refrigerated, then drained

¼ cup brandy

½ teaspoon salt or to taste

½ teaspoon poultry seasoning or to
   taste

Ground white pepper to taste

1 teaspoon fresh lemon juice or to
   taste

½ cup chopped walnuts, toasted
   (page 27)

1. In a skillet, melt 3 tablespoons of the butter over medium heat. When it begins to foam, cook the onion and shallots, stirring until golden.
2. Add the figs and cook, stirring, until tender, about 15 minutes.
3. Add 3 more tablespoons of butter and the drained liver and cook, stirring, over medium-high heat until the outsides of the livers are browned and the insides are pink.
4. Add the brandy and cook it until it evaporates.
5. Pour the liver mixture in a bowl and place in the freezer until chilled, about 30 minutes.
6. When chilled, place it in a food processor fitted with the metal blade and process until smooth, or in a mixing bowl using an electric mixer. While the machine is running, add the remaining butter, cut into small pieces, along with the seasonings and lemon juice. Taste and adjust the seasonings.
7. Process in the walnuts, using care not to destroy their texture.
8. Pack the mixture in an oiled 5-cup crock or serving container of your choice. Chill for at least 1 hour before serving.

FAST: Can prepare up to 3 days in advance and refrigerate, or freeze for up to 3 months.

FLASHY: Unmolded or served in the container with crackers and/or thinly sliced baguettes. Garnished with thinly sliced cucumbers, sprigs of watercress, walnut halves, and/or any nontoxic flower or leaves.

FABULOUS: With dried or peeled tart green apple instead of the figs.

COUNTRY HERB PÂTÉ

Robust and hearty.

Yield: about 4½ cups; 30 or more servings

2 tablespoons unsalted butter

1 large onion, minced

¾ pound ground turkey, chicken, or veal

¾ pound lean ground pork

¾ pound chicken livers, trimmed of fat, soaked in milk to cover for 1 hour or overnight in the refrigerator, and drained

¼ pound hot or sweet Italian sausage, casings removed

2 large eggs

⅓ cup dry red wine such as Cabernet Sauvignon or Zinfandel

2 tablespoons all-purpose flour

Zest of 1 lemon, finely grated

¼ cup minced fresh parsley

2 tablespoons Dijon mustard

1 teaspoon fennel seeds

1 tablespoon dried basil

1 tablespoon dried fines herbes (page 21)

2 teaspoons salt or to taste

Ground white pepper and freshly grated nutmeg to taste

½ cup heavy cream

1 pound sliced bacon

2 bay leaves

1. Preheat the oven to 350°F.
2. Melt the butter in a medium-size skillet over medium heat. When the butter foams, add the onion and cook, stirring, until golden.
3. Combine all the ingredients, except for the bay leaves, cream, and bacon, in a food processor fitted with the metal blade and process until well blended, or in a bowl using an electric mixer.
4. Add the cream and blend. Fry 1 teaspoon of the mixture until cooked all the way through to check the seasonings.
5. Line a 6-cup loaf pan, terrine, or several smaller pans with the bacon. Fill with the mixture and place 1 to 2 bay leaves on top, depending on the size of the pan. Fold the flaps of bacon over the top.
6. Cover tightly with aluminum foil and place the pâté in a larger pan with hot water that reaches halfway up the sides of the pâté pan.
7. Bake until juices run clear when a sharp knife or toothpick is inserted into the center, about 1½ to 1¾ hours.
8. Cool to room temperature and place a 2-pound can on top to weight it down. Refrigerate for at least 6 hours before serving.

FAST: Can prepare up to 3 days in advance and refrigerate, or freeze for up to 3 months.

FLASHY: With the bacon removed and discarded and served with thinly sliced cucumbers, cornichons, assorted mustards, thinly sliced baguettes, and pumpernickel squares. Garnished with sprigs of watercress, parsley, and/or any nontoxic flower or leaves.

FABULOUS: With all lean ground pork and liver or a combination of your choice. The seasonings varied. With a cup of toasted chopped nuts (see page 27) added to the pâté mixture before packing it into the terrine.

THREE MEAT AND NUT TERRINE

Yield: 20 or more servings

2 tablespoons unsalted butter

1 large onion, minced

½ cup heavy cream

2 bay leaves

½ pound chicken livers, trimmed of fat, soaked in milk or water to cover for 1 hour, and drained

½ pound ground veal

¼ pound hot or sweet Italian sausage, casings removed

1 to 2 cloves garlic, minced

½ cup minced fresh parsley

2 large eggs

¼ cup brandy or bourbon

¼ to ½ cup capers, drained and rinsed

1 teaspoon salt

Ground white pepper to taste

1 cup raw or blanched almonds, toasted (page 27) and chopped

1 pound sliced bacon

1. Preheat the oven to 350°F.
2. Melt the butter in a medium-size skillet over medium heat. When the butter foams, add the onion and cook, stirring, until golden.
3. Scald the cream in a small saucepan over medium-high heat with the 2 bay leaves. Remove and reserve the leaves.
4. Combine all the ingredients, except the almonds and bacon, in a food processor fitted with the metal blade and process until pureed.
5. Stir in the almonds. Fry 1 teaspoon of the mixture until cooked all the way through to check the seasonings.
6. Line a 1½-quart terrine or loaf pan with the bacon and place one of the bay leaves on the bottom. Fill the terrine with the puree. Fold the flaps of the bacon over and top with the other bay leaf. Cover with aluminum foil and a lid or 3 layers of foil and place in pan with hot water that reaches halfway up the sides of the pâté pan.
7. Bake for 1¼ hours, until the juices run clear when a sharp knife or toothpick is inserted into the center. Let it stand for 30 minutes, then remove it from the pan of water. Weight the terrine with a 2- to 3-pound weight or can, and chill overnight.
8. Drain off any accumulated juices and remove the lid.

FAST: Can prepare up to 4 days in advance and refrigerate, or freeze for up to 3 months.

FLASHY: With the bacon removed and discarded and served on a large platter with thinly sliced cucumbers, cornichons, assorted mustards, thinly sliced baguettes, and pumpernickel squares. Garnished with sprigs of watercress, parsley, and/or any nontoxic flower or leaves.

FABULOUS: With all lean ground pork and liver or a combination of your choice. With the seasonings varied.

BAKED CHICKEN LIVER PÂTÉ

A delightful pâté with a creamy texture and an interesting mix of subtle flavors.

Yield: 50 or more servings

2 pounds chicken livers, trimmed of fat, soaked in milk or water to cover for 1 hour, and drained

Dry sherry for soaking the liver

2 tablespoons unsalted butter

1 onion, minced

¼ cup minced shallots

2 cups minced cultivated white mushrooms

1 ounce dried shiitake mushrooms, rehydrated (page 18), stemmed, and minced

½ cup all-purpose flour

1½ cups milk

2 tablespoons minced pickled ginger or to taste (page 18)

Zest of 2 or more lemons, finely grated

¼ to ½ cup capers, drained and rinsed

½ cup minced fresh parsley

1 to 2 tablespoons minced fresh thyme or 1 to 2 teaspoons dried

½ teaspoon ground white pepper

4 large eggs, lightly beaten

Salt and freshly grated nutmeg to taste

1 pound sliced bacon

1. Place the liver in a bowl and add a goodly amount of sherry. Cover and refrigerate for several hours or overnight.
2. Preheat the oven to 300°F. Melt the butter in a saucepan over medium heat. When it begins to foam, add the onion and shallots and cook, stirring, until tender.
3. Add the mushrooms and cook, stirring, until the mushrooms' moisture cooks out.
4. Stir in the flour, reduce the heat to medium-low, cover, and let cook for several minutes. Stir in the milk gradually and cook, stirring, until thickened.
5. Drain the livers, place them in a food processor fitted with the metal blade or in a blender, and puree.
6. Add the onion mixture to the food processor and process until combined thoroughly. Add the remaining ingredients, except the bacon, and process again until combined. Fry 1 teaspoon of the mixture until cooked all the way through to test the seasonings.
7. Line pâté molds, terrines, or loaf pans with the bacon. Use two 8¼ × 4¼ × 3-inch pans or try even smaller molds and fill with the pâté mixture.

8. Place the molds in a pan with hot water that reaches halfway up the sides of the molds. Bake until the pâté reaches an internal temperature of 150°F, about 1½ to 2 hours. Remove the pâtés from the oven and water bath and allow them to cool to room temperature. Cover and refrigerate for at least 5 hours before serving.

FAST: Can prepare up to 4 days in advance and refrigerate, or freeze for up to 3 months.

FLASHY: With the bacon removed and discarded and served on a large platter with thinly sliced cucumbers, cornichons, assorted mustards, thinly sliced baguettes, and pumpernickel squares. Garnished with sprigs of watercress, minced fresh parsley, and/or any nontoxic flower or leaves.

HERBED PORK AND LIVER TERRINE
Wonderfully hearty.

Yield: about 6 cups; 50 or more servings

1½ pounds frozen spinach, thawed and squeezed dry

½ pound chicken livers, trimmed of fat, soaked for at least 1 hour in Marsala to cover, and drained

1½ pounds lean ground pork

4 large eggs, lightly beaten

⅓ cup minced fresh parsley

2 to 4 cloves garlic, minced

¼ cup packed fresh basil leaves, minced, or 1⅓ tablespoons dried or to taste

½ to 1 cup minced green onions (scallions), green and white parts

⅓ cup Marsala

Ground white pepper and freshly grated nutmeg to taste

⅓ cup heavy cream

2 tablespoons unflavored gelatin, softened in 2 tablespoons Marsala

1 pound sliced bacon

1 to 2 bay leaves

1. Preheat the oven to 350°F.
2. Place the spinach, liver, pork, and eggs in a food processor fitted with the metal blade or in a blender and process until the mixture is pureed.
3. In a saucepan, bring the parsley, garlic, basil, thyme, green onions, Marsala, and seasonings to a boil over medium-high heat and reduce by half, about 5 minutes. Stir in the cream and reduce by half again, about 5 minutes more, stirring. Reduce the heat to low and stir in the softened gelatin until it is dissolved.
4. Add the gelatin-herb mixture to the food processor and combine with the liver mixture. Fry 1 teaspoon of the mixture until cooked all the way through to check the seasonings.
5. Line an 8-cup terrine or several small terrines or loaf pans with the bacon. Let the bacon flaps hang over the sides.

6. Fill the terrine with the pâté mixture and top with the bay leaves. Fold the flaps of the bacon over the top. Cover with the aluminum foil and a lid or use 3 layers of foil.
7. Put it in a pan with hot water that reaches halfway up the sides of the terrine. Bake for 2 hours until the juices run clear when a sharp knife or toothpick is inserted into the center. Let the terrine stand for 15 minutes, then remove the lid, leaving the foil in place. Put a 4-pound weight on it and cool to room temperature. Chill it weighted overnight. Drain off and discard any accumulated juices before removing the lid.

FAST: Can prepare up to 3 days in advance and refrigerate, or freeze for up to 3 months.

FLASHY: With the bacon removed and discarded. Served on a large platter with thinly sliced cucumbers, cornichons, assorted mustards, thinly sliced baguettes, and pumpernickel squares. Garnished with sprigs of watercress, parsley, and/or any nontoxic flower or leaves.

FABULOUS: With ½ cup or more of toasted sesame seeds (page 27) added in step 2 with the spinach, meats, and eggs.

SHRIMP AND SCALLOP TERRINE

Light, delicious and simple—a.k.a. Fast & Fabulous!

Yield: about 3 cups; 25 or more servings

½ pound raw shrimp, peeled and deveined

½ pound raw scallops, rinsed and patted dry

1 large shallot or to taste

1 large egg white

Several drops hot pepper sauce

1 tablespoon minced fresh dill or 1 teaspoon dried or to taste

1½ teaspoons salt

Ground white pepper, fresh lemon juice, and freshly grated nutmeg to taste

1 cup heavy cream

Layering ingredients

Zest of 2 lemons, finely grated

Capers, drained and rinsed

Minced fresh dill

Minced green onions (scallions), green and white parts

Minced roasted red peppers (page 26)

Minced fresh parsley

1. Preheat the oven to 350°F.
2. In a food processor fitted with the metal blade combine the seafood, shallot, egg white, and seasonings and process well until smooth.

3. Add the cream and process until everything is blended and the mixture reaches a thick, smooth consistency. Fry 1 teaspoon of the mixture until cooked all the way through to test the seasonings.

4. Butter the inside of a 6- to 8-cup mold or terrine. Cut a piece of parchment paper or aluminum foil to fit the bottom and butter it well. (This will make the terrine unmold like a dream!)

5. Fill the terrine with half of the mixture. Place any or a combination of the layering ingredients on top of the mixture. Top with the remaining seafood mixture.

6. Pack the mixture well and bang the mold on the counter to release any trapped air.

7. Place the mold in a pan filled with hot water that comes halfway up the sides of the mold. Cover with a piece of aluminum foil.

8. Bake for 45 minutes to 1 hour. Test by inserting a knife in the center; it should come out clean.

9. Remove from the oven and take out of the water bath. Allow it to rest for 20 to 30 minutes before unmolding. If liquid has accumulated on the top, use a paper towel to sponge it up. Invert onto a platter.

FAST: Can prepare up to 2 days in advance and refrigerate, or freeze for up to 1 month.

FLASHY: Served hot or cold with Cold Lemon Tarragon Sauce (page 30), Dill Cream Sauce (page 31), Cold Cucumber Sauce (page 38), or Cold Smoked Salmon Sauce (page 41). Served on a bed of lettuce and garnished with watercress leaves and/or any nontoxic flower or leaves.

FABULOUS: Served as a light luncheon or supper entree.

CRAB AND VEGETABLE TERRINE WITH WATERCRESS MAYONNAISE

Yield: 20 or more servings

¾ pound zucchini, julienned, blanched (page 23) until just tender, refreshed under cold water, and drained well

Two 6-ounce jars marinated artichoke hearts, drained well and chopped

¾ pound carrots, julienned, blanched until just tender, refreshed under cold water, and drained well

5 large eggs

¼ cup ricotta cheese

¼ cup chèvre (page 20)

¾ cup milk

¼ cup medium-dry or cream sherry

2 shallots, minced

2 to 4 tablespoons minced fresh dill or to taste

¼ teaspoon salt or to taste

Ground white pepper and freshly grated nutmeg to taste

⅓ cup all-purpose flour

1 pound fresh or frozen crabmeat, picked over for cartilage

Zest of 2 lemons, finely grated

1. Preheat the oven to 350°F. Butter a 1½-quart terrine and line the bottom with buttered parchment paper or aluminum foil.
2. Dry the vegetables by placing them in a large skillet over high heat for 30 seconds and stirring.
3. Combine the eggs, cheeses, milk, sherry, shallots, and seasonings in a food processor with the metal blade or use an electric mixer, and process well. Add the flour through the feed tube or to the mixing bowl while the machine is running, and combine.
4. Add the vegetables, crabmeat, and lemon zest to the bowl and mix in with the batter.
5. Pour the batter into an oiled terrine and bang it on the counter to remove any air pockets.
6. Cover with buttered aluminum foil and place it in a pan filled with hot water that comes halfway up the sides of the terrine.
7. Bake until a skewer inserted into the middle comes out clean, about 1½ hours.
8. Remove from the water bath and allow the terrine to come to room temperature. Chill until completely cold, at least 6 hours, before unmolding and serving. Invert onto a platter.

FAST: Can prepare up to 2 days in advance and refrigerate, or freeze for up to 3 months.

FLASHY: Served with Watercress Mayonnaise (page 35) and thinly sliced baguettes. Garnished with minced fresh dill and/or any nontoxic flower or leaves.

FABULOUS: With cooked lobster, shrimp, or salmon instead of crabmeat.

PÂTÉ OF SALMON AND ARTICHOKE HEARTS

*I like to serve this mousselike pâté for spring and
summer al fresco dining.*

Yield: 24 or more servings

2 to 6 tablespoons capers, drained
and rinsed

6 to 8 green onions (scallions),
white and green parts, minced

1½ cups chicken broth, homemade
(page 11) or canned

⅓ to ½ cup dry vermouth

2 tablespoons brandy

2 envelopes unflavored gelatin

7 ounces salmon or tuna (cooked
fresh or canned—salmon baked
at 350°F for 10 minutes per inch
of thickness)

One 6-ounce jar marinated artichoke
hearts, drained

2 to 4 tablespoons minced fresh
dill

4 anchovy fillets

Juice of 1 lemon

Salt and ground white pepper to taste

1. Puree the capers and green onions together in a food processor fitted with the metal blade.
2. Combine the broth, vermouth, and brandy in a saucepan over low heat. Add the gelatin and stir until it dissolves. Set aside.
3. Add the salmon, artichoke hearts, dill, anchovies, lemon juice, and seasonings to the food processor and process until smooth.
4. Add the gelatin mixture and process until well combined. Taste and adjust the seasonings.
5. Put the mixture in a large, oiled and plastic wrap-lined mold or several smaller molds. Chill until firm, at least 6 hours. Invert onto a serving platter and remove the plastic wrap.

FAST: Can prepare up to 3 days in advance and refrigerate, or freeze for up to 1 month.

FLASHY: Served cold with assorted crackers, any Melba/Crostini (pages 263–273), and/or thinly sliced breads, and garnished with sliced cucumbers, minced fresh dill, watercress leaves, and/or any nontoxic flower or leaves.

FABULOUS: With 8 ounces of cooked shrimp or crabmeat instead of salmon.

SMOKED SALMON MOUSSE

Light and elegant!

Yield: about 4½ cups; 40 or more servings

3 tablespoons dry vermouth

1 envelope unflavored gelatin

8 ounces smoked salmon (*lox*)

½ to 1 shallot, minced, or to taste

3 tablespoons fresh lemon juice or to
   taste

¼ cup minced red or green onion
   (*scallions*), white and green parts

Zest of 1 to 2 lemons, finely grated

¼ cup minced fresh dill or 1
   tablespoon dried

Salt and ground white pepper to taste

3 cups heavy cream

1. Oil and line with plastic wrap a 5-cup mold or several smaller ones.
2. Place the vermouth in a small bowl. Stir in the gelatin and dissolve it over a larger bowl of hot water or in a microwave for about 30 seconds on low power. Allow it to cool slightly.
3. Puree the salmon, shallots, and gelatin mixture in a food processor fitted with the metal blade.
4. Add the lemon juice, onions, lemon zest, and seasonings. Process just until combined. Taste and adjust the seasonings.
5. Add the cream and process very briefly, or it will curdle.
6. Transfer to the prepared mold and chill until firm, about 2 hours in the refrigerator or 45 minutes in the freezer.
7. Invert onto a platter and remove the plastic wrap.

FAST: Can prepare up to 3 days in advance and refrigerate, or freeze for up to 3 months.

FLASHY: Served with Bagel Chips (page 272) or thin squares of pumpernickel. Garnished with a slice of smoked salmon rolled into a rose. With capers and minced fresh dill scattered on top and around the base, and/or nontoxic flowers and leaves.

FABULOUS: With prosciutto, smoked trout, or turkey instead of the smoked salmon.

FURTHER: Toss leftovers into freshly cooked pasta, rice, couscous, bulgur, etc.

SMOKED SALMON AND CHÉVRE MOUSSE

This is a mouthful of soft, subtle luxury that is the perfect
prelude to an elegant meal, and a marvelous way to
celebrate any special occasion.

Yield: about 2 cups; 10 or more servings

1 shallot

6 to 8 ounces smoked salmon (lox)

2 to 4 tablespoons minced fresh dill

Ground white pepper to taste

2 tablespoons fresh lemon juice

4 ounces chèvre (page 20)

1 envelope unflavored gelatin

2 tablespoons dry white wine

1½ cups heavy cream

Zest of 1 lemon, finely grated

1. Oil a 2- to 4-cup mold or small individual bowls of your choice.
2. Puree the shallot, salmon, dill, pepper, lemon juice, and chèvre together in a food processor fitted with the metal blade or a blender.
3. Dissolve the gelatin in the wine in a bowl set into a larger bowl of hot water, or in the microwave for 30 seconds on low power. Blend the dissolved gelatin into the salmon mixture.
4. Process in the cream with the lemon zest briefly to prevent curdling. Taste and adjust the seasonings.
5. Pour the salmon mixture into the prepared mold and refrigerate until set, approximately 4 hours. For faster results, chill in the freezer for about 2 hours. Invert onto a platter and remove the plastic wrap.

FAST: Can prepare up to 3 days in advance and refrigerate, or freeze for up to 3 months.

FLASHY: With Bagel Chips (page 272), pumpernickel squares, or thinly sliced baguettes, and/or any Melba/Crostini (pages 263–273). Garnished with minced fresh dill, whole green onions, and/or any nontoxic flower or leaves.

FABULOUS: With minced green onion or watercress leaves mixed in before molding. With fresh dill used both as a seasoning and a garnish.

COLD SPINACH MOUSSE

Simply delightful!

Yield: about 2 cups; 10 or more servings

2 tablespoons cream sherry

1 envelope unflavored gelatin

One 8-ounce package frozen spinach, thawed, and squeezed dry

½ cup sour cream

1 cup chicken broth, homemade (page 11) or canned

½ cup mayonnaise, homemade (page 13) or purchased

2 to 4 tablespoons capers, drained and rinsed

1 to 2 shallots, minced

¼ teaspoon dried tarragon, optional

Salt, ground white pepper, and freshly grated nutmeg to taste

1. Combine the sherry and gelatin in a small bowl set in a larger bowl of hot water or place in the microwave on low power for 30 seconds to dissolve.
2. Puree all the ingredients in a food processor fitted with the metal blade or in a blender. Taste and adjust the seasonings.
3. Pour the mixture into a well-oiled plastic wrap-lined 2- to 4-cup mold and chill until firm, about 4 hours. For faster results, chill in the freezer for about 2 hours. Unmold and serve.

FAST: Can prepare up to 3 days in advance and refrigerate, or freeze for up to 3 months.

FLASHY: Served with thinly sliced baguettes, crackers, Bagel Chips (page 272) or Pita Chips (page 274), and/or any Melba/Crostini (pages 263–273). Garnished with dollops of sour cream and/or any nontoxic flower or leaves.

FABULOUS: With chard, beet greens, or bok choy substituted for the spinach, and/or thyme, basil, or oregano, for the tarragon. With flaked crabmeat or chopped shrimp mixed in.

Fast & Fabulous
Hors D'Oeuvres

CAVIAR MOUSSE

*Relax, you need not blow your budget. Inexpensive caviar
is just fine for this scrumptious hor d'oeuvre.*

Yield: about 2 cups; 10 or more servings

¾ cup sour cream

¼ cup minced fresh dill

1 shallot

3 large eggs, hard-boiled (page 24)
   and cut up

¼ cup cream cheese, at room temperature

¼ cup fresh lemon juice or to taste

¼ teaspoon ground white pepper

½ teaspoon prepared horseradish or
   to taste

1½ envelopes unflavored gelatin

2 tablespoons gin

3 ounces lumpfish caviar, put in a
   fine strainer and rinsed (to remove the dyes and excess salt), or
   to taste

Salt to taste

1. Oil a 3- to 4-cup mold and line with plastic wrap.
2. Combine the first 8 ingredients in a food processor fitted with the metal blade or a blender and process until smooth.
3. In a small bowl, sprinkle the gelatin over the gin. Set the bowl in a larger bowl of hot water and stir until the gelatin is dissolved, about 5 minutes, or dissolve in a microwave for 30 seconds on low power.
4. Add the dissolved gelatin to the food processor through the feed tube while the machine is running, or add it to the blender.
5. Fold in the caviar. Taste and adjust seasonings.
6. Pour the mousse into the prepared mold and refrigerate until set, 4 hours or more. For faster results, chill in the freezer for about 2 hours. Invert onto a platter and remove the plastic wrap.

FAST: Can prepare up to 3 days in advance and refrigerate, or freeze for up to 3 months.

FLASHY: Served with squares of pumpernickel bread and/or Bagel Chips (page 272) and thinly sliced cucumbers. Garnished with sour cream on the top. Sprinkled with minced green onions, grated lemon zest, more caviar, and minced hard-boiled eggs and/or any nontoxic flower or leaves.

FABULOUS: With salmon caviar instead of black.

SEAFOOD MOUSSE

Yield: about 5 cups; 40 or more servings

½ cup medium-dry or dry sherry

1 cup chicken broth, homemade (page 11) or canned

2 envelopes unflavored gelatin

1 cup heavy cream

1½ pounds cooked shrimp (page 24), peeled and deveined, or crabmeat, picked over for cartilage

1 cup mayonnaise, homemade (page 13) or purchased, sour cream, or low-fat plain yogurt

1 teaspoon prepared horseradish or to taste

1 tablespoon capers, drained and rinsed, or to taste

3 tablespoons shallots, minced

Salt, ground white pepper, fresh lemon juice, and dried tarragon to taste

1. Oil a 6-cup mold or several smaller ones.
2. Combine the sherry, broth, and gelatin in a saucepan and heat until the gelatin dissolves.
3. Whip the cream in a food processor fitted with the metal blade until it holds soft peaks, or with an electric mixer in a bowl. Remove from the processor and set aside.
4. Combine the shrimp, mayonnaise, horseradish, capers, shallots, seasonings, and dissolved gelatin in the food processor and process until smooth. Taste and adjust the seasonings.
5. Gently fold in the whipped cream and pour the mousse into the prepared molds. Refrigerate until firm, about 4 hours. For faster results, chill in the freezer. Invert onto a platter and remove the plastic wrap.

FAST: Prepare up to 3 days in advance and refrigerate, or freeze for up to 3 months.

FLASHY: Served with Beaten Biscuits (page 296), Bagel Chips (page 272), Pita Chips (page 274), or thinly sliced baguettes, squares of pumpernickel, and/or crackers. Garnished with capers, minced fresh or dill parsley, watercress leaves, thinly sliced cucumbers, grated lemon zest, and/or any nontoxic flower or leaves.

FABULOUS: With cooked chicken, chicken livers, lobster, or salmon substituted for the shrimp or crab.

SMOKED HAM MOUSSE

I made my debut on national TV with this.

Yield: about 4 cups; 30 or more servings

6 tablespoons (¾ stick) unsalted
  butter
2 to 4 tablespoons minced shallots
2 cloves garlic, minced
2 to 3 chicken livers, trimmed of
  fat, soaked in milk or Madeira
  to cover for 1 hour at room
  temperature or refrigerated
  overnight, and drained
¼ cup Madeira
1½ envelopes unflavored gelatin
12 ounces smoked ham, trimmed
  and cut in 1-inch pieces

2 teaspoons Dijon mustard or to
  taste
1¾ cups heavy cream
¼ teaspoon dried thyme
2 tablespoons minced fresh dill or
  about 1 teaspoon dried
Salt and ground white pepper to taste
Zest of 2 lemons, finely grated
1 ounce dried shiitake mushrooms,
  rehydrated (page 18), stemmed,
  and thinly sliced

1. Melt 2 tablespoons of the butter in a skillet over medium heat. When it begins to foam, cook the shallots and garlic, stirring, until soft.
2. Add the liver and cook, stirring, until just pink on the inside.
3. Combine the Madeira and gelatin in a bowl and place in a larger bowl of hot water, or in a microwave for 30 seconds on low power to dissolve.
4. Process liver, ham, the remaining butter, the dissolved gelatin, and the mustard in a food processor fitted with the metal blade until smooth.
5. Add the cream and process until blended, being careful not to overprocess, or the cream will curdle.
6. Add the seasonings, lemon zest, and mushrooms and process briefly with several quick on-and-off motions, so as not to destroy texture of the lemon zest or mushrooms.
7. Transfer this mixture to a 6- or 8-cup oiled mold, or use several smaller molds, and chill until set, about 4 hours in the refrigerator. For faster results, chill it in the freezer for about 2 hours. Invert onto a platter and remove the plastic wrap.

FAST: Can prepare up to 3 days in advance and refrigerate, or freeze for up to 3 months.

FLASHY: Garnished with sliced cucumber, cornichons, watercress leaves, grapes, strawberries, and/or any nontoxic flower or leaves. Served with mustards, crackers, any Melba/Crostini (pages 263–273), and/or thinly sliced baguettes.

FABULOUS: With chicken broth used instead of all or some of the cream as a way to reduce the fat content. With porcini mushrooms instead of shiitake mushrooms.

CHICKEN LIVER MOUSSE

A baked mousse that makes a very light pâté.

Yield: six 4-ounce ramekins; 15 or more servings

2 tablespoons unsalted butter

1 large onion, minced

½ pound chicken livers, trimmed of
   fat, soaked in milk to cover for
   1 hour at room temperature or
   refrigerated overnight, and
   drained

2 large eggs

2 to 4 shallots, minced

2 to 4 tablespoons capers, drained
   and rinsed

3 tablespoons Madeira

½ teaspoon dried thyme or rosemary

3 tablespoons minced fresh parsley

Zest of 1 orange, finely grated

½ teaspoon salt

Ground white pepper and freshly
   grated nutmeg to taste

1 cup heavy cream

1. Preheat the oven to 325°F. Melt the butter in a saucepan over medium heat. When it begins to foam, cook the onion, stirring, until tender.
2. Place all the ingredients, except the cream, in a food processor fitted with the metal blade or in a blender and puree.
3. Add the cream and process just until blended. Do not overprocess or the cream will curdle. Fry 1 teaspoon of the mixture until cooked all the way through to test the seasonings.
4. Oil the ramekins or a 4-cup loaf pan and fill it with the mousse. Place the ramekins or loaf pan in a larger pan of hot water that reaches halfway up the sides of the ramekins or loaf pan and bake until the mousse is firm to the touch, about 1 hour. Let it cool to room temperature, then refrigerate until chilled, about 4 hours. Run a knife around the edges and invert onto a platter to unmold.

FAST: Can prepare up to 3 days in advance and refrigerate, or freeze for up to 3 months.

FLASHY: Garnished with thinly sliced cucumbers, gherkins, watercress leaves, apple slices, grapes, and/or any nontoxic flower or leaves. Served with baguettes, any Melba/Crostini (pages 263–273), or crackers.

FABULOUS: With duck or pork liver substituted for the chicken liver.

CALIFORNIA CHILE AND AVOCADO MOUSSE

A mousse with a southwestern flair!

Yield: about 6 cups; 50 or more servings

2 to 3 large, ripe avocados, peeled and pitted

1½ cups sour cream

½ cup mayonnaise, homemade (page 13) or purchased

3 green onions (scallions), white and green parts, chopped, or to taste

2 cloves garlic

¼ cup minced cilantro (fresh coriander) or to taste (I use about 1 bunch)

One 7-ounce can whole green chiles, drained, seeded, and deveined (page 20)

Fresh lime juice to taste

½ teaspoon ground cumin

¼ teaspoon chili powder

1 teaspoon salt

¼ cup dry white wine or chicken broth, homemade (page 11) or canned

2 envelopes unflavored gelatin

1. Place all the ingredients, except the gelatin and wine, in a food processor fitted with the metal blade or a blender and puree. Taste and adjust the seasonings.
2. Combine the gelatin with the wine in a small bowl set in a larger bowl of hot water or in the microwave for 30 seconds on low power to dissolve. Add to the processor or blender and combine well.
3. Oil small molds or one 6- to 8-cup mold and line with plastic wrap. Pour the mixture in and refrigerate until firm, about 4 hours. For faster results, chill in the freezer for about 2 hours. Invert onto a platter and remove the plastic wrap.

FAST: Can prepare up to 3 days in advance and refrigerate, or freeze for up to 3 months.

FLASHY: Served with breads, crackers, and/or tortilla chips. Garnished with any or all of these ingredients: sour cream, minced green onions, cilantro, green chiles, black olives, sliced radishes, and/or any nontoxic flower or leaves.

FABULOUS: With 1 cup cooked crabmeat or shrimp mixed in.

WATERCRESS MOUSSE

Astringent and refreshing, well-suited to accompany meats or to balance rich hors d'oeuvres.

Yield: about 4 cups; 40 or more servings

½ to 1 bunch watercress, stemmed

1¼ cups sour cream

¾ cup mayonnaise, homemade (page 13) or purchased

¼ cup minced fresh parsley

1 shallot, minced

1 to 3 tablespoons capers, drained and rinsed

1 teaspoon Dijon mustard

Salt and ground white pepper to taste

1 envelope unflavored gelatin

¼ cup cream sherry or chicken broth, homemade (page 11) or canned

1. Process all the ingredients, except the gelatin and sherry, in a food processor fitted with the metal blade or in a blender until pureed. Taste and adjust the seasonings.
2. Combine the gelatin with the sherry in a small bowl set in a larger bowl of hot water or in the microwave for 30 seconds on low power to dissolve. Add it to the processor or blender, and combine well.
3. Oil several small molds or one large 4- to 6-cup mold and line with plastic wrap. Pour the mixture in the molds and refrigerate until firm, about 4 hours. For faster results, chill it in the freezer for about 2 hours. Invert onto a platter and remove the plastic wrap to serve.

FAST: Can prepare up to 3 days in advance and refrigerate, or freeze for up to 3 months.

FLASHY: Served with thinly sliced roast beef, smoked salmon, ham, and Beaten Biscuits (page 296), or pumpernickel squares and thin slices of cucumber. Garnished with watercress leaves and/or any nontoxic flower or leaves.

FABULOUS: With 1 cup minced Black Forest ham mixed in after the gelatin is added.

COLD GUACAMOLE SOUFFLÉ

*This refreshing cool summer hors d'oeuvre is a more
elegant version of the classic dip.*

Yield: about 4 cups; 40 or more servings

2 envelopes unflavored gelatin

¼ cup fresh lemon juice or to taste

1 cup mashed ripe avocado (2 to 3
avocados)

1 cup sour cream

1 cup salsa, homemade (see Index)
or purchased

½ cup chopped cilantro (fresh
coriander)

¼ to ½ cup minced green onions
(scallions), white and green parts

2 to 4 dried pasilla chiles,
rehydrated (page 20), stemmed,
seeded, and minced

2 cloves garlic

1 cup grated sharp cheddar

Salt, ground white pepper, and
ground cumin to taste

1. Oil a 4- to 6-cup soufflé dish, flan tin, or container of your choice and line with
plastic wrap.
2. Dissolve the gelatin by sprinkling it over the lemon juice in a small bowl and set in
a larger bowl of hot water or in the microwave on low power for 30 seconds.
3. Combine the avocado, sour cream, salsa, and the dissolved gelatin in a food processor fitted with the metal blade or in a blender and process to a smooth consistency.
4. Process in the remaining ingredients using several quick on-and-off motions, being
careful not to destroy their texture. Taste and adjust the seasonings.
5. Pour the mixture into the prepared mold and chill until firm, about 4 hours in the
refrigerator. For faster results, chill in the freezer for about 2 hours. Invert onto a
platter and remove the plastic wrap.

FAST: Can prepare up to 3 days in advance and refrigerate, or freeze for up to 3 months.

FLASHY: Garnished with a dollop of sour cream on top and a sprinkling of minced cilantro
and/or black olives.

FABULOUS: With low-fat yogurt substituted for the sour cream for reduced fat content.
With fresh or rehydrated dried chiles of your choice substituted for the pasillas.

COLD SPINACH AND HAM SOUFFLÉ

Yield: about 3 cups; 30 or more servings

Two 10-ounce packages frozen
spinach, thawed and squeezed dry

¼ to ½ cup freshly grated Parmesan

¼ pound smoked ham, minced

¾ cup sour cream

¼ cup mayonnaise, homemade (page
13) or purchased

¾ cup minced fresh parsley

¼ cup minced shallots

Zest of 1 lemon, finely grated

¼ teaspoon dried tarragon or to taste

Salt and ground white pepper to taste

1 envelope unflavored gelatin

2 tablespoons dry white wine

½ cup chicken broth, homemade
(page 11) or canned

¼ to ½ cup raw or blanched
almonds, toasted (page 27) and
finely chopped, optional

1. Combine the spinach, cheese, ham, sour cream, mayonnaise, parsley, shallots, lemon zest, and seasonings in a food processor fitted with the metal blade or in a blender and process to a smooth consistency.
2. Dissolve the gelatin in the wine in a small bowl set into a larger bowl of hot water or in the microwave on low power for 30 seconds. Add it to the food processor or blender along with the chicken broth and process thoroughly.
3. Mix in the almonds by hand.
4. Place this mixture in a well-oiled and plastic-wrap lined 3- to 4-cup mold or soufflé dish and chill until firm, about 4 hours. For faster results, chill in the freezer for about 2 hours. Invert onto a platter and remove the plastic wrap.

FAST: Can prepare up to 3 days in advance and refrigerate, or freeze for up to 3 months.

FLASHY: Served with crackers or thinly sliced baguettes. Garnished with minced fresh parsley, sour cream, chopped almonds, and/or any nontoxic flower or leaves.

FABULOUS: With minced blanched asparagus or minced marinated artichoke hearts substituted for the spinach.

COLD BLUE CHEESE SOUFFLÉ

Rich and creamy, with a delicate flavor.

Yield: about 1½ cups; 12 or more servings

1 envelope unflavored gelatin
¼ cup cream sherry
4 to 6 ounces blue cheese, at room temperature
4 ounces cream cheese, at room temperature
4 tablespoons (½ stick) unsalted butter

1 teaspoon Dijon mustard or to taste
½ to 1 shallot, minced
Dash of Worcestershire sauce
Ground white pepper to taste
½ cup heavy cream

1. Combine the gelatin with the sherry in a small bowl and set in a larger bowl of hot water or in the microwave for 30 seconds on low power to dissolve.
2. Combine all the ingredients, except the cream, in a food processor fitted with the metal blade or in a bowl using an electric mixer and process until smooth. Transfer to a mixing bowl.
3. Add the cream and process until just combined. Do not overmix or the cream will curdle. Taste and adjust the seasonings.
4. Oil a 2-cup soufflé dish, line with plastic wrap, and fill with the mixture.
5. Chill until firm, about 2 hours. For faster results, chill in the freezer for about 1 hour. Invert onto a platter and remove the plastic wrap.

FAST: Can prepare up to 4 days in advance and refrigerate, or freeze for up to 3 months.

FLASHY: Served with thinly sliced breads or assorted crackers. Garnished with toasted sesame seeds or walnuts (page 27), minced fresh dill, green onions, and/or roasted red peppers (page 26). Served in the soufflé dish or unmolded.

FABULOUS: With green or pink peppercorns added.

COLD SMOKED SALMON SOUFFLÉ

When you want to splurge!

Yield: about 6 cups; 50 or more servings

2 envelopes unflavored gelatin

¼ cup Madeira

¼ to ½ cup minced red onion

2 to 4 shallots, minced

2 cups sour cream

Two 8-ounce packages cream cheese,
   at room temperature

Zest of 4 lemons, finely grated

½ cup minced fresh dill

Salt and ground white pepper to taste

1 pound smoked salmon (lox),
   thinly sliced, then minced

1. Combine the gelatin with the Madeira in a small bowl and set in a larger bowl of hot water or in the microwave for 30 seconds on low power to dissolve.
2. Combine all the ingredients, except the salmon, in a food processor fitted with the metal blade and process until smooth, or mix together in a bowl.
3. Add the salmon to the cheese mixture and mix well.
4. Oil a 6-cup bowl, timbale, or soufflé dish, line with plastic wrap, and fill with the mixture.
5. Cover and refrigerate until firm, 4 hours. For faster results, chill in the freezer for about 2 hours.
6. To unmold, invert onto a platter and remove the plastic wrap.

FAST: Can prepare up to 3 days in advance and refrigerate, or freeze for up to 3 months.

FLASHY: Served with Bagel Chips (page 272), Pita Chips (page 274), pumpernickel squares, or thinly sliced baguettes and Belgian endive leaves. Garnished with minced fresh dill or lemon zest, thinly sliced cucumbers, and/or any nontoxic flower or leaves.

FABULOUS: With any boneless smoked fish instead of the salmon.

Fast & Fabulous
Hors D'Oeuvres

COLD PROSCIUTTO BASIL SOUFFLÉ

Another light and luxurious appetizer course.

Yield: about 6 cups; 50 or more servings

2 envelopes unflavored gelatin

¼ cup Madeira

2 cups sour cream

Two 8-ounce packages cream cheese, at room temperature

3 to 4 cloves garlic

½ to 1 cup packed fresh basil leaves, minced, or 1 to 2 tablespoons dried

¼ cup minced fresh Italian (flatleaf) parsley

2 to 4 tablespoons capers, drained and rinsed

¼ cup walnuts, toasted (page 27) and finely chopped, optional

½ cup freshly grated Parmesan

1 pound prosciutto, thinly sliced and minced

Fresh lemon juice and ground white pepper to taste

1. Combine the gelatin with the Madeira in a small bowl and set in a larger bowl of hot water or in the microwave for 30 seconds on low power to dissolve.
2. Combine the remaining ingredients, except the prosciutto, in a food processor fitted with the metal blade and process until smooth, or combine in a bowl.
3. Add the prosciutto to the cheese mixture and mix well.
4. Oil a 6-cup bowl, timbale, or soufflé dish, line with plastic wrap, and fill. Chill until firm, 4 hours. For faster results, chill in the freezer for about 2 hours.
5. Invert onto a platter and remove the plastic wrap.

FAST: Can prepare up to 3 days in advance and refrigerate, or freeze for up to 3 months.

FLASHY: Served with thinly sliced baguettes, kiwi, cucumbers, and/or melon. Garnished with slices of kiwi, melon, and/or cucumber, minced fresh parsley, and/or watercress leaves.

FABULOUS: With smoked ham instead of the prosciutto.

COLD SUN-DRIED TOMATO, RED PEPPER, AND FETA SOUFFLÉ

Yield: about 6½ cups; 50 or more servings

2 envelopes unflavored gelatin

¼ cup Madeira

2 cups sun-dried tomatoes, softened (page 22) and minced, or to taste

¼ to ½ cup bottled marinated red bell peppers or pimientos, drained and minced

½ to ¾ cup crumbled feta cheese

2 cups sour cream

Two 8-ounce packages cream cheese, at room temperature

½ cup minced fresh parsley

¼ cup minced fresh dill or rosemary or 2 tablespoons dried

2 to 4 shallots, minced

3 to 4 cloves garlic, minced

¼ cup sesame seeds, toasted (page 27), or to taste

Salt and ground white pepper to taste

1. Combine the gelatin with 2 tablespoons of the Madeira in a small bowl and set in a larger bowl of hot water or in the microwave for 30 seconds on low power to dissolve.
2. Combine all the ingredients in a food processor fitted with the metal blade and process, using several quick on-and-off motions so as not to destroy their texture, or combine in a bowl. Taste and adjust the seasonings.
3. Oil an 8-cup soufflé dish or several smaller soufflés, line with plastic wrap, and fill with the mixture.
4. Chill until firm, about 4 hours. For faster results, chill in the freezer for about 2 hours.
5. Invert onto a platter and remove the plastic wrap.

FAST: Can prepare up to 5 days in advance and refrigerate, or freeze for up to 3 months.

FLASHY: Served with Bagel Chips (page 272), Pita Chips (page 274), pumpernickel squares, or thinly sliced baguettes and Belgian endive leaves. Garnished with watercress leaves, minced fresh dill or rosemary, and/or chopped sun-dried tomatoes or marinated red peppers.

FABULOUS: With fresh basil instead of the dill or rosemary.

GORGONZOLA PISTACHIO TORTA

Yield: about 3½ cups; 20 or more servings

½ pounds (2 sticks) unsalted butter
at room temperature

One 8-ounce package cream cheese,
at room temperature

1½ pounds gorgonzola, crumbled

1 shallot, minced

¼ cup minced fresh parsley

2 to 4 tablespoons Madeira

Ground white pepper to taste

½ cup minced green onion
(scallions), white and green parts

1 cup pistachios, toasted (page 27)
and chopped

1. Combine the butter, cream cheese, ½ pound of the gorgonzola, the shallot, parsley, Madeira, and pepper in a food processor fitted with the metal blade and process until smooth, or combine in a bowl.
2. Oil a 4- to 5-cup straight-sided mold, bowl, or pâté terrine and line with plastic wrap.
3. Add a layer of the remaining crumbled gorgonzola, green onions, and pistachios to the mold. Top with one third of the butter-cheese mixture. Repeat this until the mold is filled, ending with a layer of the butter-cheese mixture.
4. Fold the plastic wrap over the top and press gently to compress the layers. Chill until firm, at least 1 hour, before unmolding.
5. To serve, invert onto a platter and remove the plastic wrap.

FAST: Can prepare up to 5 days in advance and refrigerate, or freeze for up to 3 months.

FLASHY: Served with assorted crackers, any Melba/Crostini (pages 263–273), or thinly sliced breads. Garnished with fresh fruit slices, minced fresh parsley, crumbled gorgonzola, and/or any nontoxic flower or leaves.

FABULOUS: With all the layered ingredients mixed into the butter-cheese mixture and then molded.

FURTHER: Use leftovers tossed into hot pasta or rice, or instead of a sauce on fish and/or poultry.

CHÈVRE AND LOX TORTA

Sheer bliss!

Yield: about 4 cups; 20 or more servings

½ pound (2 sticks) unsalted butter, cut into pieces

One 8-ounce package cream cheese, at room temperature

¾ pound chèvre (page 20)

1 shallot, minced

2 to 4 tablespoons fresh lemon juice

Zest of 2 lemons, finely grated

Ground white pepper to taste

¾ pound lox (smoked salmon), or as much as your budget allows

1 cup minced green onions (scallions), white and green parts

2 bunches fresh dill, stemmed and minced

1. Combine the first 7 ingredients in a food processor fitted with the metal blade and process until smooth, or combine in a bowl. Taste and adjust flavors.
2. Oil a 4- to 5-cup straight-sided mold, bowl, or pâté terrine. Line with plastic wrap.
3. Layer in all the ingredients. I usually start with the lox, then the green onion, dill, and the cheese mixture. Repeat until container is full.
4. Fold the plastic wrap over the top, press gently to compress the layers, and chill until firm, at least 1 hour.
5. Invert onto a platter, remove the plastic wrap, and enjoy!

FAST: Can prepare up to 5 days in advance and refrigerate, or freeze for up to 3 months.

FLASHY: Served on a platter with Bagel Chips (page 272), crackers, and/or breads. Garnished with minced lox, dill, lemon zest, green or red onions, and/or any nontoxic flower or leaves.

FABULOUS: With all the layered ingredients mixed into the cheese mixture and then molded.

FURTHER: Use leftovers tossed into hot pasta or rice, or instead of a sauce on fish and/or poultry.

TOASTED PECAN AND
GREEN ONION–BRIE TORTA

Yield: about 3½ cups; 20 or more servings

½ pound (2 sticks) unsalted butter,
  cut into pieces
¾ pound brie, at room temperature
One 8-ounce package cream cheese,
  at room temperature
1 shallot, minced

2 to 4 tablespoons brandy
Ground white pepper to taste
1 cup minced green onions
  (scallions), white and green parts
2 cups pecans, toasted (page 27)
  and slivered or minced

1. Combine the butter, cheeses, shallot, brandy, and pepper in a food processor fitted with the metal blade and process until smooth, or combine in a bowl.
2. Oil a 4- to 5- cup straight-sided mold, bowl, or pâté terrine and line with plastic wrap.
3. Add a layer of green onions and pecans to the bottom of the mold. Alternate with the cheese mixture until the mold is filled, ending with a layer of the cheese mixture.
4. Fold the plastic wrap over the top and gently press down to compact the layers.
5. Refrigerate until firm, at least 1 hour. To unmold, invert onto a platter, remove the plastic wrap, and enjoy!

FAST: Can prepare up to 5 days in advance and refrigerate, or freeze for up to 3 months.

FLASHY: Served with Bagel Chips (page 272), thinly sliced French bread, or pumpernickel squares. Garnished with minced green onions or parsley and/or any nontoxic flower or leaves.

FABULOUS: With walnuts or almonds substituted for the pecans, or your favorite French cheese for the brie.

FURTHER: Use leftovers tossed into hot pasta or rice, or instead of a sauce on fish and/or poultry.

FETA AND SUN-DRIED TOMATO TORTA

Delicious indulgence!

Yield: about 4 cups; 20 or more servings

½ pound (2 sticks) unsalted butter,
cut into pieces

¾ pound feta cheese, crumbled

One 8-ounce package cream cheese,
at room temperature

2 cloves garlic, minced

1 shallot, minced

2 to 4 tablespoons dry vermouth

Ground white pepper and/or hot
pepper sauce or minced, seeded,
and deveined fresh red jalapeño
pepper (page 20) to taste

½ cup pine nuts, toasted (page 27)

8 ounces sun-dried tomatoes,
softened and minced (page 22)

1 cup pesto, homemade (page 47) or
purchased

1. Combine the butter, cheeses, garlic, shallot, and vermouth in a food processor with the metal blade and process until smooth, or combine in a bowl.
2. Season with the pepper hot pepper sauce.
3. Oil a 4- to 5-cup straight-sided mold, bowl, or pâté terrine. Line with plastic wrap.
4. Layer in all ingredients in any order you wish. I start with pine nuts, then sun-dried tomatoes, pesto, and the cheese mixture. Repeat until the mold is full.
5. Fold the plastic wrap over the top and press gently to compact the layers.
6. Refrigerate until firm, at least 1 hour. Invert onto a platter, remove the plastic, and enjoy!

FAST: Can prepare up to 5 days in advance and refrigerate, or freeze for up to 3 months.

FLASHY: Served with Bagel Chips (page 272), crackers, and/or breads. Garnished with fresh basil leaves, toasted pine nuts, minced fresh parsley, and/or any nontoxic flower or leaves.

FABULOUS: With all layered ingredients mixed into the cheese and then molded.

FURTHER: Use leftovers tossed into hot pasta, on rice, in baked potatoes, or on fish, poultry, beef, or lamb instead of an entree sauce.

FETA AND ROASTED RED PEPPER TORTA

A celebration of summer.

Yield: about 3½ cups; 20 or more servings

¾ pound feta cheese

One 8-ounce package cream cheese,
    at room temperature

½ pound (2 sticks) unsalted butter,
    cut into pieces

2 to 4 tablespoons fresh lemon juice

1 shallot, minced

1 to 2 cloves garlic, minced

Ground white pepper to taste

4 large red bell peppers, roasted
    (page 26), peeled, seeded, and
    minced or to taste

1 cup walnuts, toasted (page 27)
    and chopped

½ to 1 cup packed fresh basil leaves,
    minced

1. Combine the cheeses, butter, lemon juice, shallot, garlic, and pepper in a food processor fitted with the metal blade and process until smooth, or combine in a bowl.
2. Oil a 4- to 5-cup straight-sided mold, bowl, or pâté terrine. Line with plastic wrap.
3. Add a layer of the roasted red peppers with the desired amount of basil and walnuts to the mold. Top with a layer of the cheese mixture. Alternate until the mold is filled, ending with a layer of the cheese mixture.
4. Fold the plastic wrap over the top and gently press down to compress the layers.
5. Refrigerate until firm, at least 1 hour before unmolding. To unmold, remove the plastic wrap and place on a serving plate.

FAST: Can prepare up to 5 days in advance and refrigerate, or freeze for up to 3 months.

FLASHY: Served with Bagel Chips (page 272), thinly sliced French bread, or pumpernickel squares. Garnished with fresh basil leaves, pine nuts, minced fresh parsley, and/or any nontoxic flower or leaves.

FABULOUS: Create a caviar torta by layering 4 to 6 ounces caviar with the minced green onions and zest from 2 to 3 lemons instead of the roasted red peppers.

FURTHER: Use leftovers tossed into hot pasta or rice, or instead of a sauce on fish and/or poultry.

SESAME SCALLOP TOAST

A western touch for a Chinese classic.

Yield: about 24 toasts; 12 or more servings

6 *slices sourdough bread, or high*
quality white bread, crusts
removed and each cut into 6
fingers

8 *ounces scallops*

¼ *cup minced ham*

4 *ounces cream cheese*

1 *large egg*

2 *tablespoons minced cilantro (fresh*
coriander)

2 *tablespoons minced pickled ginger*
or to taste (page 18)

1 *clove garlic, minced*

1 *shallot, minced*

½ *teaspoon salt or to taste*

Ground white pepper to taste

1 *cup fresh sourdough bread crumbs*

½ *cup sesame seeds, toasted*
(page 27)

Chinese sesame oil, as needed

1. Toast the bread fingers in a preheated 350°F oven on an ungreased cookie sheet until lightly brown. Remove and increase the oven heat to 375°F.
2. Combine all the ingredients, except the toasted bread, bread crumbs, sesame seeds, and sesame oil, in a food processor fitted with the metal blade and process until the mixture reaches the consistency of a thick paste.
3. Fry 1 teaspoon of the mixture until cooked through to check the seasonings.
4. Spread the scallop mixture on the toast fingers. Combine the bread crumbs and sesame seeds, and dip the bread fingers in the bread crumb mixture, covering completely.
5. Place the toast on a cookie sheet and drizzle with sesame oil.
6. Bake until puffed and lightly browned, about 15 minutes.

FAST: Can prepare the scallop mixture up to 1 day in advance and refrigerate. Can assemble several hours before serving and refrigerate, or flash freeze (page 24) for up to 1 month. Do not thaw before baking. Allow several extra minutes for the cooking time. The bread can be toasted up to 2 weeks in advance and stored in an airtight jar or frozen for up to 3 months.

FLASHY: Garnished with minced cilantro, green onions, and/or any nontoxic flower or leaves.

FABULOUS: With shrimp or mild white fish substituted for the scallops, or chopped blanched almonds for the sesame seeds. Served with any cold vinegar-based Asian-style dipping sauces from Chapter 1.

CHINOISE GOUGÈRE

Gougère is a classic French hors d'oeuvre that I have
given a Chinese slant to.

Yield: about 24 puffs; 12 or more servings

¼ cup medium-dry sherry

¼ cup heavy cream

4 tablespoons (½ stick) unsalted
butter, cut into pieces

1 teaspoon Dijon mustard or to taste

¼ teaspoon salt

Pinch of sugar

1 clove garlic, minced

2 tablespoons minced pickled ginger
(page 18) or to taste

½ cup all-purpose flour

2 large eggs, at room temperature

3 Chinese sausages, cooked
according to the directions on the
package and thinly sliced
(page 17)

3 to 6 green onions (scallions),
white and green parts, minced

¼ cup sesame seeds, toasted
(page 27)

Chinese sesame oil

1. Preheat the oven to 425°F. Combine the sherry, cream, butter, mustard, salt, sugar, garlic, and ginger in a saucepan. Bring the mixture to boil and stir until the butter melts.
2. Add the flour and stir over medium heat until the mixture is thick enough to pull away from the sides of the saucepan and leaves a slight film on the bottom.
3. Transfer the mixture to a food processor fitted with the metal blade. While the machine is running, add the eggs through the feed tube, one at a time, and combine.
4. Add the sausages, green onions, and sesame seeds and combine, using several quick on-and-off motions, being careful not to destroy the texture.
5. Oil a baking sheet with sesame oil and drop the mixture from a teaspoon. Brush the tops with more sesame oil.
6. Bake for 20 minutes. Turn the heat off and let the puffs remain there for 3 minutes. They should be firm to the touch.

FAST: Can prepare through step 5 up to a day in advance, refrigerate, and bake just before serving.

FLASHY: Served hot on a platter with Asian Mayonnaise (page 36) or any of the vinegar-based Asian-style dipping sauces from Chapter 1. Garnished with minced green onions, cilantro, and/or any nontoxic flower or leaves.

FABULOUS: With ¾ cup minced ham or barbecued pork or roast duck substituted for the sausages.

MEDITERRANEAN GOUGÈRE PUFFS

Yield: about 24 puffs; 12 or more servings

¼ cup water

¼ cup milk

1 tablespoon minced shallot

4 tablespoons (½ stick) unsalted butter, cut into pieces

Pinch of sugar

½ teaspoon Dijon mustard

¼ teaspoon salt

¼ teaspoon white pepper

½ cup all-purpose flour

2 large eggs, at room temperature

½ cup sun-dried tomatoes, softened (page 22) and minced, or to taste

¼ cup crumbled feta cheese

¼ cup freshly grated Parmesan

½ cup packed fresh basil leaves or to taste

Freshly grated nutmeg to taste

1. Preheat the oven to 425°F. Combine the water, milk, shallot, butter, sugar, mustard, salt, and pepper in a saucepan. Stir while the mixture comes to a boil and the butter melts.
2. Add the flour and stir over medium heat until the mixture is thick enough to pull away from the sides of the saucepan and leaves à slight film on the bottom of the pan.
3. Transfer the mixture to a food processor fitted with the metal blade. While the machine is running, add the eggs through the feed tube, one at a time. Process well.
4. Process in the sun-dried tomatoes, cheeses, basil, and nutmeg, using several quick on-and-off motions so as not to destroy the texture.
5. Drop from a teaspoon or pipe from a pastry bag onto a greased cookie sheet.
6. Bake for 20 minutes. Turn off the heat and let the puffs remain in the oven for 3 minutes. They should be firm to the touch.

FAST: Can prepare through step 5 up to a day in advance, refrigerate, and bake just before serving.

FLASHY: Served hot or at room temperature. Garnished with minced fresh basil, parsley, and/or any nontoxic flower or leaves.

FABULOUS: With 1 cup chopped artichoke hearts mixed in at step 4 instead of the sun-dried tomatoes.

Fast & Fabulous
Hors D'Oeuvres

GOUGÈRE PUFFS

*This combination of ingredients and seasonings is
especially suited to winter entertaining.*

Yield: about 24 puffs; serves 12 or more

4 tablespoons (½ stick) unsalted
    butter, cut into pieces
¼ cup milk
¼ cup dry vermouth
1 tablespoon Dijon mustard
1 shallot, minced
¼ cup minced fresh dill or 1 to 2
    tablespoons dried

Zest of 1 lemon, finely grated
¼ teaspoon salt
Pinch of sugar
Ground white pepper and freshly
    grated nutmeg to taste
½ cup all-purpose flour
2 large eggs, at room temperature
1 cup shredded Gruyère

1. Preheat the oven to 425°F. Combine the butter, milk, vermouth, mustard, shallot, dill, zest, salt, sugar, pepper, and nutmeg in a small saucepan. Stir until the butter melts and mixture boils.
2. Stir in the flour over medium heat until the mixture is thick enough to pull away from the sides of the saucepan and forms a slight film on the bottom.
3. Transfer the mixture to a food processor fitted with the metal blade. While the machine is running, add the eggs through the feed tube, one at a time, and combine.
4. Process in the Gruyère thoroughly.
5. Drop from a teaspoon or pipe from a pastry bag onto a greased cookie sheet.
6. Bake until golden, 15 to 20 minutes. Turn off the oven and let the puffs remain inside for 3 minutes. They should be firm to the touch.

FAST: Can prepare through step 5 up to a day in advance, refrigerate, and bake just before serving.

FLASHY: Served hot or at room temperature. Garnished with minced fresh dill, parsley, and/or any nontoxic flower or leaves.

FABULOUS: Topped with extra grated cheese before baking for added flavor.

TORTILLA CHILE PUFFS

*Great for barbecues, Mexican dinners, or casual cocktail
parties.*

Yield: about 2 cups chile mayonnaise; 10 or more servings

*One 7-ounce can whole green chiles,
drained, deveined, and seeded
(page 20)*

*½ cup minced green onions
(scallions), white and green parts*

*½ cup mayonnaise, homemade (page
13) or purchased*

1 clove garlic, minced

1 cup grated jack cheese

¼ to ½ teaspoon ground cumin

*Tortilla chips, homemade (page 273)
or purchased*

1. Preheat the broiler. Combine all the ingredients, except the chips, in a food processor fitted with the metal blade, or in a mixing bowl. Taste and adjust the flavors.
2. Place the chips on a cookie sheet and spread the mixture over them.
3. Place under the broiler until golden or microwave on high for 1 minute.

FAST: Can prepare the chile mayonnaise mixture up to 5 days in advance and refrigerate.
Can assemble up to 2 hours before serving and leave at room temperature.

FLASHY: Served hot on a platter garnished with minced cilantro, green onions, and/or any
nontoxic flower or leaves.

FABULOUS: As a filling for raw mushroom caps and Tortilla Cups (page 300) or as a
dressing for potato, pasta, or rice salads.

CHUTNEY CHEESE PUFFS

Yield: about 1½ cups; 10 or more servings

*½ cup mayonnaise, homemade (page
13) or purchased*

1 to 1½ cups grated jack cheese

¼ to ½ cup chutney (see Index)

1 to 2 cloves garlic, minced

*¼ cup minced fresh parsley and/or
cilantro (fresh coriander)*

*French bread slices, melbas, or
crackers*

1. Preheat the broiler. Combine all the ingredients, except for the bread, in a food
   processor fitted with the metal blade and process until smooth, or combine in a bowl.
2. Place the bread on a cookie sheet and spread the cheese mixture generously over it.
3. Place under the broiler until hot and puffed.

FAST: Can prepare the cheese mixture up to 5 days in advance and refrigerate. Can assemble up to 2 hours in advance and leave at room temperature.

FLASHY: Served hot on a platter garnished with minced cilantro, minced green onions, and/or any nontoxic flower or leaves.

FABULOUS: As a stuffing for raw mushroom caps, spread on English muffins, or on Pita Chips (page 274). With cheese mixture spread over cooked broccoli, cauliflower, or asparagus and broiled as directed in step 3 for a delicious vegetable dish.

CHEDDARED SOURDOUGH PUFFS

*Addictive, and extremely convenient as they must be stored
in your freezer. I don't trust anyone who can eat just one!*

Yield: about 60 puffs; 30 or more servings

4 tablespoons (½ stick) unsalted
   butter
1 teaspoon Dijon mustard
1 to 2 cloves garlic, minced
½ to 1 shallot, minced
2 to 4 tablespoons minced fresh dill
Ground white pepper to taste

8 ounces sharp cheddar, grated
One 8-ounce package cream cheese,
   cut into pieces
2 large egg whites, beaten to stiff
   peaks
1 loaf sourdough bread, crusts
   removed and cut into 1-inch cubes

1. Melt the butter in a saucepan over medium heat. Add the mustard, garlic, shallot, dill, and pepper. Place over a pan of hot water or use a double boiler.
2. Add the cheeses and stir until they melt.
3. Cool slightly and stir in part of the egg whites thoroughly; then fold in the remaining egg whites.
4. Dip the bread cubes into the cheese mixture, place on a cookie sheet, and flash freeze (page 24). Bake frozen in a preheated 400°F oven until golden and puffed, 8 to 10 minutes.

FAST: Can prepare and flash freeze for up to 6 months in advance.

FLASHY: Served hot on a platter and garnished with minced fresh parsley, watercress, and/or any nontoxic flower or leaves.

FABULOUS: With Swiss, muenster, jack, or Gruyère cheese substituted for the cheddar. To create a Reuben Puff, add 1 teaspoon caraway seeds and ¼ to ½ cup minced corned beef and spread on square cubes of rye bread. Other variations: add sesame seeds, nuts, minced ham, finely chopped olives, chopped chiles, or crabmeat to the cheese mixture.

MANGO PAPER-WRAPPED CHICKEN

A wonderful and exotic summer choice!

Yield: about 20; 10 or more servings

4 chicken breast halves, boned,
  skinned, and cut into 20 bite-size
  pieces
Twenty 1½-inch-square slices smoked
  ham
Twenty 1-inch pieces of green onion
  (scallion), green part only

1 bunch cilantro (fresh coriander),
  stemmed
20 pieces pickled ginger, optional
  (page 18)
20 pieces aluminum foil, cut into
  5-inch squares
Vegetable oil for frying

Marinade

3 tablespoons soy sauce
3 tablespoons Madeira
3 tablespoons Chinese sesame oil
3 to 6 tablespoons mango chutney,
  homemade (page 15) or purchased

1 to 3 cloves garlic, minced
1 tablespoon minced fresh ginger or
  ¼ teaspoon ground
1 tablespoon sesame seeds, toasted
  (page 27)

1. Combine all the ingredients for the marinade and allow the chicken to marinate, covered, for at least 1 hour in the refrigerator.
2. On each piece of aluminum foil, place a piece of chicken, ham, green onion, cilantro, pickled ginger, and a little of the marinade.
3. Fold the foil envelope-style and seal.
4. Deep-fat fry in a pot or wok using about 4 cups of oil or cook on the barbecue until just cooked. Experiment to determine the exact time needed. When deep-fat frying, the packets will float to the top when they are done; on the grill it will take about 5 minutes. Serve them in the packets providing small plates for your guests.

FAST: Can marinate the chicken up to 2 days in advance and refrigerate, or freeze for up to 1 month. Can prepare the marinade up to 3 months in advance and refrigerate.

FLASHY: Served in a chafing dish with a sprinkling of minced fresh parsley or cilantro, or on a platter with a clump of parsley, cilantro, and/or cabbage leaves in the center, and/or any nontoxic flower or leaves.

FABULOUS: With pork, turkey, lamb, shrimp, firm-textured fish, or scallops substituted for the chicken.

DOUBLE-FRIED CHICKEN WINGS

For those who love crisp textures with bold flavors.

Yield: 6 or more servings

4 to 8 green onions (scallions),
   white and green parts, cut into
   ¼-inch lengths
3 cloves garlic, crushed, or to taste
1 walnut-size piece fresh ginger,
   peeled and minced
½ cup dry or cream sherry

½ cup soy sauce
½ teaspoon salt
¼ cup packed brown sugar
2 pounds chicken wings
Cornstarch for dredging
Peanut, canola, or avocado oil for
   frying

1. Combine all the ingredients, except the chicken wings, cornstarch, and oil, in a bowl. Marinate the wings for 30 minutes at room temperature or overnight in the refrigerator.
2. Drain the wings and dredge them in the cornstarch. Shake off the excess.
3. Fry the wings in batches in at least 4 inches of hot oil until they are pale golden. Remove the wings from the oil. Reheat the oil and fry the wings for about 2 minutes more, until crisp and golden brown. Drain with paper towels and keep warm in a very low oven.

FAST: Can prepare up to 1 day in advance after the first frying and refrigerate, or freeze for up to 3 months.

FLASHY: Served with any assortment of Asian-style dipping sauces in Chapter 1. Garnished with minced fresh parsley, cilantro, cabbage leaves, and/or any nontoxic flower or leaves.

SESAME FRIED MUSHROOMS

*These crisp-fried mushrooms are coated with a perfect
batter that you will be able to use
for almost anything.*

Yield: 8 or more servings

Batter

1½ cups instantized flour (page 21)

1 tablespoon baking powder

½ teaspoon salt

¼ teaspoon sugar

½ cup peanut oil

1 cup ice water

1 shallot, minced, optional

¼ to ½ cup sesame seeds, toasted
(page 27)

To complete the dish

Peanut or avocado oil for frying

1 pound cultivated white mushrooms

1. Combine all the batter ingredients in a food processor fitted with the metal blade, or use an electric mixer and a bowl and process until smooth.
2. Refrigerate until chilled before using.
3. Heat at least 4 inches of oil in a wok, deep-fat fryer, or a large pot over medium-high heat. The oil is ready for cooking when piece of green onion or parsley cooks rapidly.
4. Remove the batter from the refrigerator and dip the mushrooms in it. Fry the mushrooms in small batches; don't crowd. Remove the fried mushrooms to a cookie sheet lined with several layers of paper towels to drain. Keep the cooked mushrooms warm in a 350°F oven.

FAST: Can prepare the batter up to 2 days in advance and refrigerate. The mushrooms can be fried up to 1 day in advance. (Do not fully fry. Remove them from the oil before they are browned.) Finish frying before serving, or reheat them in a 425°F oven for about 10 to 15 minutes.

FLASHY: Garnished with minced fresh parsley, cilantro, cabbage leaves, and/or any non-toxic flower or leaves.

FABULOUS: This batter is perfect for all kinds of vegetables, chicken, or seafood.

REUBEN SAUSAGES

This fried sausage is well worth the effort. Let the kids help!

Yield: about 75 sausages; 30 or more servings

1 pound corned beef, cooked and
  ground

1 large onion, minced and
  browned in 2 tablespoons butter
  or oil over medium heat

¼ cup minced fresh parsley

1 to 3 tablespoons Dijon mustard
  or to taste

3 cups sauerkraut, rinsed, drained,
  and chopped

1 teaspoon caraway seeds

¼ cup minced fresh dill or 1
  teaspoon dried

2 slices rye bread, torn into small
  pieces

½ cup low-fat or regular milk

½ cup dry vermouth

1½ cups grated Gruyère

1 cup all-purpose flour

2 large eggs, beaten

⅔ cup water

3 cups rye bread crumbs

Canola oil for deep fat frying, at
  least 1 quart

1. Combine the meat, onion, parsley, mustard, sauerkraut, caraway seeds, dill, and bread in a food processor fitted with the metal blade until it reaches a smooth consistency.

2. Transfer to a skillet and heat over medium-high heat. Blend in the milk and vermouth. Cook until thickened, stirring constantly.

3. Reduce the heat to low, stir in the cheese, and cook until it melts. Taste and adjust the flavors.

4. Place the mixture in a bowl or container and refrigerate until cold, about 2 hours. For faster results, freeze for about 1 hour.

5. Combine the eggs with the water in a small bowl.

6. Shape into 1-inch sausages and roll in the flour to coat them.

7. Dip the sausages in the batter and then in the crumbs. Refrigerate the sausages for at least 1 hour or freeze for 30 minutes.

8. Deep-fat fry in about 4 inches of oil over medium-high heat for about 3 to 5 minutes until the sausages are golden. To oven fry, place the sausages on an oiled aluminum foil-lined jelly-roll pan. Drizzle the sausages with more canola oil and bake in a preheated 425°F oven for 10 to 15 minutes.

FAST: Can prepare through step 7 up to 1 day in advance and refrigerate, or flash freeze (page 24) for up to 6 months.

FLASHY: Served in a chafing dish with Dijon Sauce (page 32), a sprinkling of minced green onion tops, or on a platter with an onion, parsley, shredded red cabbage or cabbage leaves, and/or any nontoxic flower or leaves.

FABULOUS: With 2 cups more of sauerkraut instead of using the corned beef. With jack or cheddar instead of the Gruyère.

SOUTHWESTERN CHILE SQUARES

Think of this as a chile frittata. If you like chiles rellenos,
you'll love this.

Yield: about 32 squares; 15 or more servings

2 tablespoons (¼ stick) unsalted butter

5 large eggs

¼ cup all-purpose flour

½ teaspoon baking powder

2 dried pasilla chiles, rehydrated (page 20), stemmed, seeded, and minced

2 cups grated jack cheese

1 cup ricotta cheese

2 to 4 cloves garlic

¼ to ½ cup minced green onions (scallions), white and green parts

¼ cup minced cilantro (fresh coriander) or to taste

Salt, ground white pepper, and ground cumin to taste

½ cup canned whole green chiles, seeded, deveined, and chopped (page 20)

1. Preheat the oven to 400°F.
2. Melt the butter in a small square baking pan and set aside.
3. Beat the eggs, flour, and baking powder in a food processor fitted with the metal blade or in a blender, or use an electric mixer and a bowl.
4. Add the remaining ingredients, except for the green chiles, and combine well.
5. Process in the green chiles, being careful not to puree them completely, or stir in. Transfer them to the pan with the melted butter.
6. Bake for 15 minutes, then reduce the heat to 350°F and bake until a toothpick inserted into the middle comes out clean, 30 to 35 minutes. Let it sit for about 10 minutes, then cut into small squares.

FAST: Can assemble up to 1 day in advance and refrigerate, or freeze for up to 3 months. Defrost before baking.

FLASHY: Served hot or at room temperature with any of the Mexican-style dunks and/or sauces from Chapter 1. Garnished with minced cilantro and/or any nontoxic flower or leaves. With Salsa (page 66) and Mexican Cream Sauce (page 74).

FABULOUS: Cut into larger pieces for a brunch or luncheon entree.

ITALIAN SAUSAGE AND ROASTED RED PEPPER FRITTATA

Here's a solution for all of those times when your pantry is empty. As long as you have eggs in the refrigerator you can usually find enough interesting odds and ends to prepare a frittata.

Yield: 10 or more servings

2 tablespoons extra virgin olive oil

½ to 1 pound cultivated white mushrooms, sliced

1 cup minced onion

1 to 2 cloves garlic, minced

5 large eggs

2 to 4 tablespoons freshly grated Parmesan cheese

½ to 1 cup grated mozzarella or jack

¼ to ½ cup minced fresh parsley

Salt and ground white pepper to taste

1 pound sweet Italian sausage, casings removed, fried or cooked in the microwave until no longer pink, and drained well on paper towels

4 large red bell peppers, roasted (page 26), peeled, seeded, and cut into thin strips

1. Heat the oil in a skillet over medium heat. Cook the mushrooms, onions, and garlic, stirring, until the liquid from the mushrooms evaporates.
2. While the mixture is cooking, combine the eggs, cheeses, parsley, salt, and pepper in a food processor fitted with the metal blade and process until smooth.
3. Cool the cooked sausage and vegetables before adding them, or process very quickly so that the eggs do not scramble. Process until finely minced, but not pureed.
4. Pour the mixture into a heavily buttered 12 × 7-inch baking pan. Top with the red pepper strips. Bake in a preheated 350°F oven until a toothpick comes out clean, 30 minutes.
5. Cool slightly before cutting into squares.

FAST: Can assemble or fully prepare up to 2 days in advance and refrigerate.

FLASHY: Served warm or at room temperature. Garnished with minced fresh parsley, a whole or half of a red bell pepper, and/or any nontoxic flower or leaves.

FABULOUS: Experiment with different cheeses and vegetables. Here are several variations:

- Sautéed chard and sun-dried tomatoes
- Blanched (page 23) asparagus and any type cheese
- Spinach (cooked or frozen, thawed and well drained) and minced smoked ham
- Tomatoes (peeled, seeded, and sliced) and fresh basil
- Zucchini (blanched or sautéed and chopped) and Gruyère cheese
- Artichoke hearts (cooked or marinated) and brie

GRILLED POLENTA WITH SUN-DRIED TOMATOES AND GARLIC

This is my version of a wonderful Italian classic. It not only tastes greater, but is also healthy.

Yield: 6 or more servings

10 to 20 cloves garlic, peeled

½ cup minced fresh parsley

2 tablespoons extra virgin olive oil, plus extra for brushing

1 large onion, thinly sliced

½ cup sun-dried tomatoes, softened (page 22) and minced

3 cups chicken broth, homemade (page 11) or canned

1 cup dry vermouth

1 bay leaf

Ground white pepper to taste

1½ cups uncooked instant or regular polenta

1. Preheat the oven to 350°F.
2. Place the garlic in a small saucepan of salted water and bring to a boil. Drain and repeat once again. Remove the garlic and puree it with the parsley in a food processor fitted with the metal blade or in a blender.
3. Heat the olive oil in a large saucepan over medium heat, add the onion, and cook, stirring, until tender.
4. Add the remaining ingredients, and bring to a boil in a large saucepan over high heat. Stir frequently until the polenta is tender and liquid is absorbed, about 30 minutes. It should pull away from sides of pan when stirred. (Instant polenta will only take about 10 minutes to cook, regular 30 minutes.)
5. Pour the polenta onto an oiled cookie sheet. Cool to room temperature, then chill in the refrigerator. Slice into ½-inch-thick slices.
6. Brush the polenta with olive oil and place it on a hot grill or under a preheated broiler until golden, 3 to 5 minutes on each side, before serving.

FAST: Can prepare through step 5 up to 2 days in advance and refrigerate, or freeze for up to 1 month.

FLASHY: Garnished with minced fresh parsley and/or any nontoxic flower or leaves.

FABULOUS: With minced roasted red peppers (page 26), minced marinated artichoke hearts, and/or minced fresh or dried herbs added before pouring the polenta onto the cookie sheet.

GRILLED POLENTA

Italian soul food!

Yield: 10 or more servings

6 cups chicken broth, homemade (page 11) or canned

1 cup dry white wine

2 cloves garlic, minced, or to taste

¼ cup minced green onions (scallions), white and green parts, or to taste

¼ cup minced fresh parsley, or to taste

Fresh rosemary sprigs or dried rosemary to taste

3 cups uncooked regular or instant polenta

¼ cup extra virgin olive oil

1. Place all the ingredients, except the olive oil, in a large pot, and bring to a boil, stirring, over medium-high heat.
2. Reduce the heat to medium-low and continue to cook, stirring, until the liquid is absorbed and the polenta is tender and comes away clearly from the sides of the pan, about 10 minutes if using instant polenta, or 30 minutes if using regular polenta.
3. Pour the polenta onto an oiled cookie sheet. Cool to room temperature, then chill in the refrigerator. When firm, cut the polenta into desired size squares.
4. Oil the barbecue grill and brush the squares of polenta with oil. Grill until hot, or broil in the oven until golden, 3 to 5 minutes per side.

FAST: Can prepare through step 3 up to 2 days in advance and refrigerate, or freeze up to 3 months.

FLASHY: Served hot or at room temperature on a platter and garnished with fresh herbs and/or any nontoxic flower or leaves.

FABULOUS: With minced fresh basil rather than rosemary.

POLENTA WITH BAKED EGGPLANT AND ARTICHOKE HEARTS

Yield: 6 or more servings

1 cup uncooked instant or regular polenta

1 cup Ratatouille Niçoise (drained) (page 144)

4 cups chicken broth, homemade (page 11) or canned

½ cup dry white wine

¼ to ½ cup minced fresh parsley

Salt, freshly grated Parmesan cheese, and ground white pepper to taste

Olive oil for brushing

1. Combine all the ingredients except the oil in a saucepan and bring to a boil, stirring, over medium-high heat.
2. Reduce the heat to medium-low and continue to cook, stirring, until the liquid is absorbed and the polenta is tender and comes away clearly from the sides of the pan, about 10 minutes if using instant polenta, or 30 minutes if using regular polenta.
3. Season to taste and pour onto an oiled cookie sheet. Cool to room temperature.
4. Cut the polenta into small squares when it has firmed.
5. Preheat a broiler or a barbecue grill and brush the squares of polenta with some olive oil to prevent sticking. Grill or broil until golden and hot, 3 to 5 minutes per side.

FAST: Can prepare through step 4 up to 2 days in advance and refrigerate, or freeze for up to 3 months.

FLASHY: Served hot or at room temperature on a platter and garnished with fresh herbs and/or any nontoxic flower or leaves.

FABULOUS: With fresh or dried basil, oregano, or rosemary.

GRILLED POLENTA WITH ROASTED RED PEPPERS AND SAUSAGES

Yield: 6 or more servings

½ pound sweet Italian sausages

¼ cup extra virgin olive oil

½ to 1 large onion, minced or chopped

2 to 4 cloves garlic, minced

1 cup uncooked instant or regular polenta

½ cup dry red wine

4 cups chicken broth, homemade (page 11) or canned

½ to 1 cup chopped roasted red peppers (page 26)

¼ cup minced fresh parsley

Freshly ground black pepper to taste

¼ to ½ cup freshly grated Parmesan

1. To cook the sausages, prick them all over with the tines of a fork and place them in ½ inch of water or dry red wine in a pan. Cook over medium heat for about 20 minutes. The liquid will cook away and they will fry in their own fat. To microwave, prepare the same way, cover with plastic wrap, and microwave for about 10 minutes.
2. Slice the sausages into ¼-inch-thick slices.
3. For the grilled polenta, heat the olive oil in a saucepan over medium heat and cook the onions and garlic, stirring, until tender.
4. Stir in the remaining ingredients, except for the Parmesan, and bring to a boil over medium-high heat while stirring frequently.
5. Reduce the heat to medium-low and continue to cook, stirring, until the liquid is absorbed and the polenta is tender and comes away cleanly from the sides of the pan, about 10 minutes if using instant, and 30 minutes if using regular polenta.
6. Stir in the Parmesan and season to taste and transfer to an oiled cookie sheet. Cool to room temperature.
7. Cut the polenta into small squares when it has firmed.
8. Preheat the broiler or oil a barbecue grill and brush the squares of polenta with some olive oil to prevent sticking. Grill or broil the squares until hot, 3 to 5 minutes per side.

FAST: Can prepare through step 7 up to 2 days in advance and refrigerate, or freeze for up to 3 months.

FLASHY: Served hot or at room temperature on a platter and garnished with fresh herbs and/or nontoxic flowers and/or leaves.

FABULOUS: With ½ to 1 cup packed fresh basil leaves, minced and added with the Parmesan.

229

5

WRAPS

Once again, it sounds as if I've switched the topic from food to clothing. Wraps simply refers to hors d'oeuvres that are bases or enclosures for fillings or toppings. This chapter explores the complete range, from the sophisticated individual hors d'oeuvre pastries, to the informal potato skin.

Nothing could be more flattering to guests than to be served an array of individual items that reflect thoughtful attention to detail. Such flattery clearly shows that you think they deserve the best. You will learn how to accomplish this without joining the ranks of the kitchen martyrs.

First we begin with an exploration of stuffed vegetables from stuffed romaine to caviar mushrooms. They are all easy to prepare and delicious (a.k.a. Fast & Fabulous). If you have ever been at a loss for a new way to stuff a mushroom rather than using the current recipe that is circulating among your friends, you are in luck!

The next curious-sounding category is stuffed wrappers. Here we deal with the use of potsticker, sui mai, and won ton wrappers as generic pastry dough and explore countless ways for using them. The ethnic influences range from Chinese to Greek.

Substituting these wrappers for pastry not only saves time, but also allows you to prepare a tremendous variety of unique hors d'oeuvres. Have you ever considered making a tartlet shell out of a won ton or sui mai wrapper? Or, what about a mini calzone (calzette) made from a potsticker wrapper? It requires only minutes, no special skills, and results in a crisp appetizer, lower in fat than most pastries. Invest in a potsticker mold. It costs less than a dollar and makes shaping and sealing these items a breeze, plus a fun job for the kids.

Melbas, crostini, croutons . . . no matter what you call them, they are crisp bread and usually addictive. These terms are a bit ambiguous and often used interchangeably. Make no mistake about it, I am not talking about the packaged, purchased variety. Preparing them yourself is simple, healthier, and better-tasting.

The possibilities are endless; any herb imaginable can be used to season them, along with almost any cheese. They can be served plain or as a base for anything . . . and I mean anything. For ideas refer to Chapters 1 through 3. Once you develop the melbas-crostini-crouton habit, crackers will be a last resort. Keep them on hand in your freezer. You will find that even the kids love them and you'll always be ready for a party.

Croustades are another Fast & Fabulous way to create filled individual hors d'oeuvres without preparing pastry. Croustades are crisp sourdough toast cups and can be filled with anything from lobster to peanut butter. This is a job that can be given to the noncook and/or the children of the household. You'll love their versatility and I urge you, as always, to go beyond my recipes and create for yourself. Besides the fillings that I have specially designated as croustade fillings, refer to Chapter 3 for other choices.

Phyllo are paper-thin sheets of pastry from which you can produce light, flaky, and delicate results. Purchase it in Greek or Middle-Eastern delis, or in the freezer section of most supermarkets.

Phyllo items convey a special feeling to your guests and let them know you value their presence. Be sure to take the time to read all the instructions on the package. Using phyllo takes a bit of patience, but is well worth it.

Now we embark on the most sophisticated and refined area of hors d'oeuvres. Individual pastries instantly set the stage for memorable evenings. As with phyllo, they may require a bit more time but the results will justify it. If you need an elegant hors d'oeuvre but do not have a minute to spare, you can always use frozen puff pastry instead of making your own. Let me reassure you, all the pastry recipes included in this chapter are designed to help you become a fearless pastry maker. With the advent of the food processor, pastry has become a Fast & Fabulous miracle and almost child's play. It truly is effortless. This machine is the cure for "pastry phobics." For added convenience, you can prepare pastry at your leisure and freeze it.

You are going to amaze your friends and yourself!

POTATO SKINS

*A thin, crisp version of the popular restaurant appetizer
that is baked, not fried.*

Yield: about 32 skins; 5 or more servings

8 large baking potatoes   Salt to taste
Olive or peanut oil for brushing

1. Bake the potatoes in a preheated 425°F. oven until soft, about 45 minutes. When
   they are cool enough to handle, cut them in half. Scoop out the pulp and reserve it
   for another use. (Remove as much pulp as possible without tearing the skin.)
2. Cut each half in half, brush with oil, and sprinkle with salt.
3. Place them on a cookie sheet and bake in a preheated 350°F. oven until crisp, for
   about 20 minutes.

FAST: Can prepare through step 2 up to 1 day in advance and refrigerate. Can also prepare
fully and reheat before serving.

FLASHY: Served with Guacamole (page 73) or your choice of Mexican-style sauces and
dunks from Chapter 1.

FABULOUS: Topped with grated cheddar or jack cheese, herbs, browned onions, crumbled
cooked bacon, and/or minced canned green chiles (page 20).

ZUCCHINI ROUNDS MENDELSON

*When home-grown zucchini is threatening to take over
your kitchen, this recipe will rescue you.*

Yield: 8 or more servings

¼ cup minced green onions   Salt, ground white pepper, and dried
   (scallions), white and green parts   Italian herbs to taste
¼ cup minced fresh parsley   1 pound zucchini, cut into
   1 to 2 cloves garlic, minced   ¼-inch-thick rounds (fatter
Freshly grated Parmesan to taste   zucchini are perfect for this)
½ cup mayonnaise, homemade (page
   13) or purchased

1. Preheat the oven to 375°F.
2. Combine all the ingredients, except the zucchini, in a food processor fitted with the metal blade or in a bowl. Taste and adjust the seasonings.
3. Place the zucchini rounds on a greased cookie sheet and spread the cheese mixture liberally on each round.
4. Bake until hot and golden, or until they are dry and crisp, depending on your personal preference, about 15 to 25 minutes.

FAST: Can prepare through step 2 up to 1 day in advance and refrigerate.

FLASHY: Served on a platter with a marigold or zucchini blossom in the center as a garnish.

FABULOUS: Topped with toasted sesame seeds (page 27). With eggplant substituted for zucchini or dried or fresh basil for the dried Italian herbs.

STUFFED MUSHROOMS WITH BÉCHAMEL SAUCE

Appropriate for family-style Italian meals or more formal occasions.

Yield: 6 or more servings

4 tablespoons (½ stick) unsalted butter

1 tablespoon minced shallots

12 large cultivated white mushrooms, stemmed (reserve the stems and mince)

3 tablespoons chopped ham or prosciutto

3 tablespoons freshly grated Parmesan

1 cup dry sourdough bread crumbs

Salt, ground white pepper, and dried rosemary to taste

Béchamel sauce

2 tablespoons unsalted butter

½ shallot, minced

2 tablespoons all-purpose flour

1 teaspoon Dijon mustard

¼ cup dry white wine

¼ cup heavy cream

½ cup milk

Salt, ground white pepper, and freshly grated nutmeg to taste

1. Preheat the oven to 450°F.
2. Melt 2 tablespoons of the butter in a skillet over medium heat. When it foams, add the shallots and cook, stirring, until just golden. Add the minced mushroom stems and cook, stirring, until the juices they release cook away.

3. Add the ham and cook, stirring, for 2 to 3 minutes.
4. To make the béchamel, melt the butter in a saucepan over medium-low heat. When the butter foams, add the shallot and cook, stirring, until just tender; do not brown.
5. Stir in the flour and mustard and cook for 1 minute more; do not brown.
6. Remove the pan from the burner and mix in the wine. Return it to the burner and cook until thickened, about 3 to 5 minutes, stirring constantly.
7. Whisk in the cream and milk. Cook until thickened, stirring constantly.
8. Add the seasonings and cook for 1 minute more.
9. Combine in a mixing bowl the sauce, sautéed mixture, and the Parmesan cheese. Taste and adjust the seasonings.
10. Fill the mushroom caps with the mixture and place them in a buttered baking dish. Top with the bread crumbs, and dot with the remaining butter.
11. Bake until hot and the bread crumbs turn golden, for about 15 minutes, and allow them to rest for 5 minutes before serving.

FAST: Can prepare the sauce up to 3 days in advance and refrigerate, or freeze for up to 3 months. Top it with 2 tablespoons butter to prevent a skin from forming. Can stuff the mushrooms up to 2 days in advance and refrigerate.

FLASHY: Served on a platter with parsley, watercress, and/or any nontoxic flower or leaves for garnishing.

FABULOUS: With chopped toasted walnuts (page 27), roasted, peeled, seeded, and minced red bell pepper (page 26); rehydrated minced Italian or shiitake mushrooms (page 18), cooked and crumbled Italian sausage; or minced artichoke hearts added. As a dinner party vegetable dish.

STUFFED GRAPE LEAVES

Yield: about 6 dozen; 30 or more servings

½ cup extra virgin olive oil

3 large onions, chopped

3 cloves garlic, chopped

½ cup minced fresh dill

8 green onions (scallions), green and white parts, minced

Fresh or dried mint leaves to taste

½ cup chopped fresh parsley

1 teaspoon salt

½ teaspoon freshly ground black pepper

½ cup uncooked white rice

½ cup uncooked bulgur (page 20)

3 cups chicken broth, homemade (page 11) or canned, or water

1 pound ground lamb

½ cup walnuts

One 1-pound jar grape leaves, rinsed

1 cup fresh lemon juice

Parsley or dill stems from at least 2 bunches

Lemon wedges

1. Heat ¼ cup of the oil in a large saucepan over medium-low heat. Add the onions and garlic and cook, stirring, until they are translucent.

2. Stir in the dill, green onions, mint, parsley, seasonings, rice, bulgur, and 1 cup of the broth. Cook for about 10 minutes over medium-low heat until the liquid is absorbed.

3. Meanwhile cook the ground lamb in a heavy skillet over medium-high heat until no longer pink. Drain off any fat and add the meat and walnuts to the rice mixture. Mix well.

4. Place the grape leaves shiny side down. If the leaves are small, put two together.

5. Place a spoonful of the rice mixture on each leaf and roll up jelly-roll fashion, making sure to tuck in the sides.

6. Add the remaining oil, the lemon juice, and another cup of the broth to a large skillet. Arrange the rolls in the skillet, using the parsley stems to separate each layer.

7. Place a heavy plate on top and simmer over low heat for 25 minutes. Add the remaining broth and cook until the rice is tender, about 10 minutes longer. Cut a stuffed grape leave in half to check the doneness. Cook and serve with lemon wedges and Cold Cucumber Sauce (page 38) if desired.

FAST: Can fully prepare up to 4 days in advance and refrigerate or flash freeze (page 24) for up to 3 months, cooked or uncooked. If frozen uncooked, thaw before cooking.

FLASHY: Served on a platter and garnished with fresh mint leaves and/or any nontoxic flower or leaves.

FABULOUS: To create a meatless version, substitute 1 additional cup of raw rice in step 2 and the corresponding amount of additional liquid (2 cups) in step 3 for the lamb.

FAST & FABULOUS
ITALIAN EGGPLANT FINGERS

Yield: 8 or more servings

1 large eggplant, peeled and cut into ½-inch-thick and 1½-inch-long finger-shaped slices	Minced fresh parsley to taste
	Minced fresh or dried basil to taste
Extra virgin olive oil	Freshly grated Parmesan to taste, optional
2 to 4 cloves garlic, minced	Salt and ground white pepper to taste

1. Place the eggplant on an oiled cookie sheet and sprinkle generously with olive oil. Add the garlic, season to taste with the remaining ingredients, and let sit at room temperature for at least 1 hour.

2. Bake in a preheated 400°F oven until the eggplant is lightly browned and tender, about 30 to 45 minutes.

FAST: Can prepare up to 3 days in advance and refrigerate.

FLASHY: Served hot or at room temperature on a platter with toothpicks and garnished with fresh parsley, mint, and/or any nontoxic flower or leaves.

FABULOUS: With different herbs and cheeses, topped with slices of prosciutto, roasted bell pepper (page 26), or salami before serving. Sprinkle with balsamic vinegar, wine, or rice wine vinegar before serving. Served with a variety of dipping sauces from Chapter 1. With Japanese eggplant instead of the regular eggplant, sliced into ovals. Spread with a filling or spread of your choice, and rolled up jelly-roll fashion and secured with a toothpick. With the eggplant cut up into squares instead of fingers for a vegetable course.

COLD MUSHROOMS STUFFED WITH SMOKED SALMON

Classically simple, special, and well-suited for summer entertaining.

Yield: 8 or more servings

6 ounces smoked salmon (lox), minced

12 ounces cream cheese, at room temperature

4 to 6 tablespoons minced fresh dill or 1 to 2 tablespoons dried

2 tablespoons fresh lemon juice or to taste

2 to 4 shallots, minced

1 pound cultivated white mushrooms, stems removed and reserved for another use

1. Combine the first 5 ingredients by hand or in a food processor fitted with the metal blade until smooth. Taste and adjust the seasonings.
2. Fill the mushroom caps, chill, and serve.

FAST: Can assemble fully up to 1 day in advance and refrigerate.

FLASHY: Served on a platter and garnished with minced fresh parsley or dill or any nontoxic flower or leaves.

FABULOUS: With smoked trout, smoked clams, or sun-dried tomatoes substituted for the smoked salmon. With chèvre instead of the cream cheese.

CAVIAR MUSHROOMS

More instant elegance.

Yield: 6 or more servings

1 large egg, hard-boiled (page 24) and minced

1 shallot, minced

¾ cup sour cream

6 tablespoons caviar

Fresh lemon juice to taste

1 tablespoon minced fresh dill or 1 teaspoon dried

Salt and ground white pepper to taste

12 large cultivated white mushrooms, stems removed and reserved for another use

1. Blend the egg, shallot, sour cream, caviar, lemon juice, and dill in a mixing bowl. Taste and adjust the seasonings.
2. Fill the mushroom caps with the caviar mixture.

FAST: Can assemble fully up to 1 day in advance and refrigerate.

FLASHY: Garnished with hard-boiled, minced egg white, fresh dill, caviar, lemon zest, and/or any nontoxic flower or leaves.

FABULOUS: With ¼ cup of minced roasted garlic (page 26) mixed into the sour cream instead of the shallot.

MUSHROOM WRAP-UPS

This was created as a way to use up leftover rice.

Yield: 6 or more servings

12 slices bacon

2 tablespoons extra virgin olive oil

12 large cultivated white mushrooms, stems removed and minced

2 to 4 cloves garlic, minced

¾ cup cooked rice or pilaf (¼ cup raw rice)

¼ cup minced fresh dill

2 to 4 tablespoons minced parsley

1 cup burgundy or other dry red wine or to taste

Fresh lemon juice to taste

Ground white pepper

1. Cook the bacon partially (not until crisp), about 5 minutes, in a skillet over medium heat. Drain on paper towels.
2. Heat the oil in a saucepan over medium heat. Add the minced mushroom stems and garlic and cook, stirring, until the liquid they release cooks away.
3. In a large bowl, combine the rice, dill, parsley, sautéed stems, and garlic, then fill the mushroom caps with the mixture.

4. Mix the wine, lemon juice, and pepper together in a glass baking dish. Place the stuffed caps in the mixture to marinate for 30 to 60 minutes at room temperature covered with plastic wrap.

5. Wrap each mushroom with ½ to 1 slice bacon. Secure with a toothpick and return them to the same baking dish.

6. Bake in a preheated 350°F oven until the bacon is fully cooked and brown, about 35 minutes.

FAST: Can assemble fully and allow the mushrooms to marinate for up to 1 day in advance in the refrigerator.

FLASHY: Served on a platter and garnished with fresh dill, parsley, and/or any nontoxic flower or leaves.

FABULOUS: With minced fresh rosemary and green onions added to the rice. With bulgur (page 20) or couscous (page 20) substituted for the rice.

BRIE-STUFFED MUSHROOMS

This will get raves even for the noncook!

Yield: 8 or more servings

6 tablespoons (¾ stick) unsalted butter

16 medium-size to large cultivated white mushrooms, stems removed and reserved for another use

3 cloves garlic, minced

¼ cup minced fresh parsley

¼ cup minced green onions (scallions), green and white parts

Salt and ground white pepper to taste

16 pieces brie cut to fit into the mushroom caps

½ cup chopped walnuts, sautéed in 2 tablespoons butter over medium heat for about 5 minutes, stirring frequently

1. Preheat the oven to 350°F.

2. Melt the butter in a saucepan over medium heat. When it begins to foam, add the garlic, parsley, green onions, salt, and pepper and cook, stirring, for about 5 minutes.

3. Add the mushrooms and cook briefly (they should not be fully cooked), coating them well with butter mixture.

4. Remove the mushrooms to an ovenproof serving platter and place a piece of brie in each and pour any remaining ingredients from the pan over the mushrooms.

5. Place the platter in the oven and bake until the cheese melts, about 5 minutes. Sprinkle with the walnuts and serve.

FAST: Can assemble up to 1 day in advance and refrigerate.

FLASHY: Garnished with fresh parsley and/or any nontoxic flower or leaves.

FABULOUS: With different cheeses, such as teleme, whole milk mozzarella, Camembert, or chèvre, instead of the brie.

MUSHROOM-STUFFED MUSHROOMS

Specially created for mushroom devotees.

Yield: 6 or more servings

12 large cultivated white mushrooms, stems removed, minced, and squeezed dry

5 tablespoons unsalted butter, melted

Salt and ground white pepper to taste

2 tablespoons unsalted butter

2 tablespoons minced shallots

2 to 4 shiitake mushrooms, rehydrated (page 18), stemmed, and minced

2 to 4 tablespoons Madeira

½ tablespoon all-purpose flour

½ cup heavy cream

3 tablespoons minced fresh parsley

¼ cup grated Gruyère

1. Preheat the oven to 375°F.
2. Brush the mushroom caps with some of the melted butter and arrange them in a baking dish. Season with salt and pepper.
3. Melt the 2 tablespoons of butter in a saucepan over medium heat. When it begins to foam, cook the minced stems, shallots, and shiitake mushrooms, stirring, for about 5 minutes.
4. Add the Madeira and cook, stirring frequently, until it is almost evaporated.
5. Reduce the heat to low and stir in the flour. Cook for 1 minute without browning.
6. Stir in the cream and cook until it thickens, about 3 to 5 minutes.
7. Add the parsley and taste and adjust the seasonings.
8. Fill the caps with the mixture. Top each with some cheese and drizzle the remaining melted butter over the tops.
9. Bake until hot and the cheese melts, about 10 to 15 minutes.

FAST: Can assemble up to 2 days in advance and refrigerate. Bake before serving.

FLASHY: Garnished with fresh parsley and/or any nontoxic flower or leaves.

FABULOUS: Intensify the shiitake flavor by straining the reserved soaking liquid from rehydrating the mushrooms and adding it to the pan along with the wine. Cook until it reduces to about 1 tablespoon.

CRAB AND ARTICHOKE STUFFED MUSHROOMS

A luscious combination of flavors!

Yield: 8 or more servings

16 large cultivated white mushrooms, stems removed and minced

6 tablespoons (¾ stick) unsalted butter, melted

Salt and ground white pepper to taste

2 tablespoons unsalted butter

2 to 6 tablespoons minced onion

3 tablespoons minced fresh parsley

1 to 2 cloves garlic, minced

1 tablespoon all-purpose flour

½ cup heavy cream

2 tablespoons Madeira or to taste

½ cup fresh crabmeat, picked over for cartilage

One 6-ounce jar marinated artichoke hearts or bottoms, drained and minced

¼ cup grated Gruyère

3 tablespoons fresh lemon juice, or more to taste

1 teaspoon Dijon mustard

Freshly grated nutmeg to taste

Brut champagne

Grated Parmesan to taste

1. Preheat the oven to 375°F.
2. Brush the mushroom caps with some of the melted butter and season with salt and pepper.
3. Melt the 2 tablespoons of butter in a large saucepan over medium heat. When it foams, add the minced stems, onion, parsley, and garlic and cook, stirring, until the liquid given off by the mushrooms evaporates, about 10 minutes.
4. Stir in the flour and cook for 1 minute, without browning.
5. Remove the pan from the burner and whisk in the cream and Madeira. Return the pan to the burner and add the crab, artichoke hearts, Gruyère, lemon juice, mustard, and nutmeg. Cook over medium-low heat until the cheese melts and the flavors develop, about 5 minutes. Taste and adjust the seasonings.
6. Fill the mushroom caps with the crab mixture and place in a baking dish filled with 1 to 2 inches of champagne. Top the mushrooms with the Parmesan and the remaining melted butter. Bake until hot, about 10 to 15 minutes.

FAST: Can assemble up to 1 day in advance, and refrigerate. Bake before serving. Can freeze the filling for up to 3 months.

FLASHY: On a platter garnished with fresh parsley, a whole raw artichoke, and/or any nontoxic flower or leaves.

FABULOUS: With minced spinach, broccoli, or asparagus substituted for the artichoke hearts, or any seafood for the crab. Use the filling as an entree in crepes or on pasta, rice, or couscous.

CHEESE-STUFFED MUSHROOMS IN GRAPE LEAVES

Here's a playful choice for summer.

Yield: 6 or more servings

12 cultivated white mushrooms, stems removed and reserved for another use

½ cup extra virgin olive oil or more

12 cubes teleme or muenster cheese, cubed to fit mushroom caps

½ cup minced green onions (scallions), white and green parts

Minced fresh basil to taste

12 grape leaves, purchased in brine

1. Preheat the oven to 375°F or fire up the barbecue.
2. Brush each mushroom cap with olive oil and fill with a cube of cheese, some green onions, and basil.
3. Wrap the mushrooms in the grape leaves and place on an oiled ovenproof pan. Bake in the oven or grill on the barbecue just until mushrooms are hot and cheese starts to melt, for 20 minutes. Use smoke chips for a smoky flavor.

FAST: Can assemble up to 2 days in advance and refrigerate.

FLASHY: On a platter garnished with grape leaves, clusters of grapes, and/or any nontoxic flower or leaves.

FABULOUS: Served hot or at room temperature. Experiment with different cheeses and herbs for the stuffing. Feta and rosemary make a good combination.

JEWISH-STYLE SUSHI BITES

I've used the Japanese technique to produce an eclectic variation.

Yield: about 10 servings

1 cup California pearl rice (page 17), rinsed in cold water until the water runs clear

1¼ cups cold water

¾ cup dry white wine

Zest of 2 lemons, finely grated

¼ cup minced fresh dill or to taste

2 tablespoons minced red onion or to taste

2 to 3 ounces chèvre (page 20)

½ cup minced smoked salmon (*lox*) or to taste

Salt and ground white pepper to taste

1. Combine the rice, water, and wine in a heavy saucepan. Bring to a boil, reduce the heat to low, and cook, covered, until the water is absorbed, about 15 minutes. Uncover the pot and cook over high heat for about 1 minute to evaporate the excess moisture.
2. Mix the remaining ingredients into the rice. Taste and adjust the flavors.
3. Transfer to a bowl and refrigerate for about 30 minutes.
4. When the rice is chilled, shape it into balls or logs by hand. To make a sushi roll, place the desired amount of rice on a square of plastic wrap and roll it into a log of any thickness and length. Cut the logs into slices for serving.

FAST: Can prepare the sushi and sauce up to 1 day in advance and refrigerate.

FLASHY: Served topped with Cold Smoked Salmon Sauce (page 41), or serve the sauce on the side, on a platter and garnished with pieces of smoked salmon, lemon zest, fresh dill, or minced red onion.

FABULOUS: As a stuffing for pea pods, cherry tomatoes, hollowed-out cucumbers, raw mushroom caps, or artichoke hearts. On cucumber slices, topped with Cold Smoked Salmon Sauce and minced fresh dill. Wrap each log in more smoked salmon and tie a thin strand of green onion or chive around it, for the ultimate presentation.

FAST & FABULOUS ITALIAN-STYLE SUSHI BITES

Here's another variation. When I prepared this on "Hour Magazine," I splashed extra virgin olive oil all over Gary Collins!

Yield: about 10 servings

1 cup California pearl rice (page 17), rinsed in cold water until the water runs clear

1¼ cups cold water

¾ cup dry white wine

1 clove garlic, peeled

2 ounces paper-thin slices prosciutto, minced

3 tablespoons minced roasted red bell pepper (page 26)

2 to 3 tablespoons minced fresh Italian (flatleaf) parsley

2 to 3 tablespoons minced red onion

2 to 3 tablespoons minced fresh basil leaves

¼ to ½ cup minced softened sun-dried tomatoes (page 22)

Freshly ground black pepper to taste

1. Combine the rice, water, wine, and garlic in heavy saucepan. Bring to a boil, reduce the heat to low, and cook, covered until the water is absorbed, for about 15 minutes. Remove the garlic and discard. Uncover the pot and cook over high heat for 1 minute to evaporate the excess moisture.
2. Mix in the remaining ingredients. Taste and adjust the flavors.
3. Transfer to a bowl, and refrigerate for about 30 minutes.
4. When the rice is chilled, shape it into balls or logs by hand. To make a sushi roll, place the desired amount of rice on a square of plastic wrap and roll it into a log of any thickness and length. Cut the logs into slices for serving.

FAST: Can prepare the sushi and sauce up to 1 day in advance and refrigerate.

FLASHY: Served on a platter with Roasted Red Pepper Sauce (page 44) and garnished with fresh basil, minced red onion, a whole or half raw red bell pepper, and/or parsley.

FABULOUS: As a stuffing for pea pods, cherry tomatoes, hollowed-out cucumbers, raw mushroom caps, or artichoke hearts. On cucumber slices, topped with Cold Smoked Salmon Sauce (page 41) and fresh dill. Wrap each log in more smoked salmon and tie a thin strand of green onion or chive around it for the ultimate presentation.

STUFFED ROMAINE

*Great as a summer hors d'oeuvre or for an unusual salad
course. There are no amounts; just have fun and create!*

Romaine lettuce, inner leaves, washed
    and dried

Brie cheese, at room temperature

Saint André cheese, at room
    temperature

Caviar

Minced green onions (scallions), white
    and green parts

Smoked oysters

Chopped toasted (page 27) walnuts

Chopped parsley

1. Spread half of the leaves with brie and the other half with Saint André.
2. Top the Saint André with a dollop of caviar and a sprinkle of minced green onions.
3. Top the brie with a smoked oyster and sprinkle with the walnuts and parsley.

FAST: Can assemble up to 4 hours in advance and refrigerate.

FLASHY: Serve chilled or at room temperature on a large platter.

FABULOUS: Variations: brie with roasted red pepper (page 26) or pesto (page 47); Saint André or brie topped with a slice of prosciutto, chèvre, and minced sun-dried tomatoes. With Belgian endive substituted for the romaine.

PROSCIUTTO AND VEGETABLES

*An unusual variation of the classic prosciutto
with melon. There are no amounts; just
have fun and create!*

Thinly sliced prosciutto

Avocado slices squirted with fresh
    lemon juice to prevent
    discoloration

Asparagus, blanched (page 23) until
    barely tender, 3 to 5 minutes

Zucchini spears

Baby corn, blanched until barely
    tender, 3 to 5 minutes, or canned
    and drained

Cucumber spears

Jicama spears (page 21)

Tiny red potatoes, blanched until
    barely tender, 5 to 8 minutes

Wrap a slice of prosciutto around each vegetable of your choice, and voilà!

FAST: Can prepare up to 3 days in advance and refrigerate.

FLASHY: Served chilled or at room temperature on a platter.

FABULOUS: With Westphalian ham, smoked salmon, and/or pastrami substituted for the prosciutto.

PROSCIUTTO AND FRUIT

*Prosciutto is a Fast & Fabulous cook's best friend,
symbolizing opulence and style.
There are no amounts, just have
fun and create!*

Thinly sliced prosciutto

*Melon of your choice, sliced and
    skinned*

Kiwi, skinned and sliced

Apricots, sliced

Nectarines, sliced

Papayas, peeled and sliced (page 22)

Mangoes, peeled and sliced (page 21)

Peaches, sliced

Wrap a slice of prosciutto around each piece of fruit and enjoy!

FAST: Can prepare up to 1 day in advance and refrigerate.

FLASHY: Serve chilled or at room temperature on a platter.

FABULOUS: Using a large assortment of fruit. With Westphalian ham, smoked salmon, and/or pastrami substituted for the prosciutto.

BELGIAN ENDIVE STUFFED WITH SEAFOOD

Yield: about 16 stuffed endive; 8 to 16 servings

*6 ounces shrimp, cooked and shelled
  (page 24)*

*3 ounces fresh crabmeat, picked over
  for cartilage*

*1 cup mayonnaise, homemade (page
  13) or purchased*

½ cup freshly grated Parmesan

⅓ cup grated Gruyère

*⅓ cup minced green onions
  (scallions), white and green parts*

*1 teaspoon Worcestershire sauce or
  to taste*

1 teaspoon Dijon mustard

⅓ cup minced fresh parsley

2 to 4 tablespoons minced fresh dill

½ cup minced jicama (page 21)

*2 tablespoons capers, drained and
  rinsed*

*Salt, ground white pepper, and hot
  pepper sauce to taste*

2 to 3 heads Belgian endive

1. Combine all of the ingredients, except the endive, in a bowl. Taste and adjust the flavors.
2. Fill each endive with the mixture.

FAST: Can prepare filling up to 1 day in advance and refrigerate. Fill endive up to 2 hours in advance and refrigerate.

FLASHY: Served on large platter with sprigs of fresh dill and a pansy or two in the center.

FABULOUS: As a cold filling for cooked pasta shells, avocado halves, or cherry tomatoes. As a hot filling for raw mushroom caps, Tartlets (page 314), omelets, or crepes. To serve warm bake in a 350°F oven for 10 to 15 minutes.

FURTHER: Toss leftover filling into hot pasta or salad.

STUFFED WRAPPERS

WON TON CUPS

A low-calorie and low-fat alternative to pastry tartlets.

Yield: about 60 won ton cups; 30 or more servings

1 package won ton wrappers (page 19)

Extra virgin olive oil or garlic olive oil as needed

1. Oil mini-muffin tins and place 1 wrapper in each cup. Brush each with oil.
2. Bake in a preheated 350°F oven until crisp, about 10 to 15 minutes. Remove the cups from the muffin tin.

FAST: Can prepare up to 3 days in advance and store in airtight jar(s) or plastic bag(s) in the refrigerator, or freeze for up to 3 months.

FABULOUS: Filled with anything from lobster to lunchmeat. Fill the cups with the desired filling and bake at 375°F for about 10 minutes until filling is hot and bubbly. If filling frozen cups, bake about 20 minutes.

GREEN CHILE WON TON CUPS

A tasty marriage between China and Mexico.

Yield: 60 won ton cups; 30 or more servings

1 pound jack cheese, grated

1 cup sour cream

½ cup chopped pitted black olives

⅔ cup chopped canned whole green chiles (page 20), seeded and deveined

½ cup minced green onions (scallions), white and green parts

1 teaspoon ground cumin or to taste

1 teaspoon dried oregano or to taste

60 Won Ton Cups (page 246)

1. Preheat the oven to 375°F.
2. Combine all the ingredients, except the won ton cups. Taste and adjust the seasonings.
3. Place won ton cups on a cookie sheet and fill with the mixture. Bake about 10 minutes, until filling is hot and bubbly.

FAST: Can assemble up to 2 hours in advance and leave at room temperature, or flash freeze (page 24) for up to 3 months. Defrost before heating or heat frozen, adding about 10 minutes to the cooking time.

FLASHY: Served on a platter and garnished with a clump of cilantro (fresh coriander), whole green chiles, and/or any nontoxic flower.

FABULOUS: With half jack cheese and half grated cheddar cheese. With red onions instead of green onions. With a combination of green and pasilla chiles (page 20).

SEAFOOD WON TONS FLORENTINE

Yield: about 60 won tons; 30 or more servings

½ pound raw shrimp, shelled, deveined, and chilled

½ pound fresh scallops or ¼ pound scallops and ¼ pound fillet of sole, chilled

Four 1-pound packages chopped frozen spinach, thawed and squeezed dry

½ cup ricotta cheese

2 large eggs

¼ cup minced shallots

Salt, ground white pepper, dried thyme, and freshly grated nutmeg to taste

1 cup heavy cream

Sui mai (page 18) or won ton wrappers (page 19)

Extra virgin olive oil for brushing

1. Preheat the oven to 350°F.
2. Combine all ingredients, except the cream, wrappers, and oil, in a food processor fitted with the metal blade. Process until the seafood is pureed.
3. Add the cream and process only until just combined.
4. Fry 1 teaspoon of the mixture in a saucepan over medium heat until cooked through to check the seasonings.
5. Place 2 teaspoons of the filling in the middle of each wrapper and fold in half. To seal, lightly moisten the edge of one half of the wrapper with water and press the edges together. Repeat with the remaining mixture and wrappers.
6. Place on a greased cookie sheet and brush each one with olive oil.
7. Bake until crisp and golden, about 10 to 15 minutes.

FAST: Can assemble up to 1 day in advance and refrigerate unbaked on a greased cookie sheet, or flash freeze (page 24) on a floured cookie sheet for up to 1 month. Do not thaw before baking, just add about 5 minutes to the cooking time.

FLASHY: Served on a platter and garnished with fresh parsley and/or any nontoxic flowers.

FABULOUS: With ½ cup of chèvre substituted for the ricotta cheese. With frozen chard substituted for the spinach.

CHÈVRE AND SUN-DRIED TOMATO CUPS

This is so simple you will not believe the results!

Yield: 60 won ton cups; 30 or more servings

60 Won Ton Cups (page 246)
1 pound chèvre, crumbled (page 20)
½ cup minced green onions (scallions), white and green parts
¼ to ½ cup pine nuts, toasted (page 27)

1 cup minced softened sun-dried tomatoes (page 22)
½ cup fresh basil leaves, minced

1. Preheat oven to 350° F.
2. Fill each won ton cup three-quarters full with cheese.
3. Top with a sprinkling of green onions, nuts, sun-dried tomatoes, and basil.
4. Place on an ungreased cookie sheet and bake until the cheese melts, about 10 minutes.

FAST: Can assemble up to 1 day in advance and refrigerate. Bring to room temperature before baking.

FLASHY: Served on a platter and garnished with fresh parsley, basil, and/or any nontoxic flowers.

FABULOUS: The variations are endless! Try different cheeses and herbs. One of my favorite combos is teleme cheese with minced roasted red peppers (page 26) and red onion.

Niçoise Cups

Yield: 60 pieces; 30 more servings

Filling

1 small eggplant, chopped	Ground white pepper to taste
Salt	1 teaspoon dried oregano
6 tablespoons extra virgin olive oil or to taste	½ cup minced fresh parsley
1 cup minced onion	2 to 4 tablespoons minced fresh basil
2 cloves garlic, minced	
3 large, ripe tomatoes, peeled, seeded, and chopped	

Sauce

3 tablespoons unsalted butter	¼ cup freshly grated Parmesan or to taste
¼ cup all-purpose flour	
1¾ cups milk	Salt, ground white pepper, and freshly grated nutmeg to taste
¼ cup dry vermouth	

To complete the dish

60 Won Ton Cups (page 246)

1. Sprinkle the eggplant with salt and put it in a colander over a bowl. Let it drain for 1 hour.
2. Meanwhile, heat 2 tablespoons of the olive oil in a heavy skillet over medium heat. Add the onion and garlic and cook, stirring, until soft and golden, about 10 minutes.
3. Add the tomatoes and cook over medium-low heat until they are very soft and begin to lose their shape, about 20 minutes. Season with salt, pepper, oregano, parsley, and basil.
4. Dry the eggplant on paper towels. Toss it with the remaining oil. Place on a cookie sheet and bake for about 15 minutes in a preheated 400° F oven.
5. Meanwhile, prepare the sauce by melting the butter in a heavy saucepan over medium-low heat. Whisk in the flour, and cook for 1 to 2 minutes. Do not brown the mixture.

6. Remove the saucepan from the burner and whisk in the milk slowly. Return to the burner and bring to a boil. Cook until it is very thick, whisking frequently.
7. Reduce the heat to low, whisk in the wine and cheese, and cook until the cheese is melted, several minutes more. Taste and adjust the seasonings.
8. Remove the eggplant from the oven and reduce the heat to 350°F. Add the eggplant to the tomato mixture, then stir in the sauce.
9. To assemble, place the won ton cups on an ungreased cookie sheet and fill with the mixture. Bake at 375°F until the filling is hot and bubbly, about 10 minutes.

FAST: Can assemble up to 3 hours in advance and leave at room temperature, or flash freeze (page 24) for up to 3 months. Can prepare the filling up to 4 days in advance and refrigerate, or freeze for up to 3 months. Do not thaw before baking, but add about 10 minutes to the time.

FLASHY: Served on a platter and garnished with fresh basil leaves and/or nontoxic flowers.

FABULOUS: With crumbled feta cheese sprinkled over the tops of the cups. With 4 medium-size roasted zucchini or three 7-ounce jars of marinated artichoke hearts substituted for the eggplant (both without the salt). Can also use the filling without the sauce. With precooked shrimp, lamb, or chicken added to the filling, and served on couscous, pasta, or rice as an entree.

SHRIMP AND CHEESE SUI MAI

Here's California-style sui mai.

Yield: about 30 pieces, 15 or more servings

1 pound raw shrimp, shelled, deveined, and minced

1 cup ricotta cheese

1 cup grated jack cheese

6 green onions (scallions), green and white parts, minced

2 tablespoons cornstarch, plus more for dusting

1 to 2 tablespoons minced cilantro (*fresh coriander*)

½ cup toasted chopped walnuts (*page 27*)

1 teaspoon dry sherry

1 teaspoon Chinese sesame oil

1 teaspoon minced garlic

Salt and ground white pepper to taste

Sui mai wrappers (*page 18*)

1. Combine the shrimp, cheeses, green onions, 2 tablespoons cornstarch, cilantro, walnuts, sherry, sesame oil, and garlic in a mixing bowl. Fry 1 teaspoon of this mixture in a small saucepan over medium heat until cooked all the way through to check the seasonings.
2. Dust a piece of waxed paper with cornstarch.

3. Place 2 teaspoons of the filling in the center of each sui mai wrapper. Draw the edges around the filling and squeeze it a bit to allow some of the fillings to show on the top. Set it on the dusted waxed paper and repeat with the remaining filling and wrappers. Cover with a dry kitchen towel while preparing the remainder.

4. Arrange the sui mai on a steamer tray in a steamer or a large skillet filled with about 1 inch of water. Cover and steam until cooked, about 8 minutes.

FAST: Can assemble up to 1 day in advance and refrigerate unbaked or prepare through step 3 and flash freeze (page 24) for up to 3 months. Do not thaw before cooking, but add about 5 to 8 minutes to the cooking time.

FLASHY: Served hot on a platter with Balsamic Chili Sauce (page 76) and garnished with cilantro, nontoxic flowers, and/or green onion fans (page 9).

FABULOUS: Can use the filling in Won Ton Cups (page 246), Croustades (page 279), as a calzette (page 260), or in potsticker wrappers (page 18).

CHINESE CABBAGE SUI MAI WITH PORK AND SHRIMP

Yield: about 60 pieces; 30 or more servings

2 tablespoons peanut oil

2 tablespoons minced fresh ginger

2 to 4 cloves garlic, minced

1 head Chinese cabbage, shredded

Salt and ground white pepper to taste

1 teaspoon sugar

Filling

1 pound ground lean pork

½ pound raw shrimp, shelled, deveined, and chopped

½ cup raw or blanched almonds, toasted (page 27) and slivered or chopped

2 tablespoons medium-dry sherry

4 to 8 minced green onions (scallions), green and white parts

¼ cup minced pickled ginger (page 18)

2 to 4 cloves garlic, minced

½ cup minced cilantro (fresh coriander)

1 tablespoon Chinese barbecue sauce (page 16)

1 large egg

2 tablespoons cornstarch

Sugar to taste

1 package won ton (page 19) or sui mai wrappers (page 18)

Chinese sesame oil for brushing

251

1. Preheat the oven to 350°F.
2. Heat the peanut oil in a wok or large skillet over high heat. Add the ginger, garlic, and cabbage, season with salt, white pepper, and sugar, and stir fry until the cabbage wilts, just a few minutes. Remove the cabbage from the wok and place in a strainer. Allow the juices to drain out while preparing the rest of the filling. (Save the juices for adding to soups.)
3. In another mixing bowl, combine all the remaining ingredients except for the wrappers and sesame oil.
4. Press any remaining moisture out of the cabbage and then combine it with the pork and shrimp mixture. Fry 1 teaspoon of the filling to test the seasonings until cooked all the way through.
5. Place 1 teaspoon of the filling in the middle of each wrapper and fold in half. To seal, lightly moisten the edge of one half of the wrapper with water and press the edges together.
6. Place the sui mai on an oiled cookie sheet and brush the tops liberally with sesame oil. Bake until golden and fully cooked, for 10 to 15 minutes.

FAST: Can assemble through step 5 up to 1 day in advance and refrigerate unbaked, or flash freeze (page 24) for up to 3 months. Do not thaw before baking, adding about 5 to 8 minutes to the time.

FLASHY: With any Asian-style dunk, served on a platter and garnished with baby bok choy, cilantro, and/or any nontoxic flower or leaves for garnishing.

FABULOUS: When deep-fat fried. With ground turkey substituted for the ground pork.

FLORENTINE SAUSAGE SUI MAI

One of my favorites!

Yield: about 60 sui mai; 30 or more servings

½ pound sweet Italian sausages,
  casings removed

1 large onion, minced

4 to 8 green onions (scallions),
  green and white parts, minced

1 to 2 cloves garlic, minced

¼ cup dry vermouth

1 pound ricotta cheese

½ cup freshly grated Parmesan, plus
  extra for topping

One 8-ounce package frozen chopped
  spinach, thawed and squeezed dry

Salt, ground white pepper, and freshly
  grated nutmeg to taste

1 package sui mai wrappers
  (page 18)

Extra virgin olive oil for brushing

1. Preheat the oven to 350°F.
2. In a large saucepan over medium-high heat, brown the sausage meat with the onions and garlic until the meat is no longer pink. Pour off the excess fat. Add the vermouth and cook until it evaporates, about 5 minutes.
3. Place all the ingredients, except for wrappers and oil, in a food processor fitted with the metal blade and blend until it is almost smooth. Taste and adjust the seasonings.
4. Place 1 teaspoon of the mixture in the middle of each wrapper and fold in half. To seal, lightly moisten the edge of one half of each wrapper with water, and press the edges together.
5. Place on a greased cookie sheet and brush with olive oil. Sprinkle with extra grated Parmesan cheese, if desired.
6. Bake until crisp and golden, about 10 to 15 minutes.

FAST: Can assemble up to 1 day in advance and refrigerate unbaked, or flash freeze (page 24) for up to 3 months. Do not thaw before baking, just add about 5 to 10 minutes to the cooking time.

FLASHY: Served on a platter and garnished with fresh parsley, a whole raw onion, and/or any nontoxic flower or leaves. Served with Fast & Flashy Marinara (page 132) for dipping.

FABULOUS: With the sausage omitted and the onions sautéed in a few tablespoons of olive oil instead. With potsticker wrappers instead of the sui mai. Use this filling in Won Ton Cups (page 246), Croustades (page 279), or Phyllo Cups (page 294).

ONION OLIVE POTSTICKERS

Yield: about 30 potstickers; 15 or more servings

Onion-and-olive filling

4 tablespoons (½ stick) unsalted
   butter

2½ cups thinly sliced onions

2 cloves garlic, minced

One 6-ounce can pitted black olives,
   drained and chopped

¼ cup minced fresh parsley

1 teaspoon Dijon mustard

1 teaspoon dried thyme, crumbled

Salt and ground white pepper to taste

½ to 1 cup Béchamel Sauce
   (page 233)

To complete the dish

1 package potsticker wrappers
   (page 18)

Pure olive oil for brushing

1. Preheat the oven to 400°F.
2. Melt the butter in a skillet over medium heat. When it foams, add the onions and garlic and cook, stirring, until soft and golden.

3. Stir in the remaining ingredients, including just enough of the béchamel sauce to bind the mixture. Taste and adjust the seasonings.
4. Place the mixture in the freezer until chilled, about 30 minutes.
5. Place a generous teaspoonful of the mixture in the center of each potsticker. Fold in half. Slightly dampen the outer edges with cold water. Press the edges together to seal, using the tines of a fork or a potsticker mold.
6. Place on an oiled cookie sheet and brush the tops with olive oil. Bake until lightly browned, about 10 minutes.

FAST: Can assemble up to 1 day in advance and refrigerate, or flash freeze (page 24) for up to 3 months. Do not thaw before cooking, just add 5 to 10 minutes to the baking time.

FLASHY: Served on a platter and garnished with fresh parsley, a whole raw onion, and/or any nontoxic flower or leaves.

FABULOUS: With about ½ cup grated jack, Swiss, or crumbled feta, or chèvre cheese added to the fillings at step 3.

BARBECUED PORK AND RED CABBAGE POTSTICKERS

Yield: about 60 potstickers; 30 or more servings

1 cup California pearl rice (page 17), rinsed in cold water until the water runs clear

2 cups chicken broth, homemade (page 11) or canned

2 tablespoons peanut or avocado oil

½ medium-size head red cabbage, shredded

Soy sauce to taste

¼ to ½ cup minced cilantro (fresh coriander)

4 to 8 green onions (scallions), white and green parts, minced

1 tablespoon minced fresh ginger

Ground white pepper and Chinese five spice powder (page 17), optional, to taste

Szechuan peppercorns to taste (page 19)

½ pound Chinese-style barbecued pork, minced (page 17)

2 to 4 tablespoons green peppercorns, optional

2 large eggs

¼ to ½ cup sesame seeds, toasted (page 27)

Garlic, minced, to taste

1 tablespoon Chinese barbecue sauce (page 16)

2 to 4 tablespoons hoisin sauce (page 17)

2 packages potsticker wrappers (page 18)

Chinese sesame oil for brushing

1. Preheat the oven to 375°F.
2. Bring the rice and chicken broth to a boil in a small pot over high heat, then reduce the heat to medium-low and simmer until the liquid is absorbed, about 15 to 20 minutes.
3. Heat the peanut oil in a wok or large skillet over high heat. Then while the rice cooks, stir fry the cabbage, adding the soy sauce, cilantro, green onions, ginger, pepper, five spice powder and Szechuan peppercorns while you cook. Cook until the cabbage is just tender.
4. Add the cooked rice and remaining ingredients, except the potsticker wrappers and sesame oil, to the wok; stir well. Taste and adjust the seasonings.
5. Place a generous teaspoonful of the mixture in the center of each wrapper. Fold in half; slightly dampen the outer edges with cold water. Press the edges together to seal, using the tines of a fork or a potsticker mold.
6. Grease a cookie sheet with a generous amount of peanut or avocado oil.
7. Brush the top of the potstickers with sesame oil and bake until crisp and golden brown, about 15 to 20 minutes.

FAST: Can assemble up to 1 day in advance and refrigerate, or flash freeze (page 24) unbaked for up to 3 months. Do not thaw before cooking; just add 5 to 10 minutes to the baking time.

FLASHY: Served with Ginger Merlot Sauce (page 153), any of the Asian-style dipping sauces or sweet-and-sour-style sauces from Chapter 1. Served on a platter and garnished with baby bok choy, cilantro, and/or any nontoxic flower or leaves for garnishing.

FABULOUS: This filling also makes an excellent rice dish, or filling for Won Ton Cups (page 246).

NORTHERN-STYLE POTSTICKERS

Yield: about 60 potstickers; 30 or more servings

Filling

½ pound bok choy, chopped

1 pound ground lean pork

4 to 8 green onions (scallions), white and green parts, minced

2 to 4 tablespoons chopped fresh ginger

1 tablespoon medium-dry sherry

1 tablespoon soy sauce

1 teaspoon salt

2 tablespoons rice wine vinegar

2 to 3 cloves garlic, minced

1 tablespoon Chinese sesame oil

To complete the dish

2 packages potsticker wrappers (page 18)

2 tablespoons peanut oil

2 tablespoons Chinese sesame oil

1 cup chicken broth, homemade (page 11) or canned

1. Combine the bok choy, pork, green onions, ginger, sherry, soy sauce, salt, vinegar, garlic, and the sesame oil in a bowl. Mix well and fry 1 teaspoon in a saucepan over medium heat until cooked through to test the seasonings.
2. Place a generous teaspoonful of the mixture in the center of each wrapper. Fold in half; slightly dampen the outer edges with cold water. Press the edges together to seal, using the tines of a fork or a potsticker mold.
3. Place on floured cookie sheet, and cover with a clean towel until ready to use.
4. Heat both of the oils in a 12-inch skillet over medium-low heat. Add the potstickers and brown the bottoms for 2 minutes. Add the broth, cover the pan, and cook until the liquid is absorbed, about 5 minutes. Do this in several batches, transferring the cooked potstickers to a serving platter and keeping warm in a 200°F oven until ready to serve.

FAST: Can prepare the sauce up to 4 days in advance and refrigerate. Can assemble the potstickers up to 1 day in advance and refrigerate, or flash freeze (page 24) for up to 3 months. Do not thaw, just add 5 to 10 minutes to the cooking time.

FLASHY: Served hot on a platter with Chinese Dipping Sauce (recipe follows) and garnished with baby bok choy, cilantro, and/or any nontoxic flower or leaves.

FABULOUS: If you are short on time, bake the potstickers as described in the recipe for Barbecued Pork and Red Cabbage Potstickers (page 254).

CHINESE DIPPING SAUCE

Yield: about ¾ cup

¼ cup soy sauce

¼ cup rice wine vinegar

1 teaspoon Chinese sesame oil

1 to 2 cloves garlic, minced

2 to 4 green onions (scallions), white and green parts, minced

Combine all of the ingredients in a bowl, blender, or food processor fitted with the metal blade. Taste and adjust the flavors.

FAST: Can prepare the sauce up to 1 month in advance and refrigerate.

FLASHY: Served cold or at room temperature.

FABULOUS: With ¼ cup minced cilantro mixed in.

CURRIED CARROT POTSTICKERS

A great vegetarian hors d'oeuvre with an Indian influence.

Yield: about 40 potstickers; 20 or more servings

4 tablespoons (½ stick) unsalted butter

3 to 6 cloves garlic, minced

¼ cup minced pickled ginger or to taste (page 18)

1 large onion, minced

¼ to ½ cup minced cilantro (fresh coriander)

½ cup minced fresh parsley

½ pound carrots, shredded

½ cup minced dried apricots

¼ cup medium-dry sherry or Madeira

¼ cup Chinese plum sauce or to taste (page 17)

1 cup toasted (page 27) and salted peanuts

¼ teaspoon fennel seeds or to taste

½ teaspoon curry powder or to taste

¼ teaspoon ground cumin or to taste

2 tablespoons all-purpose flour

2 packages potsticker wrappers (page 18)

Peanut oil for greasing and brushing

1. Preheat the oven to 375°F.
2. Melt the butter in a skillet over medium heat. When it begins to foam, add the garlic, pickled ginger, onion, cilantro, and parsley, and cook, stirring, until tender, about 5 minutes.
3. Reduce the heat to low, add the carrots, apricots, sherry, plum sauce, peanuts, and spices, and cook, stirring, until the carrots are tender, about 10 minutes.
4. Stir in the flour and cook until the flavors develop, for several minutes, while stirring. Transfer the mixture to a bowl and refrigerate for about 30 minutes until chilled.
5. Place a generous teaspoonful of the mixture in the center of each wrapper. Fold in half; slightly dampen the outer edges with cold water. Press the edges together to seal, using the tines of a fork or a potsticker mold.
6. Place on a cookie sheet oiled with peanut oil and brush the tops with more peanut oil.
7. Bake until golden, about 15 minutes.

FAST: Can assemble up to 1 day in advance and refrigerate, or flash freeze (page 24) unbaked for up to 3 months. Do not thaw before cooking, just add 5 to 10 minutes to the baking time.

FLASHY: Served with Ginger Merlot Sauce (page 153), any of the Asian-style dipping sauces or sweet-and-sour-style sauces from Chapter 1. Served on a platter and garnished with baby bok choy, cilantro, and/or any nontoxic flower or leaves for garnishing.

FABULOUS: Use in Won Ton Cups (page 246).

GREEK POTSTICKERS

A wonderful way to use up leftover lamb.

Yield: about 60 potstickers; 30 or more servings

½ pound leftover lamb, cut into
small pieces, or ground lamb,
cooked in a skillet just until it is
no longer pink and drained on
paper towels to remove any excess
fat

½ pound ground turkey

1 cup cooked rice

½ cup crumbled feta cheese

2 cloves garlic, minced

¼ to ½ cup minced fresh parsley

6 to 12 pitted Greek or marinated
green olives

2 green onions (scallions), white
and green parts, minced

¼ to ½ teaspoon dried oregano,
crumbled

Salt and freshly ground black pepper
to taste

2 packages potsticker wrappers
(page 18)

Extra virgin olive oil for greasing and
brushing

1. Preheat the oven to 375°F.
2. Combine all the ingredients, except the olive oil and wrappers, in a food processor fitted with the metal blade, or in a mixing bowl. If necessary, process in batches and combine them in a mixing bowl. Fry 1 teaspoon of the mixture in a saucepan over medium heat until cooked all the way through to test the seasonings.
3. Place a generous teaspoonful of the mixture in the center of each wrapper. Fold in half; slightly dampen the outer edges with cold water. Press the edges together to seal, using the tines of a fork or a potsticker mold.
4. Place on a cookie sheet oiled with olive oil and brush the tops with more olive oil.
5. Bake until golden, about 15 minutes.

FAST: Can assemble up to 1 day in advance and refrigerate, or flash freeze (page 24) unbaked for up to 3 months. Do not thaw before cooking; just add 5 to 10 minutes to the baking time.

FLASHY: Served hot on a platter with Roasted Red Pepper Sauce (page 44) and garnished with fresh parsley and/or any nontoxic flower or leaves.

FABULOUS: Cook it like a traditional potsticker. See the recipe for Northern-style Pot-stickers (page 255) for directions.

Fast & Fabulous
Hors D'Oeuvres

CHINESE SAUSAGE POTSTICKERS

Yield: about 30 potstickers; 15 or more servings

¼ to ½ pound Chinese sausages,
   minced or cut into thin slices
   (page 17)
1 cup uncooked short-grain
   (Arborio) rice
¼ cup minced pickled ginger or to
   taste (page 18)
4 large dried shiitake mushrooms,
   rehydrated (page 18), stemmed,
   and minced (reserve the soaking
   liquid)
1 tablespoon sweetened chili sauce
   (page 19) or Chinese plum sauce
   (page 17)

4 green onions (scallions), white and
   green parts, minced
2 to 4 canned whole green chiles,
   seeded, deveined (page 20), and
   minced
1 cup dry white wine
Salt and ground white pepper to taste
1 package potsticker wrappers
   (page 18)
Chinese sesame oil for brushing

1. Cook the sausage in a saucepan over medium heat until some of the fat is rendered, about 5 minutes.
2. Add the rice, pickled ginger, mushrooms, chile sauce, green onions, and chiles, and reduce the heat to low. Stir and cook for a minute or two, without browning the rice.
3. Strain the reserved mushroom liquid through a double thickness of paper towels and add 1 cup of it, along with the wine, to the rice. Bring to a boil over high heat and cover. Reduce the heat to low and cook until all the water is absorbed, about 20 minutes. Taste and adjust the seasonings.
4. Transfer the rice mixture to a bowl and place in the freezer to chill, for about 30 minutes.
5. Preheat the oven to 400°F.
6. Place a generous teaspoonful of the mixture in the center of each wrapper. Fold in half; slightly dampen the outer edges with cold water. Press the edges together to seal, using the tines of a fork or a potsticker mold.
7. Place on an oiled cookie sheet and brush the tops with sesame oil. Bake until crisp, about 15 to 20 minutes.

FAST: Can assemble up to 1 day in advance and refrigerate, or flash freeze (page 24) for up to 3 months. Do not thaw before baking; just add 5 to 10 minutes to the baking time.

FLASHY: Served hot on a platter and garnished with baby bok choy, cilantro, and/or any nontoxic flower or leaves. Served with Ginger Merlot Sauce (page 153).

FABULOUS: With Chinese barbecued pork (page 17) substituted for the sausage. Cooked as a traditional potsticker, see Northern-style Potstickers (page 255) for directions.

ARTICHOKE HEART
AND GOAT CHEESE CALZETTE

Calzette is a name I coined for a mini calzone. If you happen to be unfamiliar with calzone, it is a crescent-shaped pizza turnover. The Fast & Fabulous factor here is the dough; you do not have to prepare it yourself. A calzette is made with a potsticker wrapper, which produces a lovely, effortless crust.

Yield: about 40 pieces; 20 or more servings

¾ cup crumbled feta or chèvre (page 20) cheese

1 cup grated jack cheese

½ cup ricotta cheese

1 to 2 cloves garlic, minced

¼ to ½ cup minced fresh parsley

One 6-ounce jar marinated artichoke hearts, drained and chopped

Salt, ground white pepper, and minced dill (fresh or dried) to taste

2 packages potsticker or sui mai wrappers (page 18)

Olive oil for brushing

1. Preheat the oven to 400°F.
2. Combine all the cheeses, garlic, and parsley in a food processor fitted with the metal blade or in a bowl and mix until smooth.
3. Add the artichoke hearts and process, using several quick on-and-off motions so as to preserve their texture, or mix in.
4. Taste and season.
5. Place a generous teaspoonful of the mixture in the center of each wrapper. Fold in half; slightly dampen the outer edges with cold water. Press the edges together to seal, using the tines of a fork or a potsticker mold.
6. Place on an oiled cookie sheet and brush the tops with olive oil. Bake until crisp, about 15 to 20 minutes.

FAST: Can assemble and refrigerate up to 1 day in advance, or flash freeze (page 24) for up to 3 months. Don't thaw before cooking, just add 5 to 10 minutes to the baking time.

FLASHY: Served on a platter and garnished with fresh parsley, and/or any nontoxic flower or leaves.

FABULOUS: With ¾ cup cooked chopped shrimp or crabmeat added to the filling or a can of hearts of palm substituted for the artichoke hearts.

ITALIAN SAUSAGE AND MUSHROOM CALZETTE

Assertive flavors!

Yield: about 60 pieces; 30 or more servings

1 pound sweet or hot Italian sausage, casings removed

1 medium-size to large onion, minced

1 pound cultivated white mushrooms, minced

¼ cup Madeira or medium-dry sherry

½ cup minced fresh parsley or to taste

¼ to ½ cup minced softened sun-dried tomatoes (page 22; optional; they provide nice flavor contrast)

½ cup ricotta cheese

¾ cup grated jack cheese

¼ to ½ cup freshly grated Parmesan

2 packages potsticker or sui mai wrappers (page 18)

Extra virgin olive oil for brushing

1. Preheat the oven to 375°F.
2. Cook the sausage meat in a skillet over medium-high heat until no longer pink. Remove the meat and pour off all but 2 tablespoons of the fat.
3. Add the onion and mushrooms to the hot skillet and cook over medium heat, stirring, until almost all of the mushrooms' liquid has evaporated.
4. Place all the ingredients, except the wrappers and olive oil, in a food processor fitted with the metal blade and process, using several quick on-and-off motions so as not to destroy all the texture, or combine by hand in a bowl. Taste and adjust the seasonings.
5. Place a generous teaspoonful of the mixture in the center of each wrapper. Fold in half; slightly dampen the outer edges with cold water. Press the edges together to seal, using the tines of a fork or a potsticker mold.
6. Place on an oiled cookie sheet and brush the tops with olive oil. Bake until crisp, about 15 to 20 minutes.

FAST: Can assemble up to 1 day in advance and refrigerate unbaked, or flash freeze (page 24) for up to 3 months. Do not thaw before cooking, just add 5 to 10 minutes to the baking.

FLASHY: Served hot on a platter and garnished with fresh parsley, a whole raw onion, and/or any nontoxic flower or leaves. With Fast & Flashy Marinara (page 132) for dipping.

FABULOUS: With a variety of mushrooms instead of cultivated mushrooms.

LEEK AND GOAT CHEESE CALZETTE

Sinfully delicious!

Yield: about 60 pieces

3 tablespoons unsalted butter

4 to 6 leeks, washed thoroughly and finely chopped (white and tender green part only)

¼ cup minced fresh parsley

1 cup (½ pound) thinly sliced, roughly minced smoked ham

¼ cup Madeira or medium-dry sherry

1½ cups crumbled chèvre (page 20) or feta cheese

½ cup ricotta cheese

½ cup grated jack cheese

1 clove garlic, minced

Salt, ground white pepper, and freshly grated nutmeg to taste

2 packages potsticker or sui mai wrappers (page 18)

Extra virgin olive oil for brushing

1. Preheat the oven to 375°F.
2. Melt the butter in a skillet over medium heat. When it begins to foam, add the leeks, parsley, and ham and cook, stirring, until the leeks are tender, about 10 minutes.
3. Add the Madeira and cook until it is absorbed, about 3 minutes.
4. While the leeks are cooking, combine all cheeses and garlic in a food processor fitted with the metal blade or in a bowl until smooth.
5. Combine the sautéed leek mixture and the cheese mixture in a bowl. Season with salt, pepper, and nutmeg.
6. Place a generous teaspoonful of the mixture in the center of each wrapper. Fold in half; slightly dampen the outer edges with cold water. Press the edges together to seal, using the tines of a fork or a potsticker mold.
7. Place on an oiled cookie sheet and brush the tops with olive oil. Bake until crisp, about 15 to 20 minutes.

FAST: Can assemble up to 1 day in advance and refrigerate, or flash freeze (page 24) unbaked for up to 3 months. Do not thaw before cooking, just add 5 to 10 minutes to the baking time.

FLASHY: Served hot on a platter and garnished with fresh parsley, leek flowers, and/or any nontoxic flower or leaves. Served with Creamed Tomato Sauce (page 133) for dipping.

FABULOUS: Use the filling for Croustades (page 279), Flo Braker's Magic Puff Pastry (page 309), or Tartlets (page 314). Stuffed in raw mushrooms, in omelets, crepes, or cooked pasta shells. Toss the filling into freshly cooked pasta. Add ½ cup softened and minced sun-dried tomatoes (page 22) to the filling.

Fast & Fabulous
Hors D'Oeuvres

HERBED AND CHEDDARED TOMATO MELBAS

Yield: 4 to 6 servings

1 baguette, thinly sliced

2½ pounds tomatoes, fresh or
    canned, peeled, seeded, and
    chopped coarsely

2 cloves garlic, minced, or to taste

3 tablespoons extra virgin olive oil

¼ cup minced fresh basil or 2
    teaspoons dried or to taste

½ teaspoon dried oregano or to
    taste

½ cup minced fresh parsley

1 cup shredded sharp cheddar

Salt and ground white pepper to taste

1. Place the baguette slices on a cookie sheet and toast in a preheated 350°F oven until crisp, about 15 minutes.
2. Combine all the ingredients, except the baguette, in a food processor fitted with the metal blade or in a bowl until well mixed.
3. Top the bread slices with the processed mixture and place on an ungreased cookie sheet. Bake until hot, 5 to 10 minutes.

FAST: Can assemble up to 3 days in advance and refrigerate, or flash freeze (page 24) for up to 3 months. Thaw or cook frozen, adding several minutes to the baking time. Can prepare the tomato mixture up to 4 days in advance and refrigerate or freeze for up to 3 months. Defrost at room temperature for about 4 hours before using.

FLASHY: Served at room temperature or warm in a napkin-lined basket or on a platter garnished with a whole, raw tomato, fresh basil or parsley, and/or any nontoxic flower in the center. To reheat, place on a cookie sheet in a 350°F oven for about 10 minutes.

FABULOUS: Vary the cheeses and herbs. Create tomato, bacon, and cheese melbas by adding crumbled, cooked bacon.

GARLIC FETA HERB CROSTINI

These also make a wonderful hors d'oeuvre.

Yield: about 4 to 6 servings

1 baguette, cut into ¼-inch-thick slices

Salt and ground white pepper to taste

½ cup crumbled feta cheese

¼ cup freshly grated Parmesan

2 shallots, minced

2 cloves garlic, minced

¼ cup minced fresh herbs (rosemary, thyme, dill, basil, and/or cilantro)

¼ cup minced fresh parsley

1 cup extra virgin olive oil

1. Place the baguette slices on a cookie sheet. Toast in a preheated 350°F oven until crisp, about 15 minutes.
2. Combine all the ingredients, except the baguette, in a food processor fitted with the metal blade or in a bowl until smooth. Taste and adjust the seasonings.
3. Spread the olive oil mixture over the baguette slices. Place on an ungreased cookie sheet and bake until crisp, about 15 to 20 minutes.

FAST: Can assemble up to 1 day in advance and refrigerate, or flash freeze (page 24) for up to 3 months. Thaw or cook frozen, adding several minutes to the cooking time. Can prepare cheese mixture up to 5 days in advance and refrigerate or freeze for up to 3 months. Defrost at room temperature for about 4 hours before using. To reheat, place on a cookie sheet in a 350°F oven for about 10 minutes or serve at room temperature.

FLASHY: Served at room temperature or warm in a napkin-lined basket or on a platter garnished with fresh herbs, a raw head of garlic, and/or any nontoxic flower in the center.

FABULOUS: With blue cheese or chèvre instead of the feta.

HERBED CHÈVRE CROSTINI

Another confidence-builder. You can't miss.

Yield: about 4 to 6 servings

1 baguette, cut into ¼-inch-thick
slices

8 ounces chèvre (page 20) or feta
cheese, crumbled, or more

¼ cup fresh rosemary, minced green
onions (scallions), white and
green parts, minced shallots,
chopped fresh parsley, basil, or
dill

¼ cup minced softened sun-dried
tomatoes (page 22)

1 cup extra virgin olive oil

1. Place the baguette slices on a cookie sheet and toast in a preheated 350°F oven until crisp, about 15 minutes.
2. Spread or sprinkle the cheese on the baguette slices and top with your choice of herbs and sun-dried tomatoes. Drizzle the olive oil over the top very generously.
3. Bake until hot, about 5 minutes.

FAST: Can assemble up to 1 day in advance and refrigerate, or flash freeze (page 24) for up to 3 months. Thaw or cook frozen, adding several minutes to the baking time.

FLASHY: Served at room temperature or hot in a napkin-lined basket or on a platter garnished with fresh rosemary and/or any nontoxic flower in the center.

FABULOUS: Can also prepare by combining all the topping ingredients in a blender or food processor fitted with the metal blade, and then spreading over the baguette slices.

WARM EGGPLANT AND ROASTED RED PEPPER CROSTINI

Yield: about 4 to 6 servings

1 baguette, sliced thinly on the diagonal

One 1-pound eggplant, peeled and cut into ½-inch cubes

1 large onion, chopped

¼ to ½ cup extra virgin olive oil

2 tablespoons red wine vinegar

Salt and freshly ground black pepper

2 large red bell peppers, halved, seeded, roasted (page 26), peeled, and chopped

¼ cup minced fresh parsley

¼ to ½ pound jack cheese, grated

¼ cup grated Romano

1. Place the baguette slices on a cookie sheet and toast in a preheated 350°F oven until crisp, about 15 minutes, and remove from the oven.
2. Raise the oven temperature to 425°F. In a large roasting or baking pan, toss the eggplant, onion, olive oil, vinegar, salt, and pepper together. Bake until tender, about 45 minutes.
3. Lower the oven temperature to 350°F. Transfer the roasted eggplant mixture to a mixing bowl. Add the remaining ingredients and toss well. Taste and adjust the seasonings.
4. Spread each crostini (the crisped baguette slices) with the eggplant-and-cheese mixture and return to the cookie sheet. Bake until hot, about 7 to 10 minutes.

FAST: Can prepare the crostini through step 1 up to 2 weeks in advance and store at room temperature in an airtight container or plastic bags or freeze for up to 6 months. Can assemble up to 3 days in advance and refrigerate, or flash freeze (page 24) for up to 3 months. Can freeze the eggplant mixture for up to 6 months. Thaw at room temperature for about 4 hours.

FLASHY: Served on a platter garnished with a whole red bell pepper, fresh parsley, and/or any nontoxic flower or leaves.

FABULOUS: Seasoned with fresh basil, oregano, capers, and/or minced marinated artichoke hearts.

WARM PESTO AND
ROASTED RED PEPPER CROSTINI

Yield: about 4 to 6 servings

1 baguette, thinly sliced on the
  diagonal
½ cup pesto, homemade (page 47) or
  purchased

½ pound brie, cut up
4 large red peppers, halved, seeded,
  roasted (page 26), peeled, and cut
  into small pieces

1. Place the baguette slices on a cookie sheet and toast in a preheated 350°F oven until
   crisp, about 15 minutes.
2. Combine the brie and pesto in a food processor fitted with the metal blade and
   process until smooth.
3. Spread the pesto-brie mixture over each crostini (the crisped baguette slices) and
   top with some pieces of the roasted red peppers.
4. Return the crostini to the cookie sheet and bake until hot, 7 to 10 minutes.

FAST: Can prepare the crostini through step 1 up to 2 weeks in advance and store at room
   temperature in an airtight container or plastic bags, or freeze for up to 6 months. Can
   assemble up to 1 day in advance and refrigerate covered with plastic wrap, or flash freeze
   (page 24) for up to 3 months. Do not thaw before heating.

FLASHY: Served hot on a platter and garnished with fresh basil leaves and/or any nontoxic
   flower or leaves.

FABULOUS: With muenster or teleme cheese instead of the brie.

GARLIC ROSEMARY CROSTINI

*A delicious and zero-cholesterol way to prepare garlic
bread. The seasoned oil is something you may
want to keep on hand in your refrigerator
as a cooking oil for
almost anything.*

Yield: about 4 to 6 servings

1 sourdough bread or baguette,
  thinly sliced
2 cloves garlic, minced, or to taste

1 cup extra virgin olive oil
Salt and fresh or dried rosemary to
  taste

1. Place the baguette slices on a cookie sheet and toast in a preheated 350°F oven for
   about 15 minutes until crisp.

2. Combine the garlic, oil, and seasonings in a food processor fitted with the metal blade or in a blender or a bowl. Taste and adjust the seasonings.
3. Line a cookie sheet with aluminum foil. Brush the slices of bread with the seasoned oil and place on the foil. Bake until crisp, about 15 minutes.

FAST: Can prepare oil up to 5 days in advance and refrigerate in a jar. Can prepare through step 3 up to 2 days in advance and refrigerate covered with foil or plastic wrap.

FLASHY: Served at room temperature or warm in a napkin-lined basket or on a platter.

FABULOUS: With any herb. With butter or a combination of butter and oil. Top with grated Parmesan, Romano, and/or mizithera cheese.

GARLIC OREGANO CROSTINI

Yield: about 8 to 12 servings

2 sourdough or French baguettes, thinly sliced
¼ pound (1 stick) unsalted butter
½ cup extra virgin olive oil
2 to 6 cloves garlic, minced, or to taste

¼ cup minced fresh parsley
¼ cup minced green onions (scallions), white and green parts
Salt and dried oregano to taste

1. Place the baguette slices on a cookie sheet and toast in a preheated 350°F oven until crisp, about 15 minutes.
2. Melt the butter with the olive oil in a skillet over low heat.
3. Add the remaining ingredients, except the bread, and cook, stirring, until the flavors develop to your liking, about 5 minutes.
4. Brush the mixture on the baguette slices. Place on an ungreased cookie sheet and bake until crisp, 10 to 15 minutes.

FAST: Can prepare the butter mixture up to 1 day in advance and refrigerate. Can completely assemble up to one day in advance, wrap in aluminum foil, and refrigerate. The butter mixture can be frozen for up to 3 months. Thaw at room temperature for about 4 hours. Can freeze assembled crostini and bake frozen or thawed. The time will not be noticeably affected.

FLASHY: Served at room temperature or warm in a napkin-lined basket or on a platter, garnished with green onion fans (page 9), fresh oregano, and/or any nontoxic flower.

FABULOUS: With any herb. Experiment and have fun! All sorts of grated cheeses used as toppings, including feta, Parmesan, Gruyère, or blue.

Green Onion Sourdough Melbas

East meets West on sourdough.

Yield: about 70 1½-inch squares

½ cup peanut oil

½ cup minced green onions
(scallions), white and green parts

¼ cup minced cilantro (fresh
coriander) or to taste

1 tablespoon Chinese sesame oil

¼ cup sesame seeds, toasted
(page 27)

Salt to taste

1 baguette, thinly sliced, or French
bread cut in 1½- to 2-inch
squares

1. Preheat the oven to 300°F.
2. Combine all the ingredients, except the bread, in a food processor fitted with the metal blade or in a bowl. Taste and adjust the seasonings.
3. Spread the mixture on the bread and place on an ungreased cookie sheet, bake until crisp, about 30 minutes.

FAST: Can fully prepare and store in airtight jar(s) or plastic bag(s) for up to 1 week, or freeze for up to 3 months. Rewarm in a preheated 350°F oven for about 5 minutes. If frozen add several minutes to the rewarming time.

FLASHY: Served at room temperature or warm in a napkin-lined basket or on a platter, garnished with cilantro and/or any nontoxic flower in the center.

FABULOUS: With ½ cup roasted garlic (page 26) substituted for the green onions.

Hot Cheese Fingers

Simple and zesty.

Yield: about 30 fingers

6 or more slices sourdough bread,
crusts removed and cut into long,
narrow fingers

⅔ cup grated Gruyère or extra sharp
cheddar

2 tablespoons freshly grated
Parmesan

1 teaspoon brandy

Several dashes hot pepper sauce

1 large egg

4 tablespoons (½ stick) unsalted
butter

1 teaspoon Dijon mustard or to taste

1 shallot, minced

Salt and ground white pepper to taste

1. Preheat the oven to 350°F.
2. Place the bread fingers on an ungreased cookie sheet and toast in the oven until crisp, about 15 minutes.
3. Combine the remaining ingredients in a food processor fitted with the metal blade or in a bowl using an electric mixer until smooth.
4. Test the seasonings by dipping a small piece of bread in the filling and baking it for 8 minutes.
5. Top the bread fingers with the mixture and bake until hot and the cheese melts, about 8 minutes.

FAST: Can assemble up to 2 days in advance and refrigerate covered. Can prepare the topping up to 2 days in advance and refrigerate, or freeze for up to 3 months. Thaw at room temperature for about 4 hours.

FLASHY: Served hot or at room temperature on a platter, garnished with fresh parsley and/or any nontoxic flower or leaves.

FABULOUS: With finely minced ham, cooked minced shrimp, minced marinated artichoke hearts, capers, olives, minced green onions, frozen chopped spinach (thawed and squeezed dry), or minced fresh herbs added to the cheese mixture. With rye, pumpernickel, or egg bread substituted for the sourdough.

GARLIC CROUTON ROUNDS

Serve alone or with any topping. As a rule of thumb,
crouton rounds are better suited than
crostini to more elegant events.

Yield: about 30 rounds

1 sourdough bread, sliced into 2-inch rounds, using a biscuit cutter or wineglass, or squares

4 cloves garlic or to taste
1 cup extra virgin olive oil
Salt to taste

1. Preheat the oven to 350°F.
2. Combine the olive oil and garlic in a food processor fitted with the metal blade or in a blender or a bowl. Salt to taste.
3. Brush the bread with garlic oil and place on an ungreased cookie sheet. Bake until crisp, about 15 minutes.

FAST: Can assemble up to 5 days in advance and store in airtight jar(s) or plastic bag(s), or freeze for up to 6 months. Can prepare the oil up to 1 month in advance and refrigerate.

FLASHY: Served at room temperature or hot in a napkin-lined basket, or on a platter.

FABULOUS: Made in smaller sizes and used as croutons in salads or soups. With any fresh or dried herb and/or grated Parmesan cheese. As a base for any kind of topping or instead of chips with dips.

Fast & Fabulous Focaccia

Focaccia is a marvelous pizza bread sans tomato, bathed in olive oil, herbs, and cheese. This version uses frozen bread dough, making it child's play.

Yield: 4 to 8 servings

1 pound frozen bread dough, thawed and at room temperature	*Freshly grated Parmesan*
Cornmeal for dusting	*Extra virgin olive oil*
Minced garlic	*Pesto, homemade (page 47) or purchased*

1. Preheat the oven to 450°F.
2. Roll the dough out on a board lightly dusted with cornmeal. Sprinkle with some of the garlic and cheeses. Fold the dough in half and roll out again. Repeat this process several times, adding the desired amounts of ingredients.
3. Grease a baking pan or iron skillet with olive oil.
4. Roll the dough out to a thickness of ½ inch and place on the prepared pan.
5. Drizzle liberally with the olive oil and top with the desired amount of ingredients. Bake until crisp, about 30 minutes. Cut and serve.

FAST: Can assemble up to 1 day in advance and refrigerate covered, or freeze for up to 3 months. Thaw or bake frozen, adding about 10 minutes to the cooking time.

FLASHY: Served hot on a platter and garnished with fresh basil leaves and/or any nontoxic flower or leaves.

FABULOUS: Experiment with different cheeses and herb combos—for instance, chopped green onions, dill, and crumbled feta cheese.

BAGEL CHIPS

You will love these and want to keep them on hand for nibbling. I discovered them yearsbefore they were packaged commercially, when I had a glut of bagels. These are much healthier than those available in stores.

Yield: about 18 dozen

2 cups extra virgin olive oil, grapeseed oil, or peanut oil

6 to 8 cloves garlic, smashed, or to taste

Minced dill, fresh or dried, to taste

Salt to taste

1 dozen bagels, cut into thin vertical slices

1. Preheat oven to 350°F.
2. Combine all the ingredients, except the bagels, in a food processor fitted with the metal blade or in a blender, and process until smooth. Taste and adjust the seasonings.
3. Place the bagel slices on an ungreased cookie sheet and brush with the flavored oil.
4. Bake until crisp, about 15 minutes. Watch carefully to prevent burning.

FAST: Can prepare up to 1 week in advance and store in airtight jars or plastic bags, or freeze for up to 6 months. It just takes 15 to 20 minutes to thaw. Reheat in a preheated 350°F oven for about 10 minutes.

FLASHY: Served at room temperature or warm in a napkin-lined basket, or on a platter.

FABULOUS: Seasoned with any herb, depending on what the chips are to be served with.

CHEDDARED BAGEL CHIPS

Yield: about 18 dozen

2 cups grated sharp cheddar

1 shallot, minced, or to taste

½ pound (2 sticks) unsalted butter

1 tablespoon Dijon mustard or to taste

Paprika and ground white pepper to taste

1 dozen bagels, sliced into thin vertical slices

1. Preheat the oven to 325°F.
2. Combine all the ingredients, except the bagels, in a food processor fitted with the metal blade or in a mixing bowl using an electric mixer until smooth.

3. Spread the mixture on the bagel slices, place on an ungreased cookie sheet, and bake until crisp, 20 to 30 minutes.

FAST: Can assemble up to 4 hours in advance and hold at room temperature, or flash freeze (page 24) for up to 3 months. Thaw or cook frozen adding about 10 minutes to the cooking time.

FLASHY: Served at room temperature or warm in a napkin-lined basket, or on a platter.

FABULOUS: With different kinds of cheeses substituted for the cheddar and herbs added.

TORTILLAS AND PITAS

HERITAGE NACHOS

After these, you will never eat the fast-food version.

Yield: about 96; 6 to 8 servings

12 corn tortillas or prepared tortilla
   chips
Canola or peanut oil
½ pound sharp cheddar cheese,
   grated

½ pound jack cheese, grated
1 bunch green onions (scallions),
   white and green parts, minced

1. To prepare your own tortilla chips, cut the tortillas into eighths and deep-fat fry until crisp in 6 to 8 inches of oil. Drain on paper towels. If you prefer not to fry them, brush them with oil and place on a cookie sheet in a preheated 350°F oven until crisp, 10 to 15 minutes.

2. At serving time, transfer the chips to an ovenproof platter and top with the cheeses and onions. Bake in a preheated 350°F oven until the cheese melts, 5 to 10 minutes.

FAST: Can prepare the chips up to 1 week in advance and store in airtight jars or plastic bags, or freeze for up to 3 months. No thawing necessary.

FLASHY: Served hot with Avocado Dipping Sauce (page 73) and/or Salsa Cruda (page 66).

FABULOUS: With minced cilantro and canned whole green chiles sprinkled over the cheese and onions in step 2. With any Mexican-style sauce for dipping (e.g., Mexican Cream Sauce, page 74, Guacamole, page 73).

PITA CHIPS

Yield: about 96 chips

1 package pita bread, each bread
  separated in half

½ cup olive oil

Optional seasonings

Minced garlic

Minced fresh basil

Minced cilantro (fresh coriander)

Minced fresh rosemary

Dried oregano

Minced fresh dill

Grated Parmesan

Salt

1. Preheat the oven to 350°F.
2. Combine the olive oil with the garlic and/or other optional seasonings of your choice in a food processor fitted with the metal blade or in a bowl until well mixed.
3. Brush each half with the seasoned oil.
4. Stack the pita bread and cut them into triangles using a Chinese cleaver or chef's knife.
5. Transfer the pita triangles to an ungreased cookie sheet.
6. Sprinkle them with Parmesan and/or salt if desired.
7. Bake until crisp, 10 to 20 minutes.

FAST: Can prepare up to 1 week in advance and store in airtight jar(s) or plastic bags, or freeze for up to 3 months.

FLASHY: Served in a napkin-lined basket.

FABULOUS: Prepared with any combination of your favorite oils.

Fast & Fabulous
Hors D'Oeuvres

Lamb Pita Triangles
with Cilantro

Rich Mediterranean flavors.

Yield: about 32 triangles

½ pound lean ground lamb

6 green onions (scallions), white and green parts, minced

¼ cup minced fresh parsley

1 tablespoon tomato paste

1 to 3 cloves garlic, minced

Zest of 1 lemon, finely grated

¼ cup minced cilantro (fresh coriander) or to taste

1 to 2 tablespoons Dijon mustard

1 to 2 tablespoons minced fresh mint or ½ teaspoon dried

Salt and ground white pepper to taste

2 pita breads, split open to form 4

1. Combine all the ingredients except the pita in a bowl. Mix well.
2. Fry 1 teaspoon of the mixture until cooked all the way through. Taste and adjust the seasonings.
3. Refrigerate for several hours to allow the flavors to develop.
4. Preheat the oven to 450°F or fire up the barbecue.
5. Top each pita with the lamb mixture and cut into triangles.
6. Place the triangles on an ungreased cookie sheet and bake or barbecue until the lamb is cooked to your liking, about 10 minutes. In the summer I like to use the barbecue as my oven and almost everything gets put on it. If you add some hickory chips, you'll get a marvelous smokey flavor.

FAST: Can prepare the meat mixture up to 2 days in advance and refrigerate, or flash freeze (page 24), assembled, for up to 1 month. Do not thaw before cooking.

FLASHY: Served hot on a platter and garnished with fresh mint leaves, cilantro, parsley, lemon wedges, and/or any nontoxic flower or leaves.

FABULOUS: With 4 to 8 ounces feta cheese added to the lamb mixture and/or rosemary, oregano, or thyme. With the mustard spread over the lamb mixture and topped with bread crumbs and grated Parmesan cheese before cooking.

BRIE AND WALNUT TRIANGLES

Yield: about 32 triangles

2 pita breads, separated in half and
  cut into triangles

8 ounces brie cheese, cut into 32
  small pieces

½ cup walnut halves, toasted
  (page 27)

1. Preheat the oven to 400°F.
2. Place the triangles on an ungreased cookie sheet and toast until crisp, about 15 minutes.
3. Top each triangle with a piece of brie.
4. Reduce the oven temperature to 350°F and bake until the cheese starts to melt, about 5 to 10 minutes.
5. Top each triangle with a walnut and serve.

FAST: Can prepare through step 3 up to 1 day in advance and refrigerate, or flash freeze (page 24) for up to 1 month. No thawing necessary.

FLASHY: Served hot on a platter, garnished with any nontoxic flower or leaves.

FABULOUS: With different combinations of nuts or seeds, roasted red peppers (page 26), herbs, or ham slices as toppings.

WARM GOAT CHEESE AND PESTO PITA TRIANGLES

Great for any summer entertaining.

Yield: about 32 triangles

2 pita breads, split open to form 4
¼ to ½ cup Walnut Pesto Sauce
  (page 42)

8 ounces chèvre (page 20), cut into
  32 small pieces

1. Preheat the oven to 400°F.
2. Stack the pita breads and slice them into triangles using a Chinese cleaver or chef's knife.
3. Place the triangles on an ungreased cookie sheet and toast in the oven until crisp, about 15 minutes.
4. Spread each triangle with the pesto and top with a piece of chèvre.
5. Reduce the oven temperature to 350°F and bake just until cheese starts to melt, about 5 to 10 minutes.

FAST: Can prepare through step 4 up to 4 hours in advance and hold at room temperature, or flash freeze (page 24) for up to 1 month. Thaw or cook frozen adding about 5 minutes to the baking time.

FLASHY: Served hot on a platter.

FABULOUS: With brie, jack, Camembert, or Saint André cheese substituted for the chèvre.

ARTICHOKE ALMOND PITA TRIANGLES

Another fabulous variation.

Yield: about 50 triangles

Two 6-ounce jars marinated artichoke
    hearts, drained and chopped
½ cup blanched almonds, slivered
¼ cup minced fresh parsley

2 cups grated jack cheese
3 pieces halved pita bread made into
    Pita Chips (page 274)
Grated Parmesan for topping

1. Preheat the oven to 450°F.
2. Combine the artichoke hearts, almonds, parsley, and cheese in a bowl.
3. Top the baked pita chips with the mixture and place on an ungreased cookie sheet. Sprinkle with the Parmesan and bake for about 10 minutes.

FAST: Can assemble up to 4 hours in advance and hold at room temperature, or flash freeze (page 24) for up to 1 month. Can prepare the filling up to 3 days in advance and refrigerate, or freeze for up to 3 months. Thaw or cook frozen, adding about 5 minutes to the baking time.

FLASHY: Served hot on a platter garnished with a whole raw or cooked artichoke in the center and/or with nontoxic flowers.

FABULOUS: The filling tossed into hot pasta or served as a sauce for chicken breasts.

ONION AND ZUCCHINI
PITA PIZZAS

You'll never consider using an English muffin after trying this idea.

Yield: about 32 pizzas

2 tablespoons extra virgin olive oil, plus extra for drizzling

2 large onions, sliced in half lengthwise and cut into thin slices

Minced garlic to taste

2 large zucchini, cut in half lengthwise and cut into thin slices

Salt and ground white pepper to taste

2 tablespoons minced fresh basil or ¼ to 1 teaspoon dried

2 pita breads, split open to form 4

¼ cup grated mozzarella

¼ cup freshly grated Parmesan

¼ cup walnuts, toasted (page 27) and finely chopped

1. Preheat the oven to 450°F.
2. Heat the oil in a skillet. Cook the onions and garlic, stirring until tender.
3. Add the zucchini and cook, stirring, until tender. Season with salt, pepper, and basil.
4. Place the pitas on an ungreased cookie sheet and drizzle with olive oil.
5. Top them with the cheeses and then the zucchini mixture. Sprinkle the nuts over the top.
6. Bake until golden and crisp, about 10 to 15 minutes. Cut into triangles and serve.

FAST: Can prepare the vegetable mixture up to 3 days in advance and refrigerate, or freeze for up to 3 months. Can assemble up to 2 hours in advance and leave at room temperature, or flash freeze (page 24) assembled up to 1 month. Don't thaw before cooking.

FLASHY: Served hot on a platter.

FABULOUS: With ½ cup crumbled feta instead of the mozzarella and Parmesan cheese and with toasted pine nuts instead of the walnuts.

Fast & Fabulous
Hors D'Oeuvres

CROUSTADES

*This is a quick, low-cholesterol alternative to rich pastry
tartlets.*

Yield: about 35 croustades

1 cup extra virgin olive oil

2 to 4 cloves garlic, minced

½ teaspoon salt or to taste

*1 loaf sourdough bread (must be
very fresh), sliced*

1. Preheat the oven to 350°F.
2. Combine the olive oil with the garlic and salt in a food processor fitted with the metal blade, or in a blender, or a bowl.
3. Using a cookie cutter or wineglass, cut the bread into 2½-inch rounds.
4. Roll the bread rounds out with a rolling pin.
5. Brush the mini-muffin tins with the garlic oil. Press the bread rounds into the cups and brush them with garlic oil.
6. Bake until completely crisp, about 15 minutes. Now they are ready to be filled.

FAST: Can store in airtight jar(s) or plastic bag(s) for up to 1 week, or freeze for up to 6 months. No thawing is needed.

FLASHY: Filled with anything.

FABULOUS: With fresh or dried herbs added to garlic oil. Made with any combination of peanut, canola, and/or olive oil.

HEARTS OF PALM, AVOCADO, AND SHRIMP CROUSTADES

Yield: about 60 croustades

6 to 8 canned hearts of palm, sliced into thin rounds

1 cup cooked baby shrimp (page 24), peeled

1 to 2 bunches watercress leaves

¼ to ½ cup minced fresh parsley

1 cup diced jicama (page 21)

4 to 8 green onions (scallions), white and green parts, minced

¼ cup capers, drained and rinsed

2 large, ripe avocados, peeled, pitted, and chopped

½ cup Tarragon Caper Vinaigrette (page 54) or to taste

About 60 Croustades (page 279)

1. Toss the first 8 ingredients together.
2. Add the vinaigrette and toss. Taste and adjust the seasonings.
3. Fill the croustades.

FAST: Can prepare through step 2 up to 1 day in advance and refrigerate. Can assemble up to 2 hours in advance.

FLASHY: Served chilled on a platter and garnished with johnny-jump-ups or any other nontoxic flower and/or fresh herb sprigs.

FABULOUS: With cooked lobster, tuna, crab, or chicken instead of the shrimp. With minced papaya and/or mango mixed in.

HEARTS OF PALM, FENNEL, AND SALMON CROUSTADES

Yield: about 60 croustades

¼ to ½ cup Lemon Mustard Vinaigrette (page 59)

6 to 8 canned hearts of palm, coarsely chopped

1 cup cooked salmon, fresh or canned

¼ to ½ cup sour cream

½ to 1 cup minced fennel bulb or celery

About 60 Croustades (page 279)

1. Combine the first 5 ingredients together in a bowl and mix well. Taste and adjust the seasonings.
2. Fill the croustades.

FAST: Can prepare the filling up to 3 days in advance and refrigerate. Can assemble up to 2 hours in advance.

FLASHY: Served chilled on a platter and garnished with fresh parsley, dill, and/or any nontoxic flower.

FABULOUS: With fresh cooked or canned tuna instead of the salmon. With two 6-ounce jars of marinated artichoke hearts instead of the hearts of palm. As a spread for crackers.

SHRIMP AND CHÈVRE CROUSTADES

Yield: about 60 croustades

About 60 Croustades (page 279)
About 1 cup Roasted Red Pepper
  Sauce (page 44)
About 60 small to medium-size raw
  shrimp, shelled and deveined

8 ounces chèvre (page 20) or feta
  cheese, crumbled
2 to 4 green onions (scallions),
  white and green parts, minced
½ cup packed fresh basil leaves,
  minced

1. Preheat the oven to 350°F. Place the croustades on several ungreased cookie sheets.
2. Fill each croustade with some of the pepper sauce. Add a raw shrimp or two to each croustade.
3. Combine the chèvre, green onions, and basil in a small bowl and top each croustade with some of the cheese mixture.
4. Bake until the shrimp is just cooked (opaque all the way through), about 15 minutes.

FAST: Can assemble up to 3 hours in advance, hold at room temperature, and bake just before serving. Can prepare filling up to 3 days in advance and refrigerate, or freeze for up to 3 months.

FLASHY: Served hot on a platter and garnished with fresh basil and/or any nontoxic flower or leaves.

FABULOUS: With brie, jack, Camembert, or Saint André cheese substituted for the chèvre.

FLORENTINE CROUSTADES

Next time you want to prepare creamed spinach,
remember this filling.

Yield: about 60 croustades

2 tablespoons unsalted butter

1 large onion, minced

2 cloves garlic, minced

6 ounces cultivated white
 mushrooms, minced and squeezed
 in a tea towel to remove all excess
 moisture

2 tablespoons all-purpose flour

¼ cup medium-dry sherry

¾ cup heavy cream

One 8-ounce package frozen chopped
 spinach, thawed and squeezed dry

Salt, ground white pepper, dried
 thyme, and freshly grated nutmeg
 to taste

About 60 Croustades (page 279)

½ to 1 cup grated Gruyère

1. Preheat the oven to 350°F.
2. Melt the butter in a saucepan over medium heat. When it begins to foam, cook the onion, garlic, and mushrooms until the onions are tender; do not brown.
3. Stir in the flour and cook 1 minute, without browning.
4. Mix in the sherry and cook for a minute more.
5. Remove the pan from the burner and stir in the cream. Return to the burner and add the spinach and seasonings. Cook, stirring, until flavors develop and the mixture thickens.
6. Fill the croustades, place them on an ungreased cookie sheet, and top with the Gruyère. Bake until hot and bubbly, about 10 to 15 minutes.

FAST: Can assemble up to 3 hours in advance, hold at room temperature, and bake just before serving. Can prepare filling up to 3 days in advance and refrigerate, or freeze for up to 3 months.

FLASHY: Served hot on a platter and garnished with any nontoxic flower or leaves, a whole raw onion, apple, and/or cabbage leaves.

FABULOUS: With ½ cup minced ham or prosciutto added to the filling. With fresh blanched or frozen broccoli, chard, or asparagus substituted for the spinach.

CARROT CROUSTADES

Nirvana for beta carotene seekers!

Yield: about 60 croustades

3 tablespoons unsalted butter

1 tablespoon minced shallots

1 pound carrots, blanched (page 23) for about 10 minutes until tender, peeled, and pureed

1 tablespoon all-purpose flour

2 tablespoons brandy

2 tablespoons cream sherry

2 tablespoons sesame seeds, toasted (page 27), or to taste

2 tablespoons minced fresh parsley

Dried thyme to taste

Salt, ground white pepper, and freshly grated nutmeg to taste

1 cup heavy cream

About 60 Croustades (page 279)

¼ cup freshly grated Parmesan

1. Preheat the oven to 350°F.
2. Melt the butter in a skillet over medium heat. When it begins to foam, cook the shallots, stirring, until tender; do not brown.
3. Add the pureed carrots and stir in the flour.
4. Stir in the brandy, sherry, sesame seeds, parsley, thyme, and seasonings. Cook, stirring, 3 to 5 minutes.
5. Add the cream and cook, stirring frequently, until the mixture thickens and the flavors develop, about 10 minutes. Taste and adjust the seasonings.
6. Fill the croustades, place them on an ungreased cookie sheet, sprinkle with the Parmesan, and bake until hot, about 10 to 15 minutes.

FAST: Can assemble up to 3 hours in advance, leave at room temperature, and bake just before serving. Can prepare the filling up to 3 days in advance and refrigerate, or freeze for up to 3 months.

FLASHY: Served hot on a platter and garnished with any nontoxic flower or leaves, a whole raw onion, apple, and/or cabbage leaves.

FABULOUS: With fresh or dried rosemary, marjoram, or cilantro instead of the thyme.

SPINACH AND HAM CROUSTADES

Yield: about 60 croustades

2 tablespoons unsalted butter

2 cloves garlic, minced

½ cup minced onion

2 tablespoons all-purpose flour

½ cup heavy cream

1 teaspoon Dijon mustard

3 tablespoons brandy

One 10-ounce package frozen spinach,
   thawed, squeezed dry, and pureed

¼ to ½ cup chopped ham

¼ cup minced fresh parsley

Ground white pepper and freshly
   grated nutmeg to taste

¼ cup grated jack cheese

About 60 Croustades (page 279)

¼ cup grated Parmesan

1. Preheat the broiler. Melt the butter in a saucepan over medium heat. When it begins to foam, add the garlic and onions and cook, stirring, until tender; do not brown.
2. Whisk in the flour. Cook for 1 minute without browning.
3. Whisk in the cream, mustard, and brandy and cook until thickened.
4. Stir in the remaining ingredients, except the croustades and Parmesan, and cook, stirring, until the cheese melts and the flavors develop. Taste and adjust the seasonings.
5. Fill the croustades, place them on an ungreased cookie sheet, and top with the Parmesan. Place under the hot broiler for a few minutes until the cheese melts and they are golden.

FAST: Can assemble up to 3 hours in advance, leave at room temperature, and bake at 350°F for 10 to 15 minutes; serve immediately. Can prepare the filling up to 3 days in advance and refrigerate, or freeze for up to 3 months.

FLASHY: Served hot on a platter and garnished with any nontoxic flower or leaves, a whole raw onion, apple, and/or cabbage leaves.

FABULOUS: With the same amount of frozen chard substituted for the spinach and with prosciutto substituted for the ham.

LEEK CROUSTADES

Yield: about 60 croustades

3 tablespoons unsalted butter

4 medium-size leeks, trimmed, halved
lengthwise, rinsed, and cut
crosswise into thin pieces

1 tablespoon all-purpose flour

1 cup heavy cream

2 tablespoons medium-dry sherry

2 tablespoons minced fresh parsley

Salt, ground white pepper, fresh
lemon juice, and freshly grated
nutmeg to taste

About 60 Croustades (page 279)

1/4 cup grated muenster, jack, or
Gruyère

1. Preheat the broiler. Melt the butter in a skillet over medium heat. When it begins to foam, add the leeks and cook, stirring, until tender.
2. Stir in the flour; blend well and cook for 1 minute.
3. Add the cream and sherry and simmer while stirring until the cream is reduced by about one third, about 10 to 15 minutes.
4. Add the parsley and seasonings; taste and adjust them.
5. Fill the croustades, place on an ungreased cookie sheet, and top with the cheese. Place under the broiler until the cheese melts, about 5 minutes.

FAST: Can assemble up to 3 hours in advance, leave at room temperature, and bake at 350°F for 10 to 15 minutes; serve immediately. Can prepare the filling up to 3 days in advance and refrigerate, or freeze up to 3 months.

FLASHY: Served hot on a platter and garnished with a leek blossom and/or any nontoxic flower or leaves.

FABULOUS: With blanched broccoli or cauliflower, or sautéed onions instead of the leeks.

CAVIAR CROUSTADES

*I'm convinced this is too good and too easy
to be legal!*

Yield: about 60 croustades

About 60 Croustades (page 279)

1 pound Saint André, at room
temperature, rind removed, and
cut into small pieces

3½ ounces black or golden caviar

2 to 3 large hard-boiled (page 24)
eggs, mashed

1/4 cup chives, minced

Zest of 2 to 3 lemons, finely grated

1. Fill the croustades with the Saint André. Top with caviar, a sprinkling of mashed egg and/or chives, and a pinch of lemon zest.

FAST: Can prepare up to 1 day in advance and refrigerate.

FLASHY: Served on a bed of fried Chinese cellophane noodles, or finely shredded red cabbage.

FABULOUS: With chopped toasted (page 27) almonds or pine nuts, or smoked trout substituted for the caviar.

ASPARAGUS AND SHIITAKE MUSHROOM CROUSTADES

Yield: about 60 croustades

3 tablespoons unsalted butter	1 pound asparagus, trimmed,
2 tablespoons minced fresh parsley	minced, and blanched (page 23)
1 tablespoon minced shallots	about 3 minutes
1 ounce dried shiitake mushrooms,	Grated muenster, teleme, jack, or
rehydrated (page 18), stemmed,	Gruyère to taste
and minced	Salt, ground white pepper, fresh
1 tablespoon all-purpose flour	lemon juice, dried thyme, and
¼ cup Madeira	freshly grated nutmeg to taste
1 cup heavy cream	About 60 croustades (page 279)

1. Preheat the broiler. Melt the butter in a skillet over medium heat. When it begins to foam, add the parsley, shallots, and mushrooms and cook until tender. Stir in the flour and cook, stirring, for a minute.
2. Stir in the Madeira and cream and simmer until the cream reduces and the sauce thickens nicely.
3. Stir in the asparagus, cheese, and seasonings and cook until the cheese melts.
4. Fill the croustades, place on an ungreased cookie sheet, and top with more cheese. Place under the broiler until the cheese melts, about 5 minutes.

FAST: Can assemble up to 3 hours in advance, leave at room temperature, and bake in a 350°F oven for 10 to 15 minutes; serve immediately. Can prepare the filling up to 3 days in advance and refrigerate, or freeze for up to 3 months.

FLASHY: Served hot on a platter and garnished with fresh parsley and/or any nontoxic flower or leaves.

FABULOUS: With two 15-ounce cans of hearts of palm (drained and minced) instead of the asparagus.

TOMATO CHEESE CROUSTADES

Yield: about 30 croustades

1 large, ripe tomato, peeled, seeded, and chopped, or 2 tablespoons tomato paste

½ cup sun-dried tomatoes, softened (page 22) and minced

1 cup grated teleme cheese or to taste, plus extra for topping

2 tablespoons freshly grated Parmesan

½ cup packed fresh basil, minced, or 1 to 2 tablespoons dried

1 to 2 cloves garlic, minced

¼ cup minced fresh parsley or to taste

2 tablespoons capers, drained and rinsed

¼ cup sour cream

Salt, ground white pepper, and freshly grated nutmeg to taste

Extra virgin olive oil for drizzling

About 60 Croustades (page 279)

1. Preheat the oven to 400°F.
2. Combine all the ingredients, except the olive oil and croustades, in a food processor fitted with the metal blade, or in a bowl by hand until well mixed. Taste and adjust the seasonings.
3. Fill the croustades, and place on an ungreased cookie sheet; top with more grated cheese and drizzle olive oil over the top of each croustade.
4. Bake until hot and bubbly, 10 to 15 minutes.

FAST: Can assemble up to 3 hours in advance, leave at room temperature, and bake just before serving. Can prepare the filling up to 3 days in advance and refrigerate, or freeze for up to 3 months.

FLASHY: Served hot on a platter and garnished with fresh basil leaves and/or a whole raw tomato.

FABULOUS: Use the fillings in omelets, on Beaten Biscuits (page 296), or to stuff raw mushroom caps. With fresh or dried rosemary instead of the basil. With chopped calamata olives and/or marinated artichoke hearts added.

Piperade Croustades

A celebration of all the fall harvest.

Yield: about 60 croustades

¼ cup extra virgin olive oil

2 large onions, minced

3 to 5 cloves garlic, minced

2 to 4 large red or yellow bell
   peppers, roasted, peeled, seeded,
   and chopped (page 26)

½ pound minced ham

2 large, ripe tomatoes, peeled,
   seeded, and chopped

½ to 1 cup minced fresh parsley

½ bay leaf

Fresh or dried thyme and basil to
   taste

Salt and ground white pepper to taste

1 cup grated jack cheese, plus extra
   for topping

About 60 Croustades (page 279)

1. Preheat the broiler. Heat the oil in a skillet over medium-low heat. Cook the onions and garlic, stirring, until tender.
2. Add the peppers and ham and cook, stirring, 3 to 5 minutes.
3. Stir in the tomatoes, parsley, bay leaf, and seasonings. Cook until the flavors develop and the liquid cooks away, about 15 to 20 minutes. Discard the bay leaf.
4. Stir in the cheese and cook over low heat until it melts.
5. Fill the croustades, place on an ungreased cookie sheet, and top with more cheese. Place under the broiler until the cheese melts, about 5 minutes.

FAST: Can assemble up to 3 hours in advance, leave at room temperature, and bake in a 350°F oven until hot, 10 to 15 minutes; serve immediately. Can prepare the filling up to 4 days in advance and refrigerate, or freeze up to 3 months.

FLASHY: Served hot on a platter and garnished with a whole red or yellow bell pepper, fresh basil, and/or thyme.

FABULOUS: Over pasta or couscous as an entree, or as a vegetable dish.

Italian Sausage Croustades

Yield: about 60 croustades

1 pound sweet or hot Italian
  sausages, casings removed
2 large onions, minced
4 cloves garlic, minced
2 cups ricotta cheese
½ cup minced fresh parsley
¼ cup freshly grated Parmesan or to
  taste

Salt, ground white pepper, and freshly
  grated nutmeg to taste
About 60 Croustades (page 279)
Muenster cheese, cut into small cubes
  to fit in bottom of each croustade
About 60 pitted black olives, whole or
  halved

1. Preheat the oven to 350°F.
2. Cook the sausages, breaking them up with a fork, in a skillet over medium-high heat until the meat is no longer pink. Remove the sausage meat with a slotted spoon and place it on a plate lined with several layers of paper towels to blot up the excess fat. Pour off all but 2 tablespoons of the fat.
3. Add the onions and garlic. Transfer the mixture and the sausage meat to a food processor fitted with the metal blade.
4. Add the ricotta, parsley, Parmesan, and seasonings to the food processor, and process until just combined. Taste and adjust the seasonings.
5. Place the croustades on an ungreased cookie sheet and put a piece of muenster cheese in each croustade and then fill two-thirds full with the filling. Top with an olive and bake until hot, about 10 minutes.

FAST: Can assemble up to 3 hours in advance, refrigerate, and bake just before serving. Can prepare the filling up to 3 days in advance and refrigerate, or freeze for up to 3 months.

FLASHY: Served hot on a platter and garnished with fresh parsley and/or heads of raw or roasted garlic (page 26).

FABULOUS: With turkey sausage to reduce the amount of fat.

SEAFOOD CROUSTADES

World class!

Yield: about 30 croustades

3 ounces cooked baby shrimp (page 24), peeled

3 ounces crabmeat, picked over for cartilage

1 cup mayonnaise, homemade (page 13) or purchased

½ cup freshly grated Parmesan

⅓ cup grated Gruyère

⅓ cup minced green onions (scallions), white and green parts

½ teaspoon Worcestershire sauce or to taste

1 teaspoon Dijon mustard

⅓ cup minced fresh parsley

2 to 4 tablespoons minced fresh dill

½ cup coarsely chopped jicama (page 21) or water chestnuts

2 to 4 tablespoons capers, drained and rinsed

Salt, ground white pepper, and hot pepper sauce to taste

About 30 Croustades (page 279)

1. Preheat the oven to 350°F.
2. Combine all the ingredients, except the croustades, in a bowl. Taste and adjust the seasonings.
3. Fill each croustade, place them on an ungreased cookie sheet, and bake until hot, 10 to 15 minutes.

FAST: Can prepare the filling up to 1 day in advance and refrigerate. Can fill the croustades up to 2 hours in advance and hold at room temperature; bake right before serving.

FLASHY: Served hot on a platter and garnished with fresh dill and/or any nontoxic flower or leaves.

FABULOUS: Over cooked pasta, served hot or cold. As a cold filling for cooked pasta shells, cherry tomatoes, or raw mushroom caps or on Beaten Biscuits (page 296). Used as a hot filling for Flo Braker's Magic Puff Pastry (page 309), Tartlets (page 314), or Phyllo Cups (page 294).

Fast & Fabulous
Hors D'Oeuvres

Muenstered Croustades

*Muenster is a very neglected cheese deserving
more attention.*

Yield: about 30 croustades

1 tablespoon unsalted butter

½ cup minced green onions
(scallions), white and green parts

2 cloves garlic, minced

1 tablespoon all-purpose flour

2 tablespoons dry vermouth

½ cup heavy cream

2 cups cut up or grated muenster
cheese

¼ cup minced fresh parsley

½ cup blanched almonds, toasted
(page 27) and chopped

6 to 12 slices bacon, cooked until
crisp, drained on paper towels,
and crumbled

Dash of ground cayenne pepper

Salt and ground white pepper to taste

About 30 Croustades (page 279)

1. Preheat the oven to 350°F.
2. Heat the butter in a saucepan over medium-low heat. When it begins to foam, cook
   the green onions and garlic until tender.
3. Stir in the flour and cook for a minute. Remove the saucepan from the burner and
   stir in the wine and cream.
4. Return to the burner and cook until thickened while stirring over medium heat.
5. Stir in the cheese, parsley, almonds, and bacon. Taste and adjust the seasonings.
6. Fill the croustades, place on an ungreased cookie sheet, and bake until they are hot,
   10 to 15 minutes.

FAST: Can assemble up to 3 hours in advance, leave at room temperature, and bake just
before serving. Can prepare the filling up to 3 days in advance and refrigerate, or freeze
for up to 3 months.

FLASHY: Served hot on a platter and garnished with fresh parsley and/or any nontoxic
flower or leaves.

FABULOUS: The filling tossed into freshly cooked pasta as an entree or as a filling for
crepes, to top Beaten Biscuits (page 296), or in raw mushroom caps. Seasoned with minced
fresh basil.

PHYLLO PIZZA

Designed for picnics and relaxed summer entertaining.

Yield: 4 to 6 servings

½ cup extra virgin olive oil	Salt, ground white pepper, and fresh
6 large onions, thinly sliced	or dried oregano and basil to
3 teaspoons sugar	taste
3 cloves garlic, minced	2 teaspoons tomato paste
½ cup minced fresh parsley	8 sheets of phyllo (page 22)
½ cup dry vermouth	1½ to 2 cups crumbled feta cheese
8 ripe pear-shaped tomatoes,	16 to 24 pitted calamata olives
peeled, seeded, and chopped	

1. Preheat the oven to 375°F.
2. Heat ¼ cup of the oil in a skillet over low heat. Cook the onions, stirring, until tender, 15 minutes. Add 2 teaspoons of the sugar, the garlic, parsley, and vermouth and cook 30 minutes more, until the onions are golden and glazed. Stir frequently.
3. At the same time, heat 2 tablespoons of the oil in another skillet over medium heat. Add the tomatoes, seasonings, the remaining sugar, and the tomato paste. Taste and adjust the seasonings, then cook, stirring, until the liquid is evaporated.
4. Combine the two mixtures in a mixing bowl, or in one of the skillets.
5. Oil a 10- by 16-inch cookie sheet and top with the phyllo, brushing each sheet with the remaining oil before topping with the next. Tuck the edges under neatly.
6. Cover evenly with the tomato-onion mixture, cheese, and olives.
7. Bake until it is hot and the edges are golden, about 20 to 25 minutes.

FAST: Can assemble up to 1 day in advance and refrigerate, or freeze for up to 3 months. Bake right before serving.

FLASHY: Cut into little squares. Served hot or at room temperature on a platter and garnished with fresh basil, oregano, parsley, and/or any nontoxic flower or leaves.

FABULOUS: For an Italian variation, brush the phyllo with garlic butter and top with ricotta cheese, a combination of grated whole milk mozzarella, Parmesan, and chèvre cheeses, roasted red peppers (page 26), and sautéed eggplant. Use the topping as a filling for Won Ton Cups (page 246), Croustades (page 279), Pita Chips (page 274), and/or raw mushroom caps.

GREEK CHEESE TRIANGLES

An elegant and rich classic!

Yield: about 48 triangles

½ pound ricotta cheese

½ pound jack, teleme, or muenster cheese, grated

½ pound feta cheese, crumbled

1 large egg

2 tablespoons chopped fresh dill or to taste

1 to 2 shallots, minced, or to taste

Ground white pepper to taste

½ pound phyllo pastry sheets (page 22), cut into long strips 2 inches wide

6 tablespoons sesame seeds, toasted (page 27)

½ pound (2 sticks) unsalted butter, melted

1. Preheat the oven to 425°F.
2. Combine everything in a food processor fitted with the metal blade, except the phyllo, sesame seeds, and butter, or in a bowl and mix until smooth. Taste and adjust the seasonings.
3. Brush 1 strip of phyllo dough at a time with the melted butter. Cover the remaining phyllo with waxed paper and a slightly dampened towel until used.
4. Place 1 teaspoon of the filling at one end of each strip and fold over and over into a small triangle. While folding, make sure that the bottom edge is parallel with the alternate edge. Repeat until all the filling is used. Place the triangles on a buttered cookie sheet.
5. Brush each triangle with more melted butter, sprinkle with sesame seeds, and bake until golden, 10 to 15 minutes.

FAST: Can prepare up to 1 day in advance and refrigerate, or freeze for up to 3 months.

FLASHY: Served hot on a platter and garnished with fresh dill and/or any nontoxic flower or leaves.

FABULOUS: With chopped seafood, ham, artichoke hearts, cooked chicken, spinach, bok choy, or prosciutto added to the cheese mixture. With chèvre instead of feta cheese.

PHYLLO CUPS

*Here's a faster method for using phyllo, rather than
making the traditional triangles.*

Yield: about **48** cups

½ pound (2 sticks) unsalted butter,
  melted

1 pound phyllo pastry sheets (page
  22), cut into 3- to 4-inch squares

1. Preheat the oven to 425°F.
2. Brush mini-muffin tin cups with the butter.
3. Layer the squares in the muffin cups, brushing each with melted butter, until you
   have 4 layers in each cup.
4. Bake until the cups get crisp, for about 7 to 10 minutes.

FAST: Can prepare up to 1 week in advance and store in airtight jar(s) or plastic bag(s), or
freeze for up to 3 months.

FLASHY: Served hot or at room temperature on a platter.

FABULOUS: Filled with Onion and Ham Tartlet Filling (page 119), Greek Cheese Triangles filling (page 293), Crab and Artichoke Stuffed Mushrooms filling (page 240), Spring
Mornay filling (page 128), or the filling of your choice.

CHICKEN AND PROSCIUTTO PHYLLO CUPS

Yield: about **48** cups

¼ grated Romano

2 cups ricotta cheese

½ to 1 cup cubed or grated jack,
  muenster, teleme, or mozzarella
  cheese

2 large eggs

Salt, ground white pepper, and freshly
  grated nutmeg to taste

2 tablespoons unsalted butter, melted

2 tablespoons extra virgin olive oil

1 large onion, minced

2 to 4 cloves garlic, minced

2 large chicken breast halves,
  skinned, boned, and cut up

½ cup minced fresh parsley

One 10-ounce package frozen chopped
  spinach, thawed and squeezed dry

8 thin slices prosciutto, chopped

About 48 Phyllo Cups (page 294)

1. Preheat the oven to 425°F.
2. Combine the cheeses and eggs in a food processor fitted with the metal blade, season with salt, pepper, and nutmeg, and mix until smooth.
3. Heat the butter and olive oil in a saucepan over low heat. When the butter is melted, cook the onion and garlic, stirring, until tender, 15 to 20 minutes.
4. Add the chicken and cook, stirring, just until no longer pink all the way through.
5. Add the chicken mixture, along with the parsley, spinach, and prosciutto to the food processor. Process briefly, taking care not to destroy the texture.
6. Fill the phyllo cups with the mixture and bake until hot, 10 minutes.

FAST: Can prepare the filling up to 2 days in advance, and refrigerate, or freeze for up to 3 months. Can assemble the phyllo cups up to 1 day in advance and refrigerate, or flash freeze (page 24) for up to 3 months. To cook frozen, add 5 minutes to the cooking time.

FLASHY: Served hot on a platter and garnished with fresh parsley, flowering kale, and/or clusters of grapes.

FABULOUS: With ½ pound ground veal cooked just as the chicken breast is.

PASTRIES

CAVIAR PASTRIES

So elegant and so easy!

Yield: 60 to 80 pastries

1 package frozen puff pastry, thawed
1 pound Saint André cheese with the rind removed, at room temperature
6 ounces caviar

4 to 6 green onions (scallions), minced, white and green parts as needed
Zest from 2 to 4 lemons, finely grated

1. Preheat the oven to 400°F.
2. Roll out each sheet of pastry on a lightly floured board to 1½ times its original size.
3. Cut into 2-inch circles with a cookie cutter or wineglass.
4. Place the circles on an ungreased cookie sheet and pierce with a fork. Bake until crisp and golden, 15 to 20 minutes.
5. Deflate the pastry by piercing it with the tines of a fork. Top each cooled pastry circle with a generous amount of Saint André, a dollop of caviar, and a sprinkling of green onions and lemon zest. Serve at room temperature.

FAST: Can prepare through step 4 up to 2 days in advance and store in plastic bag(s) or airtight glass jar(s), or freeze for up to 3 months.

FLASHY: Served at room temperature or chilled on a platter.

CHEESE TWISTS

A touch of understated elegance.

Yield: about 70 twists

1 package frozen puff pastry, thawed	2 shallots, minced
1 large egg white, lightly beaten	½ cup finely grated Gruyère
Salt and ground white pepper to taste	½ cup finely grated sharp cheddar
¼ teaspoon sweet Hungarian paprika	¼ cup freshly grated Parmesan

1. Preheat the oven to 400°F.
2. Roll the pastry dough out on a lightly floured board into 2 rectangles ¼ inch thick.
3. Brush with the egg white and sprinkle with the salt, pepper, paprika, shallots, and cheeses. Press this lightly into the pastry.
4. Cut into 1-inch strips (or thinner for thinner twists), twist, and place on greased cookie sheets. Bake until golden, 15 minutes.

FAST: Can prepare up to 1 week in advance and refrigerate, or flash freeze (page 24) for up to 1 month. Thaw or reheat frozen in a 400°F oven for about 5 to 8 minutes before serving.

FLASHY: Served warm or at room temperature on a platter, or in a napkin-lined basket.

FABULOUS: Top the pastry with sesame seeds and/or minced green onions, along with the cheeses, or brush with melted butter and roll in chopped walnuts before baking. Use your favorite cheese combos.

BEATEN BISCUITS

*Flaky baby biscuits that make a wonderful base
for countless mixtures.*

Yield: about 70 biscuits

2 cups all-purpose unbleached flour	¼ pound (1 stick) unsalted butter,
1 teaspoon salt	frozen and cut into small pieces
1 to 2 tablespoons minced shallots	½ cup ice water
Ground white pepper to taste	

1. Preheat the oven to 350°F and place the rack in the middle of the oven.
2. Combine the flour, salt, shallots, and pepper in a food processor fitted with the metal blade. Turn the machine on and off twice.
3. Add the butter and process until the mixture is the consistency of cornmeal.
4. While the machine is running, pour the ice water through the feed tube in a slow, steady stream. Process until the mixture forms a ball and continue for an extra 2 minutes.
5. Remove the dough and roll it out into a 1⅛-inch-thick rectangle on a lightly floured surface.
6. Fold the dough in half to make two layers. Cut through both layers with a 1½-inch round cutter or a wineglass.
7. Bake the biscuits on an ungreased cookie sheet until golden, 25 to 30 minutes. Remove from the oven and split in half immediately. If the centers are soft, return them to the oven for 3 to 4 minutes to crisp.

FAST: Can prepare up to 1 week in advance and store in airtight jar(s) or plastic bag(s), or freeze for up to 6 months.

FLASHY: Served hot, cold, or at room temperature on a platter topped with your favorite filling.

FABULOUS: With 6 tablespoons of crumbled crisp bacon, minced fresh parsley, dill, or basil, poppy seeds, sesame seeds, fried minced onions, or minced green onions, added to the dough.

POLISH SAUSAGE IN PUFF PASTRY

A great recipe when you want some gusto! This hors d'oeuvre is a wonderful brunch, lunch, or cocktail party choice.

Yield: Twelve ½-inch pieces

1 sheet frozen puff pastry, thawed
1 to 2 tablespoons coarse-grained mustard
2 green onions (scallions), white and green parts, minced

1 pound ready-cooked Polish sausage
12 small pieces caraway cheese, the diameter of the sausage and about ¼ inch thick

1. Preheat the oven to 425°F.
2. Roll the puff pastry out to a thickness of ¼ inch on a lightly floured board. Brush the top with mustard.
3. Sprinkle the green onions over the top and then place the sausage at the edge. Roll the pastry around the sausage and seal the edge, using a fork.

4. Cut the wrapped sausage into 12 slices and place on an ungreased cookie sheet. If the sausage is loose, crimp the pastry securely around it. Top each slice with more mustard and a piece of cheese.
5. Bake until the pastry is golden and puffed, 5 to 10 minutes.

FAST: Can prepare through step 4 up to 1 day in advance and refrigerate, or flash freeze (page 24) for up to 1 month. Don't thaw before baking.

FLASHY: Served hot on a platter and garnished with flowering kale, fresh parsley, and/or any nontoxic flower or leaves.

FABULOUS: With different kinds of sausages, mustards, and cheeses.

HAM AND CHEESE PASTRIES

*An elegant way to start a meal; keep a supply
in your freezer.*

Yield: about 70 pastries

*1 recipe Cream Cheese Pastry (page
301), or 2 sheets frozen puff
pastry, thawed*
2 to 4 tablespoons Dijon mustard
*6 to 8 green onions (scallions),
green and white parts, minced*

*½ pound ham or prosciutto, thinly
sliced*
*½ pound cheese slices (muenster,
jack, cheddar, Gouda, Edam, Port
Salut, or Gruyère)*

1. Preheat the oven to 400°F.
2. Roll out the pastry to a thickness of ¼ inch on a lightly floured board, then cut it into small squares about 1½ to 2 inches.
3. Brush the pastry squares with mustard, sprinkle with some green onions, and top with a piece of ham and cheese. Place the pastries on a greased cookie sheet.
4. Bake until the pastry is golden, 10 to 20 minutes.

FAST: Can assemble up to 1 day in advance, refrigerate, and bake before serving, or flash freeze (page 24) for up to 3 months. Thaw or cook frozen, adding about 5 minutes to the baking time.

FLASHY: Served hot on a platter and garnished with fresh parsley, flowering kale, savoy cabbage, and/or any nontoxic flower or leaves.

FABULOUS: With cooked eggplant or sausage substituted for the ham.

Fast & Fabulous
Hors D'Oeuvres

SOUTHWESTERN TORTILLA CUPS

Yield: about 70 tortilla cups

½ pound lean ground beef

2 cloves garlic, minced

½ cup minced green onions, white
and green parts

¼ to ½ teaspoon chili powder

¼ to ½ teaspoon ground cumin

¼ to ½ teaspoon oregano

Salt and hot pepper sauce to taste

½ cup sour cream

1 cup grated sharp cheddar

1 bunch cilantro (fresh coriander),
stemmed and minced

1 cup refried beans, homemade
(page 14) or canned

One 7-ounce can whole green chiles,
seeded, deveined, and chopped
(page 20)

½ cup pitted black olives, drained
and chopped

¾ cup tortilla chips, ground up in
the food processor

Tortilla Cups (recipe follows)

1. Preheat the oven to 350°F. Place the ground beef in a skillet with the garlic and green onions and cook over medium-high heat, breaking up the meat with a wooden spoon or fork. Season to taste while cooking.
2. When all the pink is gone, pour off all the excess fat.
3. Stir in the remaining ingredients, except the tortilla cups.
4. Fill the tortilla cups with the mixture and place on a greased baking sheet. Bake until hot, 10 to 15 minutes.

FAST: Can prepare through step 3 up to 2 days in advance and refrigerate, or freeze for up to 6 months. Can completely assemble and flash freeze (page 24) for up to 6 months. Thaw or bake frozen, adding about 10 minutes to the baking time.

FLASHY: Served on a platter and garnished with whole raw chiles, cilantro sprigs, a head of garlic, and/or any nontoxic flower or leaves.

FABULOUS: As a filling for burritos, Heritage Nachos (page 273), Croustades (page 279), omelets, and/or Won Ton Cups (page 246). With chopped hominy instead of refried beans.

TORTILLA CUPS

*Little tartlets made out of masa, adapted from
a Yucatán recipe.*

Yield: about 70 cups

6 cups dehydrated masa flour (page
21)

1 teaspoon salt

⅔ cup unsalted butter, cut into small
pieces

3 cups cold water

Olive oil for brushing

1. Preheat the oven to 375°F.
2. Combine the masa, salt, and butter in a food processor fitted with the metal blade or in a bowl until fine crumbs form.
3. While the machine is running, add the water through the feed tube and process until the dough is evenly moistened. (If necessary, prepare in 2 batches in your food processor.)
4. Shape the dough into about 1-inch balls, and cover with plastic wrap to prevent them from drying out.
5. Press the dough into oiled mini-muffin tin cups, using your fingers or a spoon to evenly cover the bottom and sides.
6. Brush liberally with oil and bake until crisp, about 20 minutes. Remove them from the muffin tin.

FAST: Can prepare up to 1 day in advance and refrigerate, or freeze for up to 6 months. To reheat before serving, bake on a greased cookie sheet in a preheated 350°F oven until hot, about 10 minutes.

FLASHY: Served empty with a selection of fillings, like: Pumpkin Seed Chile Salsa (page 65), browned and seasoned ground pork with Mexican Tomato Sauce (page 132), Gaucamole (page 73), Yucatán Sauce (page 136) with grated jack cheese, Frijoles Caliente (page 149), Avocado Dipping Sauce (page 73), Caper Sauce (page 30) with cold cooked seafood, Cold Papaya Cream Sauce (page 38) with cold cooked pork or seafood, and Chile Cheese Fondue (page 156). Served on a platter and garnished with whole raw chiles, cilantro sprigs, a head of garlic, and/or any nontoxic flower or leaves.

FABULOUS: Filled with the Southwestern Tortilla Cups filling (page 299).

Pirozhki

*A delicate but satisfying meat-filled crescent-shaped
pastry, perfect for winter parties.
You will love working with
this pastry!*

Yield: about 40 pirozhki

Cream cheese pastry

One 8-ounce package cream cheese,
    cut into quarters
¼ pound (1 stick) unsalted butter,
    frozen and cut into small pieces
Zest of 1 lemon, finely grated

1 teaspoon salt
Dash of ground white pepper
1 shallot, cut in half
¼ cup heavy cream
2½ cups all-purpose flour

Filling

3 tablespoons unsalted butter
2 large onions, minced
2 cloves garlic, minced
1 pound lean ground pork
½ cup cooked bulgur (page 20)
2 to 4 tablespoons capers, drained
    and rinsed
1 teaspoon Worcestershire sauce

¼ cup sour cream
3 to 4 tablespoons minced fresh dill
    or to taste
2 large eggs, hard-boiled (page 24)
    and chopped
½ cup minced fresh parsley
½ teaspoon salt or to taste
Ground white or black pepper to taste

Egg wash

1 egg

1 teaspoon water

1. Combine the cream cheese, butter, zest, salt, pepper, and shallot in a food processor fitted with the metal blade or in a bowl using an electric mixer until smooth.
2. While the machine is running, add the cream through the feed tube, or beat it in using the mixer.
3. Add the flour and process until a smooth dough forms.
4. Remove from the bowl, wrap in plastic wrap, and chill in the freezer for 30 minutes.
5. While the pastry chills, melt the butter in a saucepan over medium-high heat. When it begins to foam, cook the onions and garlic, stirring, until they are golden. Add the pork and brown it, breaking it up with a spoon.
6. Drain off any excess fat and mix in the remaining ingredients. Taste and adjust the seasonings.
7. Lightly beat the egg with the water for the egg wash.
8. Preheat the oven to 400°F.

9. Roll out the chilled dough between two sheets of plastic wrap to a thickness of ⅛ inch. Cut into 2- to 3-inch rounds using a wineglass or biscuit cutter. Place 1 teaspoon of the filling in each round.
10. Paint the edges with the egg wash. Fold the dough over the filling, forming a crescent. Seal the edges using the tines of a fork or a potsticker mold.
11. Place on a greased cookie sheet and brush with the remaining egg wash. Prick the top of each pastry with a fork to allow the steam to escape.
12. Bake until lightly browned, 15 to 20 minutes.

FAST: Can assemble and refrigerate up to 1 day in advance, or flash freeze (page 24) for up to 3 months. Paint on the egg wash right before baking. Thaw or cook frozen, adding about 10 minutes to the baking time.

FLASHY: Served hot on a platter and garnished with fresh parsley and/or any nontoxic flower or leaves.

FABULOUS: With ground beef and/or veal instead of the pork. With chopped pickles instead of the capers.

FETA AND SESAME CRESCENTS

*A light and delicate pastry with
a Middle-Eastern-style filling.*

Yield: about 36 crescents

Cream cheese sesame pastry

6 ounces cream cheese, cut into quarters

½ pound (2 sticks) unsalted butter, frozen and cut into small pieces

2 cups all-purpose flour

½ cup sesame seeds, toasted (page 27)

1 shallot, cut in half

¼ cup apple cider vinegar

Filling

8 ounces feta cheese, crumbled

½ cup ricotta cheese

4 to 8 green onions (scallions), white and green parts, minced

1 to 2 cloves garlic, minced

Hot pepper sauce to taste

Salt to taste

To complete the dish

1 large egg

1 teaspoon water

¼ to ½ cup sesame seeds, toasted (page 27)

1. Combine the cream cheese, butter, flour, sesame seeds, and shallots in a food processor fitted with the metal blade and process until smooth.
2. While the machine is running, add the vinegar through the feed tube and process until the mixture forms a ball.
3. Divide the pastry in half, wrap in plastic wrap, and chill in the freezer for about 30 minutes.
4. Combine all the filling ingredients in a food processor fitted with the metal blade or in a mixing bowl by hand until smooth. Taste and adjust the seasonings.
5. Lightly beat the egg with the water.
6. Preheat the oven to 400°F.
7. Roll the dough out on a lightly floured board. Cut it into two 1½-inch circles with a wineglass or biscuit cutter.
8. Place a teaspoon of the filling on each circle of dough. Fold in half and press the edges together to form a crescent. Seal using the tines of a fork or a potsticker mold.
9. Brush the egg wash on top of each crescent and coat with the sesame seeds.
10. Bake on an ungreased cookie sheet until lightly browned, 20 to 25 minutes.

FAST: Can assemble up to 1 day in advance and refrigerate, or flash freeze (page 24) for up to 3 months. Thaw or cook frozen, adding about 10 minutes to the baking time.

FLASHY: Served hot on a platter and garnished with fresh parsley and/or any nontoxic flower or leaves.

FABULOUS: With the filling seasoned with ground cumin or minced sun-dried tomatoes and fresh basil. Use the filling for Croustades (page 279), Flo Braker's Magic Puff Pastry (page 309), Tartlets (page 314), or Won Ton Cups (page 246).

CELERY ROOT AND SHIITAKE MUSHROOMS IN DILLED SHALLOT PASTRY PILLOWS

*These ravioli-shaped pastry hors d'oeuvres are lusciously
elegant and belong in the living room,
not the bedroom.*

Yield: about **48** pastries

Dilled shallot pastry

½ pound (2 sticks) unsalted butter,
frozen and cut into small pieces

1 large shallot, cut in half

1 to 2 tablespoons minced fresh dill
or 2 teaspoons dried or more to
taste

2 cups all-purpose flour

Ground white pepper to taste

½ cup sour cream or plain yogurt

1 large egg yolk

Celery root and shiitake mushroom filling

4 tablespoons (½ stick) unsalted
butter

2 cloves garlic, minced

2 shallots, minced

1 ounce dried shiitake mushrooms,
rehydrated (page 18), stemmed,
and minced

½ cup blanched almonds,
slivered

1 medium-size celery root, peeled
and finely shredded

2 tablespoons all-purpose flour

1 teaspoon Dijon mustard or to
taste

½ cup minced fresh parsley

½ cup chicken broth, homemade
(page 11) or canned

½ cup Madeira

4 ounces cream cheese, cut into
small pieces

¼ cup grated Parmesan

2 to 4 tablespoons minced fresh dill
or ½ to 1 teaspoon dried

Salt and ground white pepper to taste

1. To make, process the butter, shallot, dill, flour, and white pepper together in a food processor fitted with the metal blade or in a bowl until the mixture resembles coarse cornmeal.
2. Combine the sour cream with the egg yolk in a small bowl. Add it to the food processor through the feed tube while the machine is running, and process until a ball forms.
3. Remove the dough and divide it into 2 balls. Wrap each in plastic wrap and place in the freezer to chill for about 30 minutes.
4. Melt the butter in a large skillet over medium heat. When it begins to foam, cook the garlic and shallots, stirring, until tender.

5. Add the mushrooms, almonds, and celery root and cook, stirring, for a few minutes until the celery root is almost tender.

6. Stir in the flour and mustard and cook for 1 minute more.

7. Stir in the parsley, broth, Madeira, cheeses, and seasonings. Reduce the heat to low and cook, stirring, until thickened and the cheese melts. Taste and adjust the seasonings.

8. Preheat the oven to 400°F.

9. Roll out each ball to a thickness of ⅛ inch on a lightly floured board.

10. Place one sheet of dough in a ravioli mold and put about ½ teaspoon of the filling in the center of each square. Top with the other sheet of pastry and roll a rolling pin over the top of the mold to separate each pastry pillow.

11. Remove the pillows from the ravioli mold and place them on a greased cookie sheet. Bake until golden, 25 to 30 minutes.

FAST: Can assemble up to 1 day in advance and refrigerate, or flash freeze (page 24) for up to 3 months.

FLASHY: Served hot on a platter and garnished with fresh parsley and/or any nontoxic flower or leaves.

FABULOUS: To be Faster & Flashier, create pastry squares by cutting the pastry with a pastry cutter and topping each square with a teaspoon of the filling. Bake as directed. With the filling used in Croustades (page 279), on Beaten Biscuits (page 296), in raw mushroom caps, or in potsticker wrappers (page 19) or won ton wrappers (page 246).

Prosciutto and Saint André in Yogurt Pastry Pillows

Yield: about 48

Prosciutto Saint André filling

One 8-ounce package cream cheese,
at room temperature and cut into
pieces

½ pound Saint André cheese, at
room temperature, rind removed,
and cut into pieces

2 shallots, minced, or to taste

¼ pound thinly sliced prosciutto,
minced

One 8-ounce can hearts of palm,
drained and chopped, optional

½ cup minced fresh parsley

Yogurt sesame pastry

½ pound (2 sticks) unsalted butter,
frozen and cut into small pieces

1 cup plain yogurt

2 cloves garlic

Zest of 1 lemon, finely grated

1 teaspoon Dijon mustard

1 teaspoon salt

Ground white pepper to taste

2½ cups all-purpose flour

¼ to ½ cup sesame seeds, toasted
(page 27)

1. Combine the cheeses and shallots in a food processor fitted with the metal blade or in a bowl until smooth.
2. Process in the remaining filling ingredients, using several quick on-and-off motions so as not to destroy the texture, or stir in until combined. Set aside.
3. Combine the butter, yogurt, garlic, zest, mustard, salt, and pepper in a food processor fitted with the metal blade, or in a bowl using an electric mixer, and process until smooth.
4. Add the flour and sesame seeds and process until a ball forms. Add more flour if the dough is sticky.
5. Divide the dough into 2 balls, wrap in plastic wrap, and place in the freezer for about 30 minutes to chill.
6. Preheat the oven to 400°F.
7. Roll out each ball to a thickness of ⅛ inch on a lightly floured board.
8. Place one sheet of dough in a ravioli mold and place about ½ teaspoon of the filling in the center of each square. Top with the other sheet of pastry and roll a rolling pin over the top to separate each pastry pillow.
9. Remove the pillows from the ravioli mold and place them on a greased cookie sheet. Bake until golden, 25 to 30 minutes.

FAST: Can assemble up to 1 day in advance and refrigerate, or flash freeze (page 24) for up to 3 months. Thaw or cook frozen, adding about 5 minutes to the baking time.

FLASHY: Served hot on a platter and garnished with fresh parsley and/or any nontoxic flower or leaves.

FABULOUS: To be Faster & Flashier, create pastry squares by cutting the pastry with a pastry cutter and topping each square with a teaspoon of the filling. Bake as directed. With the filling used in Croustades (page 279), on Beaten Biscuits (page 296), in raw mushroom caps, or to fill potsticker wrappers (page 18) or won ton wrappers (see page 19).

SAINT ANDRÉ
AND SHIITAKE TARTLETS

Frozen puff pastry is a wonderful alternative to preparing your own pastry.

Yield: about 24 tartlets

1 package frozen puff pastry, thawed

2 tablespoons unsalted butter

1 ounce dried shiitake mushrooms, rehydrated (page 18), stemmed, and minced

1 tablespoon minced shallots or to taste

2 tablespoons all-purpose flour

1 teaspoon Dijon mustard

¾ cup milk

¼ cup dry white wine

4 ounces rindless Saint André cheese chunks

1 tablespoon finely grated lemon zest or to taste

Minced green onions (scallions), white and green parts, to taste

Salt, ground white pepper, and freshly grated nutmeg to taste

1 large egg yolk combined with 2 tablespoons heavy cream

1. Preheat the oven to 425°F.
2. Cut the pastry into 2½-inch circles using a wineglass or biscuit cutter. Place each circle in a mini-muffin tin cup. Cover each tartlet with a piece of aluminum foil and fill with uncooked dried beans or pastry weights to weigh the pastry down. Bake for 5 minutes.
3. When cool, remove the foil and beans and place the tartlets on an ungreased cookie sheet.
4. Reduce the oven temperature to 350°F.
5. Melt butter in a saucepan over medium heat. When it begins to foam, cook the mushrooms and shallots, stirring, until tender. Do not brown.
6. Stir in the flour and mustard and cook for 1 minute over low heat.
7. Stir in the milk and wine slowly and cook, stirring continuously, until thickened.

8. Stir in the cheese, zest, green onions, and seasonings. Continue stirring until the cheese melts and the flavors develop.
9. Stir 2 tablespoons of the sauce into the yolk mixture, then mix back into the sauce. Cook, stirring, for about 1 minute. Do not boil or the yolk will curdle.
10. Fill the tartlets with the filling. Bake until firm, 10 to 15 minutes, and serve hot.

FAST: Can assemble up to 2 days in advance and refrigerate, or flash freeze (page 24) for up to 1 month. Do not thaw before baking.

FLASHY: Served hot on a platter and garnished with fresh parsley and/or any nontoxic flower or leaves.

FABULOUS: With 4 ounces minced ham or 6 ounces cooked shrimp, 6 ounces hearts of palm, 7 ounces artichoke hearts, or 6 ounces crabmeat substituted for the shiitake mushrooms.

ITALIAN SAUSAGE AND SUN-DRIED TOMATO TARTLETS

Yield: about 12 tartlets

1 sheet frozen puff pastry, thawed

1 large or 2 small Italian sweet sausages

1 cup ricotta cheese

¼ cup grated Parmesan or to taste, plus extra for topping

½ cup sun-dried tomatoes, softened and minced (page 22)

12 pieces jack or mozzarella cheese cut to fit the tops of the tartlets

1. Preheat the oven to 425°F.
2. Cut the pastry into 2½-inch circles using a wineglass or biscuit cutter. Place each circle in mini-muffin tin cups.
3. Prick the sausages with a fork, wrap in a paper towel, place on a plate and microwave them for 2 minutes on high. To prepare in a regular oven, place in a baking dish and cook fully in a preheated 350°F oven for about 20 minutes. Slice the sausages into ¼- to ½-inch-thick slices.
4. Combine the ricotta cheese with the Parmesan and tomatoes. Place some in each pastry cup, top with a little more Parmesan, a sausage slice, and a piece of the jack cheese.
5. Bake until hot and the cheese is melted, about 8 minutes.

FAST: Can assemble up to 1 day in advance and refrigerate, or flash freeze (page 24) for up to 1 month. Do not thaw before baking.

FLASHY: Served hot on a platter with a whole raw tomato, fresh parsley, and/or fresh basil in the center.

FABULOUS: With minced fresh basil or rosemary mixed in with the ricotta and Parmesan.

MUSHROOM AND CANADIAN BACON TARTLETS

Flo Braker is my hero, and she'll be yours after you try her pastry! The recipe comes from her book
The Simple Art of Perfect Baking
(William Morrow and Company).

Yield: about 9 dozen tartlets

Flo Braker's Magic Puff Pastry

2 cups all-purpose flour

½ pound (2 sticks) unsalted butter, frozen and cut into small pieces

½ cup sour cream or plain yogurt

1 large egg yolk

Mushroom and Canadian bacon filling

4 tablespoons (½ stick) unsalted butter

4 to 6 shallots, minced

¼ pound Canadian bacon, minced

2 cloves garlic, minced

Salt, ground white pepper, and fresh or dried thyme to taste

¼ cup minced fresh parsley

1 pound cultivated white mushrooms, minced

2 ounces dried shiitake mushrooms, rehydrated (page 18), stemmed, and minced

2 tablespoons all-purpose flour

½ cup heavy cream

¼ cup medium-dry or cream sherry

6 ounces Saint André cheese, rind removed, or brie, cut into small pieces

½ cup pumpkin seeds, toasted (page 27) and chopped

1. Process the flour and butter in a food processor fitted with the metal blade until the mixture resembles coarse cornmeal, or combine in a bowl using a pastry blender.
2. Combine the sour cream with the egg yolk in a small bowl and add it to the processor. Process until blended and the dough begins to form a ball.
3. Remove the dough and divide it into 2 balls. Wrap it in plastic wrap and place it in the freezer to chill for about 30 minutes.

4. Melt the butter in a skillet over medium heat. When it begins to foam, cook the shallots, Canadian bacon, garlic, seasonings, and parsley, stirring, until the shallots and garlic are tender.

5. Add the mushrooms and cook, stirring, until the liquid released by them cooks away.

6. Mix in the flour and cook for a minute; do not brown.

7. Stir in the cream and sherry. Cook until thickened, while stirring.

8. Add the cheese and seeds and cook, stirring continuously, until the cheese melts. Taste and adjust the seasonings. Set aside.

9. Preheat the oven to 400°F.

10. Roll out each of the balls to a thickness of ⅛ inch on a lightly floured board.

11. Cut into 2½-inch squares or circles and place each one into a mini-muffin tin cup.

12. Place the desired amount of filling in each tartlet.

13. Bake until fully cooked and golden, 25 to 30 minutes. To reheat, place in a 350°F oven for about 10 minutes.

FAST: Can assemble up to 1 day in advance and refrigerate, or flash freeze (page 24) unbaked for up to 3 months. Thaw or bake frozen, adding about 5 minutes to the baking time.

FLASHY: Served hot on a platter and garnished with fresh parsley and/or any nontoxic flower or leaves.

FABULOUS: Use this technique for tartlets with any filling in this book. There is no end to what you can fill these tartlets with! Create Wellington Tartlets by sautéing small cubes of beef fillet in butter with shallots. Cool and place 1 cube of beef along with the mushroom filling in each tartlet and bake as directed.

SPRING TARTLETS

A perfect way to celebrate the rites of spring.

Yield: about 36 tartlets

2 tablespoons unsalted butter

1 onion, minced

1 clove garlic, minced

3 tablespoons all-purpose flour

¼ cup dry sherry

½ cup heavy cream

2 tablespoons Dijon mustard

3 tablespoons minced fresh dill or
   1 tablespoon dried

Salt, ground white pepper, and freshly
   grated nutmeg to taste

¼ cup sesame seeds, toasted
   (page 27)

1 cup chopped smoked ham

½ cup grated Romano

1 cup grated sharp cheddar

1 cup asparagus tips, minced and
   blanched (page 23) until just
   tender, about 2 minutes

1 recipe Flo Braker's Magic Puff
   Pastry (page 309) or 1 package
   frozen puff pastry, thawed

1. Preheat the oven to 400°F.
2. Melt the butter in a saucepan over medium heat. When it begins to foam, cook the onion and garlic, stirring, until softened. Whisk in the flour and cook over low heat for 1 minute. Do not brown.
3. Remove from the burner and whisk in the sherry, cream, mustard, dill, and other seasonings. Return the pan to the burner and whisk until thickened, about 10 minutes.
4. Add the remaining ingredients, except the asparagus and pastry, and cook over medium heat, stirring, until the cheese is melted. Taste and adjust the seasonings.
5. Roll out the pastry into a thin rectangle about ⅛ inch thick on a lightly floured board and cut into 2½-inch squares or circles.
6. Place each square in a mini-muffin tin cup and place a teaspoon of the filling into the center of each square. Fold the opposite ends of the pastry up to meet in the center, or leave open.
7. Bake until golden, 25 to 30 minutes.

FAST: Can assemble up to 1 day in advance and refrigerate, or flash freeze (page 24) for up to 3 months. Do not thaw before baking. When baking frozen tartlets, bake at 350°F for 10 minutes to thaw, then raise the temperature to 400°F and bake until golden, 25 to 30 minutes.

FLASHY: Served hot on a platter and garnished with fresh parsley, strawberries, watercress, and/or any nontoxic flower or leaves.

FABULOUS: With minced, blanched spinach, chard, or broccoli substituted for the asparagus.

SUN-DRIED TOMATO
AND FETA TARTLETS

Yield: about 24 tartlets

1 package frozen puff pastry, thawed

1 to 2 cloves garlic, minced

Ground white pepper to taste

2 to 4 tablespoons chopped fresh
basil or 1 teaspoon dried

½ cup mayonnaise, homemade (page
13) or purchased

¾ cup milk

¼ cup Madeira

3 large eggs

1 tablespoon all-purpose flour

2 ounces sun-dried tomatoes,
softened and minced (page 22)

4 to 6 green onions, white and green
parts, minced

¼ pound feta cheese, crumbled, or to
taste

1. Preheat the oven to 425°F.
2. Cut the pastry into 2½-inch circles using a wineglass or biscuit cutter. Place each circle in a mini-muffin tin, cover each with a piece of aluminum foil, and fill with uncooked dried beans or pastry weights to weight the pastry down. Bake for 5 minutes.
3. When cool, remove the foil and beans and place the tartlets on a greased cookie sheet.
4. Reduce the oven temperature to 350°F.
5. Meanwhile, combine the garlic, pepper, basil, mayonnaise, milk, and Madeira in a food processor fitted with the metal blade or in a bowl and mix until smooth. Add the eggs and flour and process until just blended.
6. To each tartlet add some sun-dried tomatoes, green onions, and crumbled feta cheese, then fill each tartlet two-thirds full with the egg-and-milk mixture.
7. Bake until set, about 30 minutes.

FAST: Can prepare through step 6 up to 1 day in advance and refrigerate, or flash freeze (page 24) for up to 1 month. Do not thaw before baking, just add several minutes to the baking time.

FLASHY: Served hot on a platter and garnished with fresh basil, parsley, and/or any nontoxic flower or leaves.

FABULOUS: With Gruyère, gorgonzola, or jack cheese substituted for the feta or roasted red or green peppers (page 26) for the sun-dried tomatoes.

GARLIC AND FETA TARTLETS

This is an hors d'oeuvre with world-class flavor!

Yield: filling for about 36 tartlets

10 to 12 cloves garlic

¾ cup medium-dry sherry

½ cup heavy cream

2 large eggs and 2 large yolks

10 ounces feta cheese

Freshly ground black pepper to taste

Tartlet Shells (recipe follows)

½ cup sun-dried tomatoes, softened
and minced (page 22)

1. Preheat the oven to 350°F.
2. Put the garlic in small saucepan and cover with the sherry. Simmer over medium heat until the garlic is tender and has mellowed, about 5 minutes.
3. Stir in the cream and cook, stirring, until the mixture is thickened and reduced by one half.
4. Meanwhile, combine the eggs and feta in a food processor fitted with the metal blade, or in a blender, or a bowl until smooth.
5. While the machine is running, slowly add garlic-sherry mixture and mix until fully combined. Season with pepper.
6. Fill each prebaked tartlet shell two-thirds full with a piece of sun-dried tomato, then top with the feta mixture. Bake until a toothpick comes out clean, about 30 minutes.

FAST: Can prepare the filling up to 2 days in advance and refrigerate. Can flash freeze (page 24) assembled for up to 3 months. Thaw or cook frozen, adding about 10 minutes to the baking time.

FLASHY: Served hot on a platter and garnished with a head of garlic or fresh parsley and/or with any nontoxic flower and/or leaves.

FABULOUS: Seasoned with minced fresh basil, oregano, dill, rosemary, green chiles, or crushed Szechuan peppercorns (page 19).

TARTLET SHELLS

Using the food processor makes this
unbelievably easy!

Yield: about 36 tartlets

⅔ cup unsalted butter, frozen and
    cut into small pieces

2 cups all-purpose flour

¼ teaspoon salt

¼ cup ice water

1 large egg white, lightly beaten

1. Combine the flour, butter, and salt in a food processor fitted with the metal blade until it resembles coarse cornmeal.
2. Slowly add the ice water through the feed tube while the machine is running. Process until the pastry begins to form into a ball.
3. Wrap the pastry with plastic wrap and chill in the freezer for 10 to 15 minutes.
4. Preheat the oven to 450°F.
5. Roll the pastry out on a lightly floured surface to a thickness of about ¼ inch.
6. Cut the pastry into 2½-inch circles using a wineglass or biscuit cutter. Fit the circles into mini-muffin tin cups.
7. Brush with the beaten egg white and bake until almost fully baked, about 8 minutes.

FAST: Can prepare up to 2 days in advance and refrigerate, or freeze for up to 3 months. Thaw or cook frozen, adding about 10 minutes to the baking time once frozen.

FLASHY: Serve hot or at room temperature on a platter garnished with anything from parsley to nontoxic flowers in the center, depending on the nature of the party and the filling used.

FABULOUS: Filled with anything.

Fast & Fabulous
Hors D'Oeuvres

Index